# Crafting Luxury

**Mark Bloomfield** is a designer and visiting professor in the School of Creative Arts at the University of Hertfordshire, UK. He has worked in film and TV making jewellery for *Titanic*, *Judge Dredd*, *Tolkien*, *Gentleman Jack* and *The Crown*.

**Shaun Borstrock** is a luxury brand strategist, and Associate Dean, Business, Innovation and Projects, founder and head of In Pursuit of Luxury and the Digital Hack Lab in the School of Creative Arts at the University of Hertfordshire, UK.

**Silvio Carta** is an architect, associate professor and head of art and design in the School of Creative Arts at the University of Hertfordshire, UK.

**Veronica Manlow** is professor in the Department of Business Management at the Murray Koppelman School of Business at Brooklyn College.

# Crafting Luxury

## Craftsmanship, Manufacture, Technology and the Retail Environment

Mark Bloomfield, Shaun Borstrock,
Silvio Carta and Veronica Manlow

 **intellect**

Bristol, UK / Chicago, USA

First published in the UK in 2022 by
Intellect, The Mill, Parnall Road, Fishponds, Bristol, BS16 3JG, UK

First published in the USA in 2022 by
Intellect, The University of Chicago Press, 1427 E. 60th Street,
Chicago, IL 60637, USA

A catalogue record for this book is available from
the British Library.

Copy editor: MPS Limited
Cover designer: Nick Lovegrove
Layout design: Nick Lovegrove and Aleksandra Szumlas
Production manager: Sophia Munyengeterwa
Typesetter: MPS Limited

Hardback ISBN 978-1-78938-533-5
Paperback ISBN 978-1-78938-580-9
ePDF ISBN 978-1-78938-534-2
ePUB ISBN 978-1-78938-535-9

Printed and bound by CPI

To find out about all our publications, please visit our website.
There you can subscribe to our e-newsletter, browse or download
our current catalogue and buy any titles that are in print.

www.intellectbooks.com

This is a peer-reviewed publication.

# Contents

# Preface:
# The Hand of the Maker

*Crafting Luxury* takes an independent view of the global luxury market, its idiosyncratic definitions and its constantly changing position in defining products and services.

The authors – a designer of product and jewellery, a brand strategist and a fashion designer, an architect, and a sociologist and specialist in business management – are practitioners and academics. Their approach to dissecting the complex world of luxury brings distinct viewpoints to the debate, offering different perspectives, thoughts and interpretations of luxury. While their voices might, by the nature of their expertise, sometimes present a different tone, it is the merging of that expertise and knowledge that gives deep understanding and nuance to the convictions they share and that shape the book.

The authors do not see craft as the starting point in the design and creation of luxury, but as a continuum. The act of making is present at every phase, from concept to the presentation of merchandise in stores or online. How a product is made defines whether or not it could be considered a luxury good. The hand of the maker is ever present, whether or not one has direct knowledge of that maker.

Purveyors of luxury goods, whether they are independent artisans or multinational conglomerates, understand that the crafting of luxury is the defining feature of each product showcased to an audience. Some customers may be quite discerning, seeking out luxury and capable of making judgements about quality and pricing. Others rely on information provided by the artisan or the brand to make their decision.

While the individual artisan selling his or her creations has a more direct relationship to the product they create and with the consumer to whom it is sold, in larger establishments the process by which luxury goods are crafted is less direct. In the largest firms, the customer relies on messages communicated through merchandising and marketing, and through his or her interaction with salespersons.

The location of the store, its architectural features, the arrangement of merchandise within the store, the website, messages communicated by the brand about its heritage and identity and indeed, statements made about the quality and craftsmanship of products and their prices – all contribute to the knowledge a customer has, as well as to his or her opinions about the value of the brand's products. It is often taken for granted that the brand is a purveyor of luxury goods and that the products are well made, unique in their design features and created from the highest quality materials.

Still, this knowledge could recede into the background of a consumer's consciousness or not even be a consideration on which they dwell or think of at all. The shopper's knowledge could merely stem from the associations he or she has of the brand and what that brand's universe represents. A luxury customer absorbs information about the quality of the goods they consider buying. Perhaps an influencer played an important role, or the brand's marketing messaging resonated with them.

Our image of ourselves is frequently caught up in what we wear, or drive, the items we surround ourselves with, where we live or vacation, the gifts we bestow on others. Everything resonates. As such, thinking about and shopping for luxury products is an emotional experience. What is in the mind of that person as he or she decides to explore or shop at that particular establishment? Probably the sensations evoked as they walk into a store or visit a website and have an experience defined as exceptional and worthy of the luxury designation.

The way goods are displayed and handled by the salesperson, the fact that the price is not mentioned or obscured – all these convey the message that the product has been carefully made. Some brands go so far as to blatantly misrepresent the process by which products are crafted. An advertisement, for instance, could show a contemplative artisan sewing a handbag by hand in a workshop when in fact anonymous workers make them in factories at a rapid rate.

Others take for granted that merchandise is hand crafted. The 'Made In...' label confers on it a heritage and alludes to it being constructed according to practices that have not changed, or at least which uphold certain standards. Even those referred to as mass-market luxury brands rely on consumers making these associations and not making others. The worst association a consumer can make is to align that brand with mass marketed methods, and with marketing strategies aimed at obscuring the true nature of the products. This is a conclusion brands do not want, and many luxury businesses are built around leading the consumer away from making such judgements.

This work concludes with a number of pointers for future research and for readers to reflect upon. In the Final Thoughts chapter, key aspects are identified that are inextricably related to the luxury world and its creation.

The first one is the impact of the luxury industry on the planet and how people with ethical and sustainable perspectives perceive this.

Second, the role of technology in the creation and consumption of luxury is discussed highlighting the discrepancy between aspirations, promises – and reality and perception.

Third, a reflection on the fluid notion of luxury underpins how difficult it is to categorize with a fixed definition. It is, instead, an idea influenced by a number of factors – including financial, societal, and political, as well as a complex system of trends.

The changing nature of physical spaces and their digital extensions, where luxury products are experienced and sold, is discussed, concluding that the dichotomy of the physical and virtual is far from resolved, with a growing number of attempts by many luxury brands to offer exciting as well as disappointing experiences.

Some of the case studies analysed in this book pave the way for a promising direction, one where customers are part of the creation of the luxury process. Customers who are deeply involved in the luxury experience are likely to share more personal data, a development luxury companies benefit from and try to cultivate. But this does pose questions on the privacy and ethics of this kind of surveillance, questioning the extent to which customers are aware of the ways in which their personal information is used.

While some sections and chapters may have started out as the work of one author, each writer has brought his or her perspective to bear on the entire book, discussing it, writing and rewriting it collaboratively. In this way, the book can be called a collaborative project, representing collective thinking on the matter of luxury in all its manifestations.

The aim of the Final Thoughts chapter is to highlight these salient points to the reader in the hope that future work and discussions will continue to scrutinize the important questions raised.

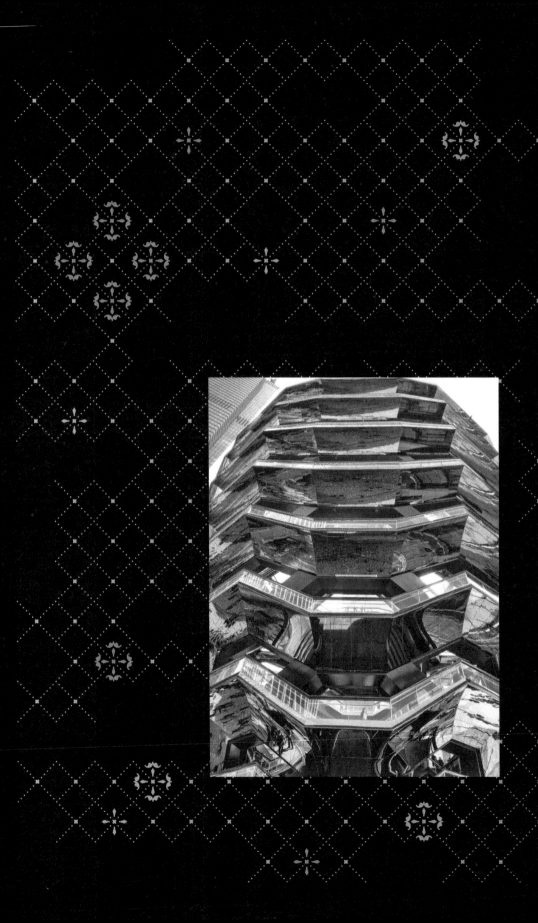

# 1

# The Luxury Journey
# of Discovery

*Discovery is instrumental to the realization of the translation of one material state into a different state. This transition of a material state generally becomes more valuable to us because it may make a mundane process easier, more beneficial or the combined effort of material, tool and the expertise of the individual using them creates something wonderful to be admired, sought after and coveted as an item of value.*

Taking a philosophical view, this chapter explores the connections between luxury and technology. In the first instance, we discover how the move towards a luxurious existence has always been in parallel to the discovery of tools, which has in turn allowed us to realize the potential of materials. Sometimes it is the material that inspires the need for the tool; sometimes it is the tool that transforms the material into something unexpected.

Looking at the historical origins of tools and how they were used to build empires that transformed civilization to give rise to the modern world and technology today, we examine the practical, philosophical and psychological impact of how luxury and technology continue to make our lives easier, more comfortable and something to be valued. We pitch early discoveries, which came about by simply observing the world around us, against contemporary unseen methods of real-ization, production and delivery. For example, how does something simple like the wheel drive a global automotive industry that is worth an estimated $5 trillion. What separates one car from the next when all cars could be considered a luxury?

Luxury's foundation was built on discovery, on excellence in craft and material execution as it transformed the world around us.

How, then, does it adapt to a new technological era constructed around the value of information and the rise of dataism? Will luxury as we recognize it today survive, or will luxury simply meld into technology? What is the practical, philosophical and psychological impact of how luxury and technology continues to make our lives better, more comfortable and something to be valued?

As technology becomes increasingly entwined in managing our complex lives – regardless of whether we actively engage with it or not – we question how our values are changing. Microchips and computer code begin to take control, organizing and delivering a plethora of possibilities through complex discovery processes such as artificial intelligence, which is accessible to all but really only understood by the few.

Technology, or tools, have enabled people to manipulate materials and build the modern world. Luxury's foundation of great comfort, ease and wealth was constructed out of our ability to utilize these tools to create objects, both useful and useless, by those whose intention it is to enable people to express their existence as something of value through their material wealth. As technology advances, the means to express and value our own complex lives has become a simple transaction as these tools focus on delivering convenience with the touch of a button. Where tools were once easier to understand through observing the craftspeople at work, new technologies are more difficult to comprehend as what they do and the impact they have goes largely unnoticed. They are almost invisible. This disconnection from historical, tangible and observable mechanisms distances us from what is really happening and we seldom question it, unless its impact is felt as a disturbance due to societal and environmental conditions dramatically and/or dynamically changing.

This same technology connects us to a degree never before experienced. Where once unnavigable landmasses and seas separated us, the boundaries and differences between the entire populations of the globe are now navigable through the small phone most of us carry around in our pockets. The devices expedite the potential to unite us through the many ways digital technologies connect us to the world and each other. And, even if we consider ourselves to not be direct users of the technology, it still impacts our lives indirectly through the products and services we do engage with.

Part of this new global landscape is being defined by brands using digital strategies to conquer new territories, fuelling their growth as they strive for a ubiquitous existence supported by technologies such as the cloud, an all-encompassing network of information intent on delivering possibilities.

As corporate borders expand, technology becomes the only way to manage these complex new lands, most of them residing in virtual space where growth can infinitely expand beyond the physical space where their headquarters may reside. As our dependency on network technologies expands beyond the real world, new worlds are opening up in rapid succession inside a virtual domain. This transformation has always been part of life, but in contemporary society, it is the pace of change that continues to rapidly redefine everything. We're now part of a constantly accelerating state of adjustment, refinement and changing conditions become normalized. This promotes uncertainty, as we seem to be constantly exposed to things we do not really understand and have no control over, as we are continuously encouraged to make quick decisions during our everyday lives.

It could be argued that luxury is also transformative. When people are attracted to luxury goods and services their lives, along with their perception of the world around them, change. This is due to luxury's appeal, as participants feel connected to something of value. Often this connection is based on material goods and services driven by an aspirational narrative, one where time is also considered a luxury. But without technology – from cloud services to manufacturing techniques – enabling and supporting this aspirational existence through products and services, there is no transformation. The physicality of existence is tied to the objects in the physical environment; these objects connect us to a reality. Without them, only an ethereal quality remains.

Technologies and the people who invent them are key to the process of change. It is a mechanism giving forward momentum to our existence by giving the impression these products, services and inventions improve our lives, supposedly by being better than the previous version. And as change is the only constant, it is almost as though it is a conditional part of our very being. As technology has become embedded in society it shapes us and defines us by giving new meaning to our existence. We always seem to be searching for what that could mean.

One of the defining aspects that set human beings apart from most other forms of life lies in our ability to use tools. Our tool making could be seen as the means to interface with our immediate environment, helping us to understand it and the wider world through extending our core capabilities. Early discoveries such as the wheel probably came about through observing natural phenomena. A log or a boulder rolling down the hill under the influence of gravity took place before we even realized there was such a thing as gravity. From the perspective of early Neanderthals, gravity didn't even exist, yet these rolling objects must have sparked the imagination and triggered a response.

Reacting to changing conditions in an intentional manner gave rise to an early intellectual process that connected events to possibilities through the translation of an otherworldly sensation such as a thought or simply by an emotional response to a situation. This practice is more likely to have been instinctively discovered through observations and direct experience with the conditions of the time. If you were cold perhaps an animal skin kept you warm. Or if it was raining, you sheltered under a tree.

These early, simple reactions needed no understanding of where the rain came from, of weather fronts or how the fur of animals could trap air and regulate body temperature. These expanded qualities and properties grew in conjunction with language and gave rise to the means to explore and explain in a deliberate, inventive fashion. This began to materialize as humans and some animals realized they could manipulate their environment to make their existence within it easier, more comfortable and most importantly, ensure their survival. And they could do so in such a way that these newly found abilities and observations could be distributed, discussed and debated.

# Tools of the trade

The principle of the wheel was discovered prior to its invention during the Neolithic period or the new Stone Age. But its practical application was invented c.3500 BCE; a wooden disc with a hole at its centre, connected to an axle, allowed it to be fixed to a cart so more things could be transported over greater distances. And when livestock were introduced to pull the cart, it became a relatively easier operation for people and made their lives more comfortable. A similar arrangement of wheel and axle could also be used to manipulate clay, like a potter's wheel, enabling the potter to shape clay into round vessels and plates, still a signature of most crockery and glassware today. These technologies enabled the early mechanization and later industrialization of tasks, and the production of products on a mass scale.

Flint tools probably came about via a similar process of discovery through observation and subsequent refinement in order to use the material's sharp edge to kill, cut and process animals, skins and meat. The edge of the flintstone could be chipped away to produce a sharp cutting edge and with practice, the material could be fashioned into all manner of implements from arrowheads to axes. José-Manuel Benito Alvarez (2016) contends that examples from the Middle Palaeolithic period are still as sharp and useful today as they were when first made over 60,000 years ago.

Tools enabled our technological transition from acting instinctively to acting with purpose as we began to realize our mental and physical effort could translate into something valuable. Initially, it was a value necessary to our survival during those early formative ages as we manipulated stone and iron, through to the development of value that underpins our current capitalist system that is instrumental in contemporary mechanisms of value creation and wealth.

These transformational routines are still prevalent as raw material is stripped from the planet to fuel a consuming and expanding population. Materials – natural or synthetic – are processed into a vast array of objects, some of which we can't live without, others that could be described as unnecessary. But even those so-called 'useless' objects have carved out a position for themselves, a position created by those companies or individuals looking to develop markets for their products and services. Value creation is frequently unlocked through the stories those purveyors tell potential customers about the benefits of what they are offering. The narrative is often imaginatively woven into the very fabric of the materials used to construct the company's products and is ultimately carried through the business's entire operation in what has become known in contemporary business jargon as a company's DNA.

A company's DNA is now contained on a microdot or a Radio Frequency Identification (RFID) tag attached or integrated into the company's product. These markers can be interrogated through a range of technological scanning devices that reveal the hidden data concealed on the tag. This digital interrogation discloses all kinds of information about the product, the company and even the owner. The technique effectively embeds provenance into products, and can be deployed in many ways.

A product's provenance is particularly important when buying antiques and art. It is the story of where it comes from and the reason for its value, often given through its association with completely unrelated situations. A product can attain a much sought-after value. The background metadata acts as proof of the product's exclusive nature; it is one of a kind because X owned it. The digital version of product profiling is already being implemented through emerging technologies such as blockchain.

This identification mechanism becomes increasingly entwined as a business evolves, and the commercial landscape changes. It is capable of responding through customer engagement, the introduction of new legislation and supply chain management. The collected data can be used to hone and focus the business's operations to deliver its core values.

In the luxury goods market, this value is all about instilling desire with intention. A desire that those companies then service as part of life, often presented to us in a way that makes us believe it will make our lives more comfortable. In short, the stories and the provenance behind the luxury company and its products make them desirable and accessible.

# Tools and technologies

The relatively simple tools that first enabled us to manipulate materials have become increasingly sophisticated over time. And now these advanced toolsets and technologies are entwined and necessary to the point where the modern developed nations would find it difficult to return to the old ways and methods. Just as luxury has come to symbolize a pinnacle of expertise and endeavour, technologies have become paramount to our very existence.

As the world becomes more complex, technologies are relied upon, and in most cases are an absolute requirement to enable the systems creating and managing the demand for all goods and services. Technologies are required to achieve efficiency to deliver precision as effectively as possible. These systems maximize the value proposition and allow all who participate to reap the rewards as companies and consumers create an innovation landscape built on that value.

Discovery is being augmented with search engines that align individual needs, wants and desires with the plethora of products and services available. Invisible technological networks of inquiry, and the resulting returns, are becoming more complex by the second. It is this complexity that outstrips any single person's capability to fully understand it and to recognize the patterns to be discovered in the bigger picture.

This complexity also creates the need for additional technologies. As these complex situations are beginning to be analysed and managed by machine learning routines, a so-called artificial intelligence is evolving, an intelligence supposedly guided by wants and needs, which exists to provide appropriate solutions by making the emerging complexity easier to probe and understand. Its intent is to provide insight into that which we may have missed.

The analysis or mining of these massive data sets highlights patterns, behaviour and other insights relevant to those doing the digging. Or the process reveals something unexpected that takes the excavation in a different direction. Big data contain billions of unique points of reference and each can be contrasted, compared and calculated to create a different set of results. Often patterns emerge where there is a similarity but unique arrangements will appear when multiple data sets are taken into consideration. A customer may spend money at a regular time each day for lunch, along with thousands of others but what they buy reduces the similarity. The payment method they use reduces it further. Compare that with a credit score reference, and the differences become more extreme. As more and more data points are collected and analysed, a unique profile is realized and people naturally become a rarity due to the very specific details that describe who they are. This ordered occurrence describes their existence and the uniqueness of their experience and can be used to predict what they may do or need next.

Analytical procedures are undertaken to assess the state of the end customer. Market research will be carried out and feedback from forums, chat rooms and ratings all be used to better understand the product, its position, customer engagement, how they use and feel about products and the range of activities the company may be involved in. Data analysis contributes to a company's customer service strategy, which is tailored accordingly. It also feeds back into the company's business strategy and informs the product development cycle. Materials are transformed to create things. In the luxury goods industry, this emphasis focuses on how to create a one-of-a-kind thing in a mass-market context, and sell as many as possible while taking the time to make each customer feel as though they are the only one.

Generally, all product development results in a pre-production sample, the first of its kind that starts the whole process. Buyers, customers and marketing teams then react to this sample as a sales strategy, the product's commercialization is built around it to maximize its impact on the open market. The product is then sold until it will sell no more. Anything left from the production run is marked down to clear the stock. The whole process then starts again, but insight from this previous activity will contribute to the next iteration.

This activity and compilation and analysis of data are creating technologies focusing on personalization. Indeed, all the tech companies are already implementing these services to tailor e-mail, messaging, advertizing and product suggestion services. Suddenly we are being made more aware of the rarity and uniqueness of our own selves. After all, there is only one you!

Luxury, too, is often sold as something of rarity and not readily available, and this context describes conditions that create an opportunity and a subsequent market. The luxury industry is founded on these principles and when combined with technological analytical tools that give insight into customer behaviour, need and desire, the supply of luxury goods and services can be delivered with pinpoint accuracy.

Luxury goods may be constructed from materials that are hard to come by, difficult to extract and process, or from materials that do not exist in large quantities. They command a high price that restricts consumption either because the price is controlled or because the company making those products chooses to market them as expensive. All of these aspects are designed to embody uniqueness and appeal to a special rare quality that speaks to the customer.

What is this rare quality so many luxury companies rely on to separate what they do from others making the same or similar things? Is it simply the technology used that establishes this difference? Or is the projected rarity of what they are making that reflects our own notion of our uniqueness and specialness?

# Historical context

Life, since it first emerged, possibly from hydrothermal vents, has been constantly challenged by the conditions within which it exists. Overcoming these challenges to survive and become the apex life form it is today, humans have predominantly secured their position through the use of tools and technology. The discovery and utilization of these tools have also been accompanied by stories serving to bond what we've accomplished to narratives we tell each other in order to make lasting sense of our endeavours and connect them to a wider audience.

The reasons why we have an instinctive need to create can seem mysterious, but often it is simply triggered by our direct observation of local conditions, building experiences with our immediate environment. Materials are all around us and natural occurrences of these materials can prompt a new way of seeing the world, enabling us to transform it into something that better suits our needs.

A cave formation, for example, provides shelter from changing weather conditions like rain, sun and wind. A cave protects us and is something we discovered early on; suddenly extreme weather conditions could be softened and made tolerable, making our existence more certain but also more comfortable. An early idea of a luxurious existence was born, and when taken as a relative experience to the conditions early sapiens had to endure, the difference was monumental, but probably not seen as a luxury as the language didn't exist at that time. As we've evolved, our cave has become an architectural wonder, a palace, an extreme example of our technological understanding and ability to manipulate material on a massive scale in order to make our lives more comfortable.

With this experience and insight, our propensity for adjusting things to suit our needs became the norm. Everything became malleable: fallen trees could be used to make shelters, different kinds of clay could be used as a seal between the logs and the huge array of leaf, bracken and twig properties could be used to fashion all sorts of useful objects that would make life easier and more comfortable. This played an important part in the realization that we could not only build things but also the things we built could alter our very existence.

Developing in conjunction with this ability to manipulate material was the discovery that tools were equally valuable. Suddenly, if you could extend your hands, teeth, indeed any bodily function through its augmentation via devices, then you became better equipped to process materials, increasing your efficiency and accuracy. You became more effective at these tasks and improved not only your existence but also that of those around you. This would increase the likelihood of your immediate social group's survival. Suddenly technology and the things we would make with it, and use it for, became symbiotic to our very existence.

Our lifestyle changed and continued to change as each new material was discovered, along with the new technologies invented to manipulate that material, and the skills people developed with each new expression of that material using those tools.

# Travel and discovery

Treasures from overseas were discovered through humans designing sailboats; a technology that captured the wind and enabled travel to previously undiscovered regions of the planet. Humans never even knew of the existence of other landmasses until boat technology was invented. With it came the invention of a range of other supporting technology such as navigation aids that formed the foundation of modern-day GPS. As humans traversed the globe, new materials were discovered, along with indigenous communities that had already transformed that material into wonders of the ancient world. Some were sought after, treasured, and traded, ultimately establishing mechanisms of exchange realized and managed through technology.

Perceptions of reality changed with each new discovery by opening up the understanding of the world around us. Mechanisms enabling us to maximize the potential of our new understanding were established as a result. Sometimes they were enabled through technology, but their success was primarily driven by the social constructs that emerged as humans organized themselves to live effectively, efficiently and in comfort. A luxury that began within a humble framework of intuitive observation aiding our survival would ultimately become divisive, as the capital created and resources required to fulfil future endeavours spiralled. These early hierarchies formed the foundations for the modern world, probably without any knowledge of what would transpire due to this early mechanization of trade as it was set in motion.

Were the hierarchical structures established through those that observed and saw potential or were they simply invigorated by the novelty of these new objects, materials and processes offered, which captured the imagination? As these commodities were made accessible to all, those at the pinnacle of the discovery process began to realize their true value. They realized the untapped potential of these materials. The products and services that came into existence through these materials were made accessible to the wider population, and the markets grew. Those skilled in the techniques required to work the materials into something extraordinary did so for royalty, nobility and the wealthiest of families and individuals in an effort to further enhance their social standing. This became increasingly important as the global market opened up.

This, in turn, resulted in the founders' own value spiralling and servicing this growth which resulted in task creation. Suddenly people could work and earn a wage, but they also needed managing. Ledgers were used to record all this new activity and connect it to value. Record keeping began as a collection of symbols cut into stone or clay tablets, the mark making being representative of the technology of the time around 3400 BCE. This was further developed with the invention of papyrus and implements to make marks on it c.2550 BCE (Mark 2011).

Sticks, and then quills, carried pigments held in suspension, laid carefully onto the flexible sheets of the reed fibre to represent the physical products and agreements as they were traded among the community. The benefit of the papyrus sheets over the stone tablets was that they were easier to update, and being flexible and lightweight, they were more convenient to transport and store. This development of what we would consider from a contemporary perspective, as very basic technology was actually life changing for those who could wield a pen to record transactions of the day. Indeed, some of these early documents have survived and exist as a reminder of how our modern trading systems came into existence. As technology began to open the world to trade through global telecommunications networks, the paper and the pen were replaced with spreadsheets, which became connected through network technologies to form a complex web of transactions that happen every millisecond of every day (LLFOURN 2018).

Technologies are inextricably linked to every part of our life and go hand-in-hand with enabling us to realize our adaptive capacity. Where once the focus of our adaptation was on survival, it shifted to the apparent betterment of humanity. Most of us are fortunate enough to live comfortably when compared to the rocky floor of a cave that gave humans much-needed shelter 100,000 years ago. But now the perception of what is comfortable is influenced by a luxury industry built on excess, and which encourages us to aspire.

When considering physical comfort against psychological comfort the difference is one of the relative perspectives. Each of us has a subjective set of preferences based on our individual experiences. Connoisseurship may influence our response to a given situation as the so-called expert draws on a wealth of experience and knowledge. But most of the time, those qualities a connoisseur may highlight to separate one thing from another are based purely on taste or opinion. They use new knowledge, or re-emphasis, to imbue a product with characteristics setting it apart from the other competing versions. Sometimes connoisseurs are also linked to the company making the product they are representing. Today, these individuals have become known as influencers whose prime objective is to promote products through their social media networks.

When imbued with the benefits of a narrative, even the most mundane can take on a special quality. These features, differences in material quality or even the company's origin and apparent association to other brands or individuals, along with the kind of treatment the parts have been subjected to and the wellbeing of the workforce, can set apart one product over the next, even if they are practically identical in their function. Our command of images and text and the messages they communicate have become more sophisticated since the earliest examples of paintings on a cave wall or sales messages painted onto papyrus. Products, services, companies and even individuals have become brands, and the accompanying stories distributed through technological media connect with the narratives they depict.

This book addresses all these questions, providing research, case studies, opinions and ideas giving insight into the possible futures of luxury.

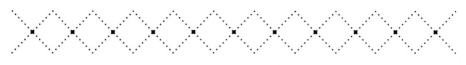

# 2

# The Luxury Domain

*Luxury in all of its manifestations was once purely the domain of the rich and powerful that travelled the world in search of treasures from afar. Today, it encompasses a much broader base. In fact, the world of luxury products and services has changed so significantly it has become increasingly difficult to determine what is and what is not luxury.*

Definitions of luxury are in question. Discussions on what does or does not merit the luxury designation are more prevalent in the face of luxury becoming pervasive. Customers now question how and where luxury-branded products are manufactured, and whether they merit their exorbitant prices. Many – included among them artisans, designers, academics, journalists and customers themselves – are calling into question the mass manufacture of luxury goods, forcing leaders in the sector to defend the quality and authenticity of their products.

   Within the sector itself, there is disagreement on whether luxury goods can be mass-produced, and sold at a discount, and whether the purveyors of luxury products can continue to achieve significant growth through ecommerce. The concept and the existence of luxury as a sector are demonstrably unstable. Several factors contribute to this instability, including market conditions influenced by unforeseen factors, political change, changing consumer attitudes and preferences, technological innovation, the increased influence of social media and a new landscape where retail, manufacturing and marketing strategies need to be rethought as environmental concerns are increasingly taken into account.

   The field of luxury and luxury brands includes established companies with a long heritage – from conglomerates to small independents – to 'new' luxury, and emerging models using innovative practices. The industry structures with respect to production as well as the hierarchies that exist, and the impact these have on internal and external perceptions of luxury from the makers to the sellers and consumers are in a state of change. Further attention is given to the working structures of the ateliers, production facilities, the origins of materials and manufacturing, and the impact of technology on consumption, manufacture and sales. This provides a true insider's view of this complex world.

# Democratization of luxury: The antithesis of luxury?

The emergence of a new movement, one in which quality handcrafted items – one-offs or those made in small batches – are available to a larger audience at more accessible prices outside of a corporate context. The role of craftspeople and the value they bring to a product or service provide context when they compete with global corporations that control entire ecosystems of supply, manufacture and sales. The role of the maker is often invisible or mythologized. All these factors stack up to make for a subject of pressing concern and febrile debate.

The irony of the 'democratization' of luxury is subject to analysis as are the myths surrounding production techniques, the impact of advertising and marketing and online presence. Contentious issues surrounding perceptions of luxury and its relationship to contemporary branding as created by marketers has an impact on the consumer and their purchasing habits.

Describing and defining the contemporary luxury model dictated by luxury brands, and their business models which require ever larger segments of the global population to consume luxury, in faster fashion cycles provides further insight into luxury as a sector of the economy. The impact of these cycles now sees the removal of seasonal showcases with mass production and immediate access to products, thus, removing the notion of seasons to capitalize on sales, revenue and profit. The industry plays a crucial role in defining and maintaining perceptions of luxury, all of which are addressed in a new approach to defining luxury today.

We present the reader with the practice of luxury – luxury as a habit, within which is the complexity of experience and the production of knowledge which occurs within boundaries and constraints, be they academic, professional, historical or cultural. The concept of habitus is a means to organize experiences that are shared, for example, by members of a social class who draw on certain convictions and experiences. In short, a system of collective knowledge is produced which at the same time allows for variation, such as a 'personal style' (Bourdieu 1990: 60).

Luxury as a habitus draws on a common history or foundation that must be taken into account (even when challenged or rejected) but within which its 'agents' – be they brands, designers, consumers, etc. – can incorporate new information and respond variably. It is this shared framework through which we explore diversity and themes such as sustainability, and come to conclusions that deepen our understanding of luxury.

Luxury requires a certain type of consciousness to emerge, one at first which responded to the environment in an 'intentional manner'. The invention and the use of tools gave rise to early intellectual processes. These tools became more advanced, leading to new technologies. The emergence of markets and a push towards more innovative thinking are inevitable as new problems arise and new needs emerge.

Artisans today who work in the factories of large luxury firms or conglomerates often begin their work as unskilled factory workers with little training. This is a far cry from the skilled artisans who worked during the reign of Louis XIV under the direction of Jean-Baptiste Colbert, his Minister of Finance. Specialized manufacturers run by experts, sometimes brought in from other countries, were instrumental in shaping luxury as an enterprise and cementing the King's absolute power. He brought French traditional artisans into a codified and regulated system in which luxury items such as lace and tapestry were manufactured.

If we think of the spark of creativity and intellectual advancement occurring in prehistory when humans began to create and refine objects, and compare it to the situation of artisans in many of the luxury factories described in this chapter, the opposite force is at work: deskilling versus the building of skills and abilities. Should the artisans enter factories with skills, in many cases, these are not cultivated but destroyed. What is fostered is an ability to perform one function as quickly as possible. Any knowledge or intelligence possessed by the artisan as he or she learns to do his or her task may be seen not only as useless to the company, as we will see in Chapter 3, but as something forbidden. This, however, is not the case in all luxury environments.

Branding revolves around storytelling, myth creation and creating spectacular environments such as luxury flagship stores. This is a means of distracting the customer from the realization that many of the 'luxury' items they are presented with are mass-produced and mass marketed. This strategy is far removed from the notion of luxury as being rare and of the highest quality. Calling essentially unskilled labourers in factories 'artisans' or stretching the term to include those who are not fully able to realize their potential as artisans in the full meaning of the term is an important part of the mythology of global luxury brands.

The benefits of the brand story elevate the purveyor of any goods and services. These stories of authentic heritage or contemporary objectives such as 'make the world a better place' become the focus of determining the value of the products and services sold and the company selling them. Products begin to become and mean more than their actual physical rendition as the story behind the outcome successfully connects it to the minds and lives of those customers who choose to participate in this reveal.

The luxury domain encompasses fashion, travel, jewellery, horology, beauty products, homeware, fragrance, real estate, aviation, automotive, home furnishings and spirits, to name the major categories. Certainly, many products within a full range of sectors claim luxury status. For instance, food items such as chocolate or tea may be described as luxury. Within the domain of architecture and the construction, trade materials from flooring and tiles to bathroom fittings and fixtures and kitchen cabinetry have a luxury designation. Star architects and designers market themselves as providers of luxury lifestyles that extend beyond the physical space to products and services: Peter Marino, Rem Koolhaas and Philippe Starck are just a few examples. Establishments from fitness clubs and spas to wedding venues define themselves as providers of a luxury experience. The list goes on as the reader can well attest.

In this book, we consider luxury as a concept and material object falling within certain parameters related to its design, manufacture and unique properties. This may be in the form of a retail space, aircraft design, fashion items or a piece of jewellery. In all these sectors, the luxury designation is attributed to goods and services regardless of quality and/or price. We also consider luxury as a service and experience that unfolds in a variety of settings – including that of a physical purchase, a service provided by a concierge, or personal shopper, all of which happen within carefully constructed spaces of luxury.

The scale of the market for anything luxury is testament to its success. The term 'luxury', owing to its historical meaning, has always been held in the highest esteem. It drives sales of products and encourages the adoption of services. Due to the sheer volume and variety of products (be they yoghurt, chocolate, cars or clothing) and the wide range of services and companies positioned as luxury, the term is diluted and compromised. As the market for luxury has grown to global proportions, linking it to exclusivity seems ironic. Modern western society has everything it needs to prosper, and excess is the norm. Searching for a product or service can now be conducted instantaneously from the palm of your hand; discovery has become an algorithm linked to search engine optimization.

Luxury today is affected by the global economic climate. Recessions, global incidents, wars and pandemics all continue to impact the global luxury market but in ways they did not in the past when only a minority of privileged members of society availed themselves of luxury goods. Today through a globalized, connected and disseminated market, changes in economic climate resonate more profoundly. Most recently, the Covid-19 pandemic had a significant impact on the manufacture, distribution and consumption of luxury-branded products as factories and stores around the world were forced to close and customers in many locations had to stay at home. It is during these challenging times that the fragility of the luxury ecosystem is exposed, and, more, its purpose called into question.

# The scale of luxury businesses

The luxury market was predicted to grow exponentially in early 2020. Suggestions indicated that it would 'top €1.3 trillion ($1.5 trillion) by 2025, with experiential luxury [dining, hotels, cruises, resorts, wine and spirits, furniture, lighting, cars, boats, smartphones and technology] growing, faster at five per cent than personal luxury goods at three per cent' (Danziger 2019: n.pag.). This suddenly changed as the world went into lockdown. The value of the global luxury market was reassessed with Bain & Co saying, 'in the first quarter of 2020, we predict that global luxury sales will suffer a year-over-year decline of 25 per cent to 30 per cent, although there are signs of recovery in China' (D'Arpizio et al. 2020: n.pag.).

However, these predictions were limited to global luxury brands, those owned by conglomerates and dependent on a constant stream of fashion conscious aspirational consumers, many from emerging markets. What these brands (Louis Vuitton, Prada, Chanel, Hermès, Dior, Gucci, etc.) have in common is the need to shift large amounts of seasonal stock. With physical stores closed for a significant part of the season, and shopping limited to online purchases, they ended up with a glut of unsold merchandise that had to be heavily discounted or otherwise disposed of (Arnett 2020).

Morgan Stanley projected that LVMH's sales would decrease 49 per cent in the second quarter compared to 17 per cent in the first.

Its stock price as of 25 May 2020 was down 13 per cent and Kering's declined to 26 per cent (Sherman 2020). By January 2021, their stock price had regained momentum and continues to rise. Sales in fashion and leather goods (largely attributable to the Louis Vuitton and Dior brands) grew 18 per cent in the last three months of the fourth quarter, exceeding expectations (Guilbault 2021).

When dealing with uncertainty in the market, the scale of the luxury business also comes into play. Smaller providers of fashion-led luxury goods and services are more prone to disruption but are agile and can quickly pivot and adapt, while larger conglomerates have the financial stability to weather the storm but are more cumbersome and slower to react. There is little or no reference by analysts or the press to the designer makers who are not as reliant on the fashion-led shopper. But the larger the concern, the greater the dependence on maintaining and increasing sales within this target market.

The wealthy remain wealthy and in times of strife, more often than not tend to benefit from the misfortune of others. They have access to private travel, customized products and services and on-demand requests. Companies at the very top of the pyramid servicing this clientele will fare better than those who must sell in volume, appease shareholders and rely on a global supply chain to produce goods. The increased frequencies of sudden changes in the world that shift customer behaviour or disrupt supply chains expose their fragile position. Societies have always faced unexpected change and the survivors are those that adapted to new circumstances. That said, luxury is an integral part of society and its purveyors will always find ways to adapt and to thrive no matter what.

# The patina of the elites

A recurring question regarding how luxury is defined arises whether dealing with the long span of history and philosophical thought (Berry 1994; Lipovetsky and Roux 2003) or a focus on contemporary manifestations of luxury (Armitage and Roberts 2016) and its strategic management (Kapferer et al. 2017; Serdari 2020; Cantista and Sadaba 2019). We touch on this, and, in each chapter, this question will be revisited in relation to the topic addressed.

Thorstein Veblen in 1899 posited three basic, defining features of luxury: scarcity, extra value and high quality. Even in prehistory, there is evidence of the precursors of luxury as man sought to escape from the toils of everyday life. It is society's elites who, for a long time, defined the parameters around these variables but in today's world, luxury brands, to a large extent, control the discourse on luxury.

Luxury brands are economically and symbolically powerful entities that continually make significant strides to expand their scope of influence. They claim the most expensive and important locations for their flagship stores in the world's capitals. Their strategy is significant as not only do they occupy retail spaces in the most expensive shopping destinations in the world – Madison Avenue in New York, Avenue Montaigne in Paris, Bond Street in London, Ginza in Tokyo and Myeong-dong in Seoul – but they also tend to move to what may be less obvious locations in trendy areas such as SoHo in New York and Shoreditch in London. The location and the association made in the minds of consumers, particularly as property value in these areas is at the top end, create an impressive foundation for luxury to build upon, being both physical and psychological. As brands invest more in their digital presence, significant resources are allocated to the creation of an exceptional online experience.

The most well-known brands – Chanel, Louis Vuitton, Gucci and Prada, for example – occupy a great deal of space in the consciousness of the global consumer population whether or not they actually buy the products. With the rise of influencers and celebrity endorsers (those paid to promote particular products) and the use of social media, these influencers and a wider range of consumers contribute to defining and sustaining the luxury mystique.

The parameters of how luxury is defined will of course broaden as we consider not only our own views but also those of people holding a variety of cultural and political ideals. Nevertheless, it is the elite – and by this we mean those who hold the highest rank (including the titled and wealthy, intellectuals and others who possess cultural capital) – in a given society and, to an extent, those designated tastemakers whether fashion editors, buyers, critics, celebrities or bloggers, who deem whether or not something is seen as luxury. For luxury brands, the opinions of those who enjoy high status associated with longstanding economic position and family background are the most coveted. They are followed by many who more recently acquired their economic, social and cultural capital, as well as influencers, celebrities and those who have large followings. Historically, these individuals have been the mainstay in popularizing and enabling the growth of the luxury industry.

Interestingly, social media influencers do not need any previous knowledge and/or experience with a product or service. Influencers play a part in consecrating products and services as luxury without typically having any real and ongoing engagement with a particular brand. This can devalue and even undermine a brand. As both Veblen and Georg Simmel ([1904] 1957) discussed, luxury status can also be lost; something that has been elevated can fall from grace when it is widely adopted. It is this that poses the biggest risk for purveyors of luxury goods.

If designated tastemakers, once regarded as makers of fashion, are now nothing more than followers of fashion whose role it is to sell mass-produced products, they will continue to lose credibility with a desired luxury clientele. This approach is traced back to the first decades of the 1900s when people like Edward Bernays (Bernays 1947) pioneered (mass) consumption as an act of public and individual freedom. In his famous 'The engineering of consent', he explains the impact media has on people (as masses): 'We must recognise the significance of modern communications not only as a highly organised mechanical web but as a potent force for social good and possible evil' (Bernays 1947: 113).

This idea is analysed in detail in the 2002 BBC documentary on Bernays, *The Century of the Self* (Curtis 2002). The tier system currently in place, and one that has continued to grow since the late 1980s has in effect democratized luxury through the creation of a pyramid structure that has the untouchable (bespoke) at the top and the mass produced at the bottom (luxury brands). Nearly anyone with some disposable income or credit can buy into the world of a luxury brand. No longer are the products destined only for 'elites' as they are increasingly made available to the masses.

However, as a fundamental part of the consumption mechanism of luxury, the idea of desire and something unachievable still needs to be present in certain market segments. Luxury-branded products are no longer just for the elite, but they need to retain their elitarian patina in order to convince customers to continue to purchase them and to maintain that element of desire.

# Of cultural capital and influence(rs)

There may or may not be consensus on luxury both on the definition or its domain, particularly as the numbers of those joining the ranks of the elite expands, and the number of cultural influencers grow. In simple terms, there is no absolute evidence that the cultural capital of this expanding moneyed class is itself expanding. It is simply that their wealth has increased, as has their spending power. James

Twitchell suggests that 'in a world in which so many different brands compete for our attention, the prestige of one seemingly overnight luxury soon cancels out another, and "the best" is simply the latest, the hottest, the most talked about' (2002: 25). This reflects the similarities among contemporary luxury brands, their fluctuating social and cultural value and distinct lack of staying power as defined by the media, social media clout and fashion trends. Twitchell suggests: 'The new luxury is the ineluctable result of a market economy and a democratic political system' (2002: 25). He quotes Thomas Beer who wrote, 'money does not rule democracy. Money is democracy' (cited in Twitchell 2002: 25).

Where luxury was once reserved for those who could afford it, new capitalist systems encourage the consumption of luxury-branded goods and services marketed as luxury by anyone, even by those who cannot afford it. What is clear is that with an emergent, new, monied class, the value of luxury and its definitions are constantly changing. Within this ever-changing landscape, we see how value and street credibility defined by users and influencers is amassed or dissipated as trends change. One could also see how different social groups or 'tribes' actively adopt or appropriate brands and the responses to this by the brand should it not comply with their brand strategy.

Famously adopted by 'chavs' in the United Kingdom in the late 1990s, Burberry opted for a complete rebrand to remove negative publicity generated by its 'undesirable' clientele. This is typical of a fashion system that promotes democracy as long as it fulfils the ambitions of the brand. Where luxury resists change, it is less likely to have to respond to fashion and fashion trends.

## What is scarcity?

And as fashion dictates, the seasons change with new products released in vast quantities resulting in more products on the market and more opportunity to make a purchase. This raises questions about scarcity if one is to consider luxury products as scarce. The idea of limiting the amount of something probably stems from the early fourteenth century when spices and exotic novelties were discovered as explorers sailed the high seas and established the trade routes to make that limited supply available to more people at great expense.

But what is scarcity? When Hermès begins farming its own crocodiles in America and Australia and steps up production to keep up with demand for its coveted bags, do they cease to be scarce? Are their prefabricated waiting lists simply there to create demand for products that are in fact in mass circulation (Reuters staff 2017; Aloisi and Spencer 2021)? Compared to other luxury brands producing and selling exponentially more, perhaps Hermès is safe. It depends how one defines scarcity. Luxury brands define scarcity through self-imposed assessments. Furthermore, they assign definitions that may imply scarcity. These include limited editions, special editions and exclusive offers, which could simply take the form of an exclusive colourway that make an already mass-produced item coveted.

Vertical integration allows the manufacturer to increase or reduce supply at will. Selective distribution is an enabler in that the luxury brand has further control over the market. A product may be scarce in one country but in mass supply in another. Typically, a product marketed as 'scarce' demands a higher price. This creates further demand not only for the product in question but also for other products sold by the company. If one takes the notion of mass production out of the equation and considers the Aston Martin One-77 or a watch made by R. W. Smith, where every component is handmade or finished by a craftsperson, it is clear that there are distinct differences in approach. On the one hand, there are hundreds of thousands of the same product mass produced and sold as luxury, and, on the other hand, a limited series of products handmade and sold in single numbers also sold as luxury.

As far as luxury brands go, more questions are asked than can be answered. They are notoriously lacking in transparency where product is concerned. Do they produce 'limited' quantities to preserve their image or do they satisfy shareholder demand for profit and consumer demand for more merchandise? It goes without saying it would not be financially viable to produce all products in limited production runs. This will change with technological advances in manufacturing, as there will be an increase in efficiency for the manufacturer to produce goods on demand that can be customized and personalized without any additional costs.

What is unquestionable is that the production and sale of goods operates on a logic that appeases the shareholders. For example, putting a limited quantity of merchandise on the shop floor while maintaining a massive stockpile behind the scenes in stockrooms is a common approach to illustrate exclusivity where it does not exist. People whose opinions matter and on whom the brand's image relies might accept this narrative. Once a threshold is crossed, one's top clients and advocates may drop the brand.

Value and quality are also relative to a given context and to a variety of factors. Mass-produced items can approach the quality of luxury and substances; laboratory made fragrances, for example, that have been artificially produced may take on the actual qualities of a natural substance or appear to be something they are not. Diamonds can be artificially produced, presenting a huge dilemma for an industry whose existence relies on scarcity, extra value and high quality for profit. Mary Frances Gerety coined the phrase 'A diamond is forever' for De Beers in 1947 as part of a revival marketing campaign to increase diamond sales. De Beers continue to use the slogan today as it has successfully encouraged growth in the market. The slogan cleverly circumvents the quality criteria associated with diamonds and creates an impression that all diamonds – regardless of their size, cut, colour or clarity – are of value. Of course, this is of great financial benefit to De Beers, which sells relatively common small stones alongside the larger, unique specimens. No longer is a diamond forever unless it is rare, very large and of the highest quality FL/D (flawless/completely colourless). Despite the complexity of the diamond market, stores selling diamond jewellery are not that dissimilar to those selling fashion or leather goods.

Inflated prices tend to accompany the marketed superior product. A large flawless diamond from Tiffany & Co. differs considerably if one were to compare the same purchase from a Hatton Garden wholesaler in London or a 47th Street seller in New York. It is the brand that adds the value to what is essentially the same product. To give one example, Heine (2012) speaks of price, quality, aesthetics, rarity, extraordinariness and symbolism. If man-made diamonds could be bought cheaply on the market, would they have the same value to consumers as a De Beers diamond or as a diamond engagement ring purchased at Tiffany & Co.? We see in this example how price, symbolism, extraordinariness and aesthetics come into play. Receiving the De Beers diamond in the iconic Tiffany's box with its blue ribbon tied in a certain way and perhaps even having the chance to view it in one of its artfully designed flagship stores in a major city centre, assisted by an attentive, knowledgeable and professional salesperson all the while being conscious of the long and venerable history of this brand adds a dimension to this purchase that transcends the physical properties of the diamond, as spectacular as it may be in its own right.

The man-made diamond may be indistinguishable even to a jeweller and the Tiffany setting can be easily reproduced but for the owner of this ring, it may not feel as valuable, special or rare stripped of these commercially constructed features, particularly if it is also produced in a laboratory. However, as with all things luxury and the perceptions associated with it, time will tell. Synthetic diamonds are indistinguishable from those mined and made from the same material as those that are mined – carbon. If a mass marketed and moderately priced purse or pair of shoes appears to be of the same quality as those from Louis Vuitton, would a significant number of customers forego the logo and prefer to do something else with their hundreds or thousands of pounds, dollars, euros or other currencies? Or would the LV logo, the branding and the store experience be more important?

Each brand is focusing more intently on its intellectual property (IP). This is in part as a reaction to the constant and growing threat of counterfeiting in the luxury goods industry. The IP legal framework is also used as an important mechanism enabling brands to distinguish what they do from their competitors. The expression of IP extends the brand's reach to encompass not only the product but also the marketing and promotional materials they generate. This activity stretches the brands' 'world of' and is becoming an accepted technique to justify the high price points of luxury-branded products. This storytelling, as is discussed later in the book, although intangible as a physical object, adds much needed value to products the brands sell. The scales can be tipped in many directions.

Is the future of luxury precarious or is it secure, relying as it does on fundamental aspects of human nature and the need to distinguish oneself? To be sure, the future of any one brand, even those who now appear to be the strongest, is precarious, particularly as the high street is under threat and many new players are replicating successful brand DNA.

The idea of luxury has secured a place in contemporary western culture and the term is now part of the common parlance in established and emerging economies. The contemporary concept of luxury has been influenced by historical and social factors. These include when and where the concept of luxury emerged, its evolution in a variety of contexts, and its complex material history as an object of beauty, desire and commerce. Each of these facets has impacted contemporary definitions of luxury, which in turn influence practices by a variety of agents.

While luxury has long been a marker of social status and class, it does not necessarily have to remain the preserve of the few who are able to afford rare objects. Indeed luxury has entered a more 'democratic' phase. The factors, which contribute to an object or experience being defined as luxury, have expanded. Traditionally, high-quality materials, craftsmanship and exclusivity were requisite features of luxury, but more recently mass-produced products have attained luxury status, sometimes entirely through branding and promotional strategies. This is the complete antithesis of what luxury historically represented.

In a global context, where consumption is increasing exponentially at the same time as the world's resources are diminishing, luxurious consumption can be seen as politically and/or ethically suspect. The political implications of conspicuous consumption take on greater resonance.

What is the future of luxury in a world beset with financial turmoil, and characterized by an increasing gap between the rich and the poor? This gap in equality will continue to be exacerbated by global events. It will force us to focus on the global economies, the ways in which we shop, our reasons for shopping and, at the same time, force us to focus on what we really need and why. Will the consumer acknowledge the impact of their actions should they choose to continue to consume in the way that they are used to? Or will they adopt a more selective approach to shopping?

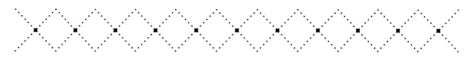

# 3

# Contemporary Notions of Luxury

*The contemporary luxury industry has undergone a metamorphosis. The transition from typically small and very specialized providers of bespoke products at the high end to a global industry is a major shift. Luxury is a significant contributing sector to the global economy with a variety of important segments, including core businesses such as personal luxury goods (apparel, accessories, beauty products, jewellery and timepieces), automotive (its most lucrative sector), aeronautical and yachts, wine and spirits, homeware and luxury experiences (which encompass travel and fine dining).*

## Luxury today

Many of the most prominent luxury brands are publicly held and traded entities – like Ferrari – or part of conglomerates like LVMH, Kering and Richemont. As such, they are tracked and analysed. Discussing the emergence of the global luxury brand industry, Tim Jackson points to the 1990s as the time when brands that had been smaller family enterprises grew and merged to become a consolidated economic sector. These enterprises were founded on the 'premium quality and the aesthetic value of their goods' (Jackson 2002: 161). Steven Greenhouse reflects on Louis Vuitton's past, just two years after it became a part of the LVMH conglomerate:

> For more than a century, the Vuitton name remained magical, thanks to a clientele that included Emperor Hirohito, Douglas Fairbanks, Coco Chanel, Charles Lindbergh and various Vanderbilts.

Vuitton built a trunk with a fold out bed for Savorgnan de Brazza, explorer of the Congo, and a trunk with a fold out altar for Pierre Teilhard de Chardin, the theologian.

(1989: n.pag.)

The focus of attention on a select clientele shifted to a primary emphasis on global marketing and branding efforts. As Dana Thomas puts it, '[l]uxury fashion was in the throes of a transformation from smaller, founder run companies that catered to a niche clientele to global publicly traded corporations headed by business tycoons with no previous links to the industry' (2016: 170).

Bernard Arnault previously ran his family's construction company, then '[i]n 1989, [he] became the majority shareholder of LVMH Moët Hennessy – Louis Vuitton, creating the world's leading luxury products group. Mr. Arnault has been Chairman and CEO of the company since that date' (LVMH 2020: n.pag.). LVMH owns 75 brands including Louis Vuitton, Dior, Fendi, Loewe and Fred. Richemont was founded in 1988 by Johann Rupert and owns Cartier, Dunhill and Yoox/Net-a-Porter. Francois Pinault founded Pinault SA in 1988, which changed its name to Pinault-Printemps-Redoute (PPR) in 1994 and became Kering in 2014. This group acquired Gucci and Yves Saint Laurent in 1999 and later, other notable brands such as Bottega Veneta and Balenciaga. It is solidified as a global luxury conglomerate.

The acquisition of individual brands, which were run in a very different way, was quite contentious as were the battles between Arnault and Pinault for the acquisition of Gucci. From the 'unceremonious' firing of Dior's couturier, Marc Bohan, to reducing the family members of the Vuitton brand to tears after securing control of Louis Vuitton, Arnault developed a reputation as the 'wolf in cashmere' (Thomas 2016: 170–71). Henry Racamier, who headed a steel company, married the great-granddaughter of the founder of Louis Vuitton and transformed a company that seemed according to Steven Greenhouse (1989) stuck in the nineteenth century with two stores – one in Paris and one in Nice – into a billion-dollar company after he took control in 1977. As he explains: 'Racamier has put Vuitton in the tiny elite of companies that can boast net profit margins of 19 cents on each dollar of sales' (Greenhouse 1989: n.pag.). At the time he wrote his *New York Times* article in 1989, there were 135 stores with 20 in Japan. Racamier says he understood the changes that were needed to ensure the success of the business. 'The clientele that would buy products grew immensely in the 1960s and 1970s. We saw this sleeping potential'; but, he adds: 'We would not be happy if everyone in the world owned a Louis Vuitton purse' (cited in Greenhouse 1989: n.pag.). Greenhouse goes on to say that as Arnault became the dominant shareholder of LVMH, Racamier was stripped of his title of deputy chairman and later removed as the head of Vuitton. Alain Chevalier, the president of Moët Hennessy who executed the merger with Louis Vuitton, was forced to resign. 'They did not foresee the new era, in which aggressive entrepreneurs using arcane financing structures could pounce on even the largest and most glamorous prey. That was his opening' (Greenhouse 1989: n.pag.).

In just 40-odd years, Louis Vuitton went from owning two stores to having over 400 worldwide. Since the merger with Moët Hennessey and the formation of LVMH, the concern has grown to some 75 companies in five sectors from around the world (LVMH 2019). This takes them worlds away from Racamier's comment, '[w]e would not be happy if everyone in the world owned a Louis Vuitton purse', to the current state in which they act as if they do want everyone in the world to own a Louis Vuitton purse. Global dominance, which ultimately leads to greater product diffusion, is a clear ambition for the LVMH group. It is not only good for business; it is good for the shareholders.

Today, luxury is big business and is not limited to just fashion, accessories and beauty products. The automotive industry has also undergone an extensive transformation. Like fashion, there are suppliers of affordable goods and those that remain the preserve of the very wealthy. But contemporary luxury in the supercar world is much more clearly defined than in fashion. In most instances, craftsmanship and price play a decisive role. But there are some similarities. Most luxury carmakers also began as small concerns. As times changed and moved on, global automotive companies such as BMW and Volkswagen acquired rights to Rolls Royce, Bentley, Ferrari, Maybach, Bugatti and Lamborghini. The attention invested in these high-end car brands, not only to aesthetic detail and subsequent desirability but also, very importantly, to technological advancement relating to performance, plays a critical part. In this world, the designer craftsperson works closely with the engineers to ensure all component parts work together to provide the optimal driving experience for the customer and their passengers.

At this level of purchase, where the most expensive of all automobiles is the Bugatti La Voiture Noire, costing $18.7 million, the expectation would naturally be for perfection (Chang 2019). In some extreme cases, the ownership and rights to manufacture of distinctive high-end cars (such as BMW, Rolls Royce, Bugatti and Lamborghini to name but a few) is not immediately clear but, despite this, these car companies maintain their distinct presence in the marketplace. They do not necessarily compete for customers, as the super-wealthy typically own more than one supercar.

Engineer and inventor Ettore Bugatti founded the car company in 1909 in Molsheim in the Alsace region of France. Ettore Bugatti was 20 when he made his second automobile for which he won a prize. Bugatti entered into various contracts with automakers before and after founding his company. In 1911, he made racing cars for Peugeot. Bugatti's cars were legendary, winning 1851 victories including the first Monaco Grand Prix and the Le Mans. By the time of his death, fewer than 8000 Bugatti cars were made. Volkswagen acquired the company in 1988 (Craddock 2016; Sansome 2011). The company describes itself as 'the world's most powerful, fastest, most exclusive and luxurious production hyper sports cars' (Bugatti 2019: n.pag.). The Divo, with a production limit of 45 cars, costs $6 million. The Bugatti Chiron, of which only a total of 500 will be made, starts above $3 million. In 2019, the company announced it sold 80 cars in total (Bugatti 2019). To secure an order, one pays half the price as a deposit and the rest seven months later once the car is finished and delivered. Customers visit the headquarters in France to personalise their automobiles. About 20 engineers and technicians work on each car. Every year the car is picked up for servicing from wherever in the world the owner happens to be. Bugatti's CEO Stephan Winkelmann describes the customer as 'a self-made man' who collects cars and has, on average, at least 30 in his garage; this is likely in addition to owning a private jet and a yacht (Nicoletti 2018: n.pag.). Says Cedric Davy, CEO in the US: 'Our goal is to be the benchmark'. And he goes on to say: 'If it is comparable, it's no longer a Bugatti' (Taub 2020: n.pag.). Board member Christopher Piochon says: 'Each vehicle is unique, in no way comparable to a fellow member of the Chiron family' (Bekker 2020: n.pag.). This is a result of the level of customization. Unlike fashion, there is no seasonal cycle. The manufacture is defined as an edition (the total number of cars produced in any one series).

The luxury market is one of contradictions and contrasts. All manner of products and services are designated luxury. It could be a multi-million-dollar car or a handbag. What is relevant is the maker's commitment and artistry.

# The luxury spectrum

Atelier Renard, founded in Paris in the 1930s, is a small leather shop specializing in hand-made leather goods. Customers can purchase directly from the store, personalise an item or commission one of their artisans to create something bespoke. *Le Figaro* readers were told in its *Madame* magazine supplement, they could choose anything from a small 'crocodile skin case' to 'hand-sewn cabin trunks' and 'the range of creations signed by Atelier Renard is impressive and limitless' (2019: n.pag.) Owner Brigitte Montaut was asked about how their creative process works.

> Creating an exclusive piece for a customer necessarily involves metaphorically stepping into their world in order to advise them on the choice of shapes, leathers, colours and even thread: all the details that make a bag unique and of exceptional quality. For me, real luxury is exactly that: an alliance between the time that can be unstintingly devoted to each individual, the rare quality of leather, and the joy of inventing your own object – all coupled with expertise conveyed through a perfectly skilled touch, right the way through to the smallest stitch.
>
> (*La Resérve Magazine* n.d.: n.pag.)

We selected Bugatti and Atelier Renard to illustrate the extreme spectrum of luxury. What the companies have in common, despite their differences, is an underlying principle of luxury – to produce high-quality products using the finest materials, made by artisans. Their approaches are obviously different but this illustrates their common values. These companies produce luxury products significantly different in type and price range, and appeal to a different demographic – but both provide a unique experience to their customers, including exceptional service focused on their needs and desires. They produce items in a limited quantity, but of the highest quality made by experts who are afforded the time necessary to make each item, either alone or in collaboration with others.

At the top of the luxury brand pyramid, there will always be the exception where the bespoke offer is a remarkably different experience to that of walking into the store. It is unlikely a customer would ever meet the maker of their bespoke artefact in any of the luxury brand environments. What has become clear is that the overarching luxury brand business is founded on the principles of the top end of service and then watered down to appease the aspirational consumer of mass-produced products. When it comes to the number of items produced, the speed at which they are made, and the connection the customer has to the products they buy, the experience is completely different depending on the level at which they purchase.

For example, Hermès bears more resemblance to a traditional luxury company than Prada, as their bespoke service is more extensive. In keeping with its tradition of made-to-measure leather and other goods, Hermès runs its Le Sur-Mesure workshop where custom orders are designed and made. Director of Design and Engineering, Axel de Beaufort, says he does not involve himself with retail matters, illustrating the division between levels of design, production and retail. The design and engineering staff at the workshop take on about 300 projects per year. Le Sur-Mesure has a varied portfolio of activity, producing products such as a skateboard ($2975), boxing gloves ($44,100) and a fishing rod ($11,800). In addition, the workshop undertakes more elaborate private commissions including the interior of a Bugatti Chiron and an Airbus ACJ 319 private jet.

Hermès has an interesting way of working in that there are clear divisions between labour and product categories. At the very top end is the Le Sur-Mesure, in the middle are the Kelly and Birkin bags, and below that are the mass-produced, predominantly machine-made products sold in their stores. There is, however, some confusion and apparent mystique around the production of both the Kelly and Birkin bags. Apparently the most coveted of all Hermès products. Their prices differ, depending on what one orders, ranging between $9000 and $35,000+, respectively. The price depends on which of the thousands of options of leather or finishes the client selects. In the most extreme circumstances, one could be purchased at auction for upwards of $300,000. Hermès bags are the biggest selling, and the most popular handbag at auction and on resale anywhere in the world. Sometimes, thousands of bags are sold at any time (Ryan 2020).

Some say they are handmade in a workshop, others say they are made on a production line. Some say it takes 48 hours to make one bag, and others say it takes twelve hours. In the press, we are told you can buy one on the odd occasion in a Hermès store, that they are on a waiting list, that there is no waiting list if you are wealthy, and that they are made in limited numbers. Another area of dispute. What we are told is the production of both bags is in the region of 12,000–120,000 each year. One has to wonder if any of the information forthcoming is reliable and or true or simply a marketing ploy to keep the mythology of these handbags alive. Hermès maintains its silence presumably to perpetuate the story around a product like any other produced in the thousands and sold at hugely inflated prices.

In contrast Prada's iconic bag, the Galleria, apparently takes six hours for artisans to make (Todd 2020). The price for a micro-sized Galleria bag is about $2000. One could compare this to the Hermès 2002 – 20 bag, which costs $9000. It is not abundantly clear why at this level there are such dramatic differences in price. For the most part, there is no rationale between price, time taken to make the product, quality of the materials used and the ability of the artisan. What is clear is that visual language, opacity and self-generated hype create the stories perpetuating the sales of products – regardless of cost.

# The changing tide: Luxury from then to now

Luxury is something we can trace back to prehistory. Georges Bataille says: 'The history of life on earth is mainly the effect of a wild exuberance; the dominant event is the development of luxury' ([1949] 1988: 33). Humans turn to luxury to represent status and honour, the superiority of man over the animal world, and over other men and indeed, to display victory. For luxury objects to be capable of conveying such glory, excellence must be displayed in their construction. A boy and girl buried around 24,000 years ago were discovered in a cave in Sunghir, Russia, each holding a carved ivory spear. Red ochre, fox teeth and about 5000 ivory beads, probably sewn to their ornate clothing, surrounded their skeletal remains (Wesler 2012: 41). The luxury bequeathed upon those children was an indication of their importance and wealth in that society and reflected their family status. As another example, in a cave in Botswana, 70,000-year-old spearheads of various colours – including white and red – were left as offerings in a pit in front of a 6 × 20 foot rock styled to look like a python with indentations made to resemble scales and a mouth (Doyle 2007; The Research Council of Norway 2006). This archaeological find is the oldest indication of religious ritual. Significant too was that these well-constructed spearheads, described as 'beautiful', and were burned as a sacrifice to the python. They were not merely utilitarian items; they were jewel-like luxury objects perhaps constructed specifically to honour this deity by people who had travelled great distances (Vogt 2012).

Dietmar Neufeld (2009: 674) speaks of the way in which deities are portrayed in Ancient Near Eastern texts. In the Descent of Ishtar, deities are 'adorned in robes of grand splendour and glory' (Neufeld 2008: 674). Their splendour is embodied in part in their clothing and the Sumerian word *melammu* signifies 'a bright garment of flame and light, covering the person dressed in it or endowed with it' (Emelianov 2010: 1112). It was only gods and beings possessing divine attributes, such as dragons, which were endowed with such radiance, explains Elena Cassin (1968: 66). The oldest king in the Assyrian empire, associated with being radiant and shining, is Sargon of Akkad. Neufeld discusses the account given by Titus Flavius Josephus of King Agrippa who 'intentionally amazed the crowd' in a garment 'woven completely of silver so that its texture was indeed wondrous' (2008: 669). He explains that in the sun it became 'wondrously radiant and by its glitter inspired fear and awe on those who gazed intently upon it' (Josephus cited in Neufeld 2008: 669). Louis XIV, who believed in his divine right, chose to associate himself with the sun, making it his emblem. The symbol is connected to Apollo, the sun god of the Greeks and Romans.

Whether we consider prehistory or some time in between, or an imaginary post-history, certain factors remain constant. People make sense of the social world through verbal and non-verbal communication. Societies are built on symbols with significant meaning to members. The clothes people wear and the objects they display shape and announce their identity. One's role and status is communicated through extravagant displays of luxury. In contemporary society, this is accomplished through the display of recognizable brands, such as displaying the interlocking back-to-back Cs or the double Gs in the Chanel and Gucci logos, or by more subtle codes deciphered only by knowledgeable others. Supercars do not even need a logo, and discreet whispers of membership to an exclusive club also communicate status, superficial or not. In an interview with shoemaker Olga Berluti (2009) she says of luxury: 'It's not education, but it's to teach somebody to respect the deep profound state of the artwork and to feel attached and to feel linked to an object is "being in luxury", there's a special relationship.' Luxury need not be opulent, it can be understated or it can take on new meanings depending on the values of a given society.

Meaning is dynamic and always subject to change. As Robert Perinbanayagam puts it: 'The production of meaning must be viewed then as an act, albeit an act that demands completion from self and/ or others, whether it is a speech act or a written act' (1985: 12). The emergent nature of meaning is also embodied in social acts, in which people take part in everyday life. Simmel captured this in his 1904 essay 'Fashion', describing the cycle of change initiated by those at the top who abandon styles when those who are inferior to them with respect to social class adopt them. Veblen also raises related issues when he discusses conspicuous consumption in the *Theory of the Leisure Class*. In various stages of barbarism in which a leisure class is present, there is a rigorous adherence to class-based distinctions. Men of the upper classes are 'debarred, from all industrial occupations' (Veblen [1899] 1953: 3). As societies advance and become more complex, conspicuous consumption becomes an important indicator of status to a larger circle of others – hence one needs an ornate carriage and other extensions of self, not just an estate. Women of the leisure class serve as a means of displaying their family or husband's status. Poor women had to work outside the home for an income as well as inside the home to provide for the needs of husbands and children. For middle-class women, work inside the home may have been one's sole occupation. Veblen speaks of how high heels and the skirt 'hampers the wearer at every turn and incapacitates her for all useful exertion' ([1899] 1953: 172). As a woman was under her husband's domination, wives of upper-class men could be found wearing corsets described by Veblen as a 'mutilation' rendering females 'permanently and obviously unfit for work' and hence an object of leisure. He calls the display of 'refined tastes, manners, and habits of life' the 'voucher of a life of leisure' ([1899] 1953: 48–49).

The meaning of luxury itself has changed conceptually and in its material existence. The idea that a man would use a walking stick to display that he is a gentleman of leisure is rooted in the symbolism of the stick as a weapon and its user having strength, power, authority and social prestige and has since been replaced by a more active notion of leisure involving sporting activities and physical fitness (Hovailo 2020: n.pag.). The only physical representation here is physique, and perhaps the accessories that endorse an intention through their association to an activity. As David Hume wrote in 1742:

> Luxury is a word of uncertain signification, and may be taken in a good as well as in a bad sense. It signifies great refinement and gratification of the senses: and any degree of it may be innocent or blameable, according to the age, or country, or condition of the person.
>
> ([1972] 1875: 268)

While it has certain boundaries, luxury can also display a great deal of fluidity, inhabiting contradictory spaces and drawing condemnation or praise. Luxury theorizing took the form of moral arguments focused on the polis, and civic life and responsibility, and the necessary control of luxury as a vice (Socrates, Plato, Aristotle) or was aimed at curtailing luxury, associating it with greed and lust (Aquinas). Economic arguments emanated from Hume, Smith, Mandeville and Keynes, who wanted to vindicate commerce, and Veblen and Marx, who wanted to control or transform it. Luxury has become a subject explored in a variety of disciplines spanning from the humanities and social sciences, to art, design and business.

Christopher Berry's (1994) historical and philosophical exploration and categorization of luxury through the ages; David Cloutier's (2015) polemical analysis tracing luxury's history and focused on Catholic theology; Maxine Berg's (2005) economic, technological and cultural history of luxury in Britain; and Gilles Lipovetsky's and

Elyette Roux's (2003) exploration of the evolution of thought on luxury and its role in civilization from the religious to the hyper-commercial realm, explore the profound role luxury has played in shaping history, contemporary society and global economies.

And despite all the commentary about luxury's characteristics, it remained for most of history in the hands of the haves, not the have-nots: the wealthy, aristocratic classes, who had the means to partake of a luxurious lifestyle – however it was defined. The notion of vice and virtue as expressed by Mandeville in the *Fable of the Bees* in 1714 dominated the eighteenth century. Up to the nineteenth century, luxury followed an aristocratic, artisanal model where the most skilled artisans created objects for the aristocratic class, who collected antiquities that were passed down to the next generation, thereby extending their investment and its associated value. Luxury has evolved from a craft with artistic dimensions into a multi-sectoral global industry.

# Luxury and fashion

There were, and in fact, still are so many different views as to what luxury is and is not, whether it is a good or an evil, a form of artistry or a business, but despite this opinion has shifted.

> [...] luxury as it had been viewed for centuries underwent a lasting devaluation: from myth to a fiction, from an ethic to a prejudice, and from an essential general element of moral theory to a minor, technical element of economic theory.
>
> (Sekora 1977: 112)

As times changed, what has dominated the luxury market is the economic value and market growth. And as the twenty-first century has unfolded, luxury and its democratization saw the connection with fashion become inextricably linked.

Lipovetsky and Roux (2003) speak of the phases of luxury and say it is entering a modern phase. Severed from the realm of the eternal, and later from an existence in this world where it is tied to traditional social systems, and once wedded to fashion, it is now free to become superficial – a novelty. With couture, a commercial logic based on limited production emerges. The couturier or couturière creates a collection or a line of clothing with several styles clients can purchase and have a custom fit. Each salon has 'forms' built in the size and shape of their clients, they are offered fittings, and like the Bugatti customer, can be 'serviced' anywhere in the world. This is a highly specialized business comprising skill and craftsmanship. What we see is a transition from the dressmaker who made one-of-a-kind clothing exclusively for one client to, decades later, an industry – in this instance, fashion – adopting the term 'luxury' to add value to widely available fashion goods.

Haute couture lays the seeds for mass-produced fashion. This methodology is not dissimilar to the automotive industry. Mercedes Benz, BMW and Audi follow the same trajectory. Once the pinnacle of luxury cars, they too have effected change through the introduction of smaller, more affordable cars. At the very top end, the Mercedes Benz S Class is typically the most expensive starting at about $95,000. But if ownership of a Mercedes is an aspiration, one could buy an A Class at $30,000 – however, with cars, the list price is always negotiable and finance options are always available to the customer. Regardless of how a product is paid for, the symbolism remains.

We live in a symbolic environment in which meaning has to be assigned and interpreted. Objects become commodities in a consumer society. Roland Barthes (1957) speaks of semiological systems that tell a story and have their own codes or structures of meaning. They draw on meanings that can be determined and are based on universal truths in a social system shaping values and behaviours. The luxury industry creates myths drawing on a traditional craft heritage founded on the place of origin and its history.

As society becomes organized around consumption, Jean Baudrillard (1996: 87) sees it as entering a new realm. The process of symbolic exchange had once been anchored in values backed by tradition and significations were thus clear. As society moves to a second and then third order of signification, the distinctions between reality and representation continue to break down. In the second order, we enter an age of mass production where copies are indistinguishable from the original. The distinction between reality and representation vanishes. Simulacra are detached from meaningful signifiers and we have a reality driven by simulation in the third order. The Birkin bag is more akin to a second-order simulacra pointing back to a heritage, which Hermès no longer fully possesses, or which was compromised as the brand grew. A Michael Kors bag is closer to the third-order simulacra, where as Baudrillard says when speaking of fashion, 'signifieds come unthreaded', and 'the parades of the signifier [...] no longer lead anywhere' (1996: 87). We are faced with a 'liquidation of meaning'. Michael Kors, whose career includes having been creative director at Céline, understands the luxury industry, uses signifiers associated with luxury and calls itself a luxury brand. Yet products are cheaply made in factories in China and workers have nothing in common with artisans (Li 2018).

# It wasn't how we shopped but where

Luxury has come to be seen as something to be branded and marketed in such a way so as to elicit emotions – not because of the innate characteristics of a luxury item but because of something outside of or separate from products: an advertising campaign, merchandizing, the store design, the website or social media platform experience. All this is relatively new. In the late 1990s and reaching a peak in the early 2000s, star architects were called on to design flagship stores in fashion capitals around the world. Frank Gehry, Rem Koolhaas, Renzo Piano, Peter Marino, Eric Carlson, Christian de Portzamparc and others built hundreds of stores for the major luxury fashion brands. This heralded the start of destination shopping as well as shopping as an experience on a much larger scale.

New tactics have been employed to entice customers back into stores. They focus on an enhanced experience and include a number of additional services such as private events, customised and technologically enabled shopping experiences and the smarter use of data analytics to personalise the shopping experience. Special 'salons' continue to be built to offer privacy and to accord exceptional service not only to the existing high-value customer but to a wider range of clients to make them feel appreciated and extend the brand's VIP experience. This experiential approach to selling is replicated at all levels along the luxury continuum. Exceptional service is not limited to the luxury experience, it is found in all sectors of the market including the high street. Whether one is purchasing a supercar, private jet, couture or anything bespoke, the experience is critical.

# The new elites and other players

The new elites in society are not as easy to define. There are many variations and contradictions in their consuming behaviour, and their consumption manifests itself in different ways. For example, there are conspicuous consumers who spend unashamedly on high profile, highly visible products and services. And there are those who consume luxury more discreetly and are more interested in true quality and heritage, not just the signifiers of wealth and status. Financial crashes and pandemics may deter some but not all of these consumers who are intent on living the high life – conspicuously or inconspicuously. It is these consumers, along with the aspirational consumer, who sustain the fortunes of the luxury conglomerates and independent giants. And, finally, there are those who are less concerned with material objects, and care more about environmental and social issues.

In discussing Texas millionaires and the newly rich, C. Wright Mills points out that there is a conspicuous display of wealth in the latter, but that in

> established local society, the men and women of the fourth and fifth generation are quietly expensive and expensively quiet; they are, in fact, often deliberately inconspicuous in their consumption with unpretentious farm houses and summer retreats, they often live quite simply, and certainly without any ostentatious display of vulgar opulence.
>
> ([1956] 2000: 59)

Elizabeth Currid-Halkett speaks of how the new elites, termed the 'aspirational class', have adopted more subtle ways of displaying the privilege they very much want to preserve through cultural capital versus consumption (2019: 18, 22). As consumers, they invest in things that make them smarter and more socially aware and make them feel ethical and enlightened. In fact, members of this new elite are not necessarily wealthy as their class position is dependent on cultural capital: 'they are educated and they prize knowledge and engage in consumer practices that reflect these values' (Currid-Halkett 2019: 22). Currit-Halkett (2019) argues that in the United States today, conspicuous consumption – and she mentions the purchase of a Louis Vuitton bag as an indication of this – is more likely to be practiced by those who are struggling financially while the new dominant class invests in building himself or herself professionally, socially and culturally and passing advantages on to their children.

# Craft, the intimate connection between hand and head

At present, there is a degree of interest in knowing more about not only star designers but also about craftspersons who make products that are viewed if not as a luxury, then as one-of-a-kind creations. Sennett extols the 'craftsman' for his 'skill, commitment, and judgement' focused on 'the intimate connection between hand and head' (2008: 9). There are inherent differences between the work of a craftsperson and one who works on a production line, even if the goods both produce are presented as luxury. During production, costs may be cut, workers deskilled and labour subject to techniques found in the mass market. Karl Marx sees the working class reduced to meeting 'animal' needs, while the dominant classes have the time, the freedom and the discernment to seek refinement. It is this condition Pierre Bourdieu defines as 'luxury'.

Artisans create luxury products for the dominant classes, providing justification for this group's dominance and enabling the continuation of hierarchies. They are far removed from the privileged classes who partake of luxury and from the cultural intermediaries within corporate offices who shape tastes. Neither the consuming public nor cultural intermediaries have contact with those loosely defined as 'artisans' who possess expertise and knowledge and who work backstage to produce goods coveted by luxury consumers.

Bourdieu defines cultural intermediaries as tastemakers working in fields such as advertising or fashion who infuse goods with symbolic meaning. Within this new bourgeoisie, one finds 'masters of the economy' who hold high-level positions in marketing and management and a petit bourgeoisie who provide necessary support in sales and service positions and in new occupations such as stylists, bloggers and coaches. Those who work at the level of production may mediate between the realms of production and consumption, for example, a designer or artisan who has created a small brand and is actively involved in the creation of his or her product and its sale alongside others.

Those artisans working for large commercial brands have no access to the world of consumption. They have no power to make decisions and thus remain locked in the hidden world of material labour. Many academics and theorists have dismissed this as no longer relevant in the post-industrialist capital economy. In large luxury companies there are indeed artisans who are recognised for their craft but they represent the minority and their numbers are declining.

Workers provide products that take on luxury status and bring enormous profit to companies. While the value of labour may be determined based on its exchange value, wages are calculated before products become commodities. There is no relation between their contribution to the company, the quality of the work they are producing and the prices that these products are sold for. In some instances, artisans are not being paid much more than those receiving subsistence from the French government (the SMIC allowance, the French guaranteed minimum wage, is €1188 a month and the beginning salary for a Louis Vuitton worker is €1700). Jacques Techer speaks of luxury ateliers as 'back offices' where stagnant salaries approach the level of SMIC, as profits increase (Djabali 2018b). In a surprising comment comparing employees to this most unfortunate segment of society, Emmanuel Mathieu, industrial director of Louis Vuitton, is quoted as saying employees earn a salary well above SMIC (*L'Usine Nouvelle* 2011). Interestingly, Mathieu suggests the salaries Louis Vuitton pay their 'artisans' justify the quality of the work they are doing and the prices charged for each of their products. This is a questionable rationale as it undermines the value of both the artisan and the products they make on behalf of the company/luxury brand. One could argue this is the basis upon which the luxury brand industry is built, to keep production costs low while maximizing the retail value and profit.

Fabrice Giracasa speaks about the stark contrast between salaries paid to employees and the selling price of the products they produce. 'Imagine that they are producing crocodile sacs at 25,000 euros. I'll let you imagine what the price of a suitcase will be' (Djabali 2018a). Jean-Marc Damelincourt, who like Giracasa has been employed for 30 years, only earns €2000 a month despite his years of services and skills in working with exotic skins (Djabali 2018 a). A factory industry journal reveals that thanks to advanced industrial technology and automation techniques, production in the Marsaz, France factory increased by 50 per cent. Despite Louis Vuitton referring to their production workers as 'artisans', it chooses not to hire those experienced in the relevant craft in its factories. One worker was a dog groomer and another previously worked in a factory mincing beef. An applicant with 20 years' experience in the luxury craft was rejected for her proud attitude. Yves Carcelle, former LVMH CEO, lowered his voice when he uttered the word 'production'. The author notes lean manufacturing has been practiced for close to three years (*L'Usine Nouvelle* 2011).

Through our own research, we've obtained a paystub from an 'artisan' working for a European luxury brand in their factory located in the United States. At the time of writing, an 'artisan' is paid $13.50 per hour for the day shift and $15.00 for the night shift (see also Dalton 2015). This clearly substantiates numerous claims made over the years about the level of pay received by factory workers in the luxury brand industry.

The contribution factory workers make to the manufacture of luxury brands is not to be underestimated. Saying that, it is also important to differentiate the notion of craftsmanship and the traditional interpretation of the term 'artisan' and the value those words add to the overall descriptions of products. A product made by an artisan and or craftsman carries with it an implicit understanding that it is made by someone who is skilled and has learned their trade over time. This process differs from the one of factory workers, as we have explained in this chapter, despite them being referred to as artisans. There is a little artisanal process about the mass production of products. The following chapter considers craft and design and the integral component of luxury and its definitions and applications.

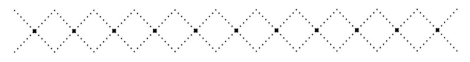

# 4

# Craft and Design

*The notion of luxury is examined through a comparative and critical analysis of contemporary theories and accounts of luxury and luxury brands. Here, we will address the changing luxury landscape and how technology influences and impacts on the producer, customer and their ultimate experience. This chapter clarifies and establishes the differences between perceptions, interpretations and implementation of luxury today. We question the illusory forms of luxury that are phenomena of the contemporary luxury brand marketplace, in favour of an authentic notion of crafted luxury. This chapter also defines the characteristics of luxury within a contemporary and continuously changing manufacturing and consumer-based landscape.*

Existing definitions of luxury are unstable because of an ever-changing cyclical market, exacerbated by continuous redefined interpretations of luxury in an expanding global consumer market. Luxury brand heritage – communicated through advertising, social media platforms, architecture, philanthropic gestures that include the setup of museums – all attempt to preserve the terminology that defines a luxury product or service. This despite the shifts in the production of specialized luxury products to those that are mass-produced.

    Craftsmanship is inextricably linked to luxury. Examples of luxury products could be an haute couture dress or a bespoke piece of jewellery, which may be made to order by highly skilled craftspeople using the finest materials. Scarcity, quality and innovation, too, are characteristics defining a luxury product. But as technological advances impact on manufacturing, distribution and retail environments, the notion of craftsmanship goes beyond product. To define luxury purely as a method to produce products negates the impact technology has on the overall supply chain. As such, it diminishes the skills through which luxury is defined. Coders, architects, service designers, specialists in computer-aided design (CAD) and the development of new materials all play crucial roles in contributing not only to the production of physical products but also to the overall implementation of craftsmanship to enhance the luxury experience.

Advertising is a physical manifestation of luxury and is articulated through marketing, branding and social media portals. It is important to remove the façade of marketing and branding to reveal a perspective that acknowledges the change and importance of fashion business methodologies to ensure business growth. At the same time, it is vital to recognize the fundamental significance of luxury brand heritage and the convenient message this sends to the consumer via these portals. Concepts of luxury will continue to be defined and redefined as part of a complex structure of understanding and interpretation. In light of this, one must not lose sight of the importance of the knowledge of the craftsmen and women and their ability to communicate the intricacies of their skills in order to provoke and challenge the perpetuating luxury debate.

The distinction is created between luxury products and luxury branded products. The former is based on principles of craftsmanship, materials and rarity, while the latter is based on mass production and consumption, and fashion. Now fashion is undeniably the catalyst through which luxury brands are defined. They change their narratives with each passing season to market their products.

Advertising strategies, narrative techniques and marketing methods are used to influence how a product and or service is perceived. Advertising is a critical tool, and the primary aim is to sell more products. A prerequisite is the capacity to increase production efficiently and expediently. The discussion takes place in relation to mass production and the extraordinary lengths to which the luxury conglomerates go to ensure their supply chain is tightly controlled. It has to have the ability to service all the brands under the respective group's 'umbrella'. The relationship between mass production and craftsmanship is often deliberated when comparing a product created in a workshop by one person, and those made on a 'piece work' production line. The distinct qualities of craftsmanship are explored and defined to ensure clarity and to preserve the true essence of what makes a luxury product as opposed to a luxury brand product.

While taking all this into consideration, it is also important to differentiate between the characteristics of crafted luxury versus mass-produced luxury, products and services. Defining luxury through clear markers addresses the misrepresentation of luxury brands that do not adopt the traits found in a luxury product and or service but are nevertheless marketed and sold as luxury. Typically, companies such as Louis Vuitton, Dior, Gucci and Chanel have historical relevance predating the luxury brands market that emerged in the late 1980s with the advent of the designer label. Their original intent was to produce specific products. In the case of Louis Vuitton and Gucci, the focus was on producing luggage, while Dior and Chanel made clothing. Their products were considered luxury because of the craftsmanship, the materials used and the bespoke nature of the production process. Today, these companies are no longer 'sole traders' after being consumed by global conglomerates whose intent is wholly financial. With that comes expansion and with expansion comes mass production and consumption. The manufacturing processes have changed beyond all recognition. But the luxury label remains and the 'brand' heritage retains the aura of luxury through extensive aspirational marketing and advertising campaigns.

# The luxury brand

Without a doubt, there was a continuing trend of growth within the luxury goods market until the global pandemic struck in early 2020. As we previously noted, according to Bain and Company (2019), in 2018 the luxury market grew 5 per cent to an estimated €1.2 trillion and is expected to continue to grow on average by 3 per cent to 5 per cent until 2025. These figures account for an increase of spending by generations Y and Z[1] who account for 47 per cent of luxury consumers. Unsurprisingly, there's been an increase in online sales with the expectation that online shopping will represent 25 per cent of the market's value by 2025 (D'Arpizio et al. 2019). Therefore it goes without saying that as the luxury market continues its global expansion through its many retail portals, the products and services rendered will reach an increasingly wide and diverse consumer group. More products, more consumers. That was the projection.

But all of that changed significantly when the global market in effect shut down as a result of the global pandemic. What then became the most pressing issue was predicting when the markets would reopen. The luxury brands, those with a global presence, felt the brunt of the impact. Many did not want to respond so as to be seen to be opportunistic and profit from the crisis. Instead, they showed compassion and concern by producing hand sanitizer, masks and personal protection equipment for frontline workers. There was an acute awareness that consumer shopping habits would change. Some customers questioned their need to consume luxury. Others could not afford to do so or decided to redirect or conserve their resources. Clothing, and or fashion goods, the core product offer of luxury brands, were no longer wanted or needed. This raises interesting questions about luxury. Is what is being produced really luxury, or simply an exercise in adding value to luxury brand products that are nothing more than fashion in disguise? And as luxury goods tend to have some substance in that their lifespan extends beyond a fashion season, how would, not only the manufacturer but also the customer, view and respond to the product offer and whether or not to make a purchase?

A quote from Berry's book, *The Idea of Luxury*, remains as relevant now as it was when first published. He suggests

> luxury can without hesitation be tacked on to almost any article of merchandise from pizzas to handbags, from a fountain pen to a dressing gown and done so presumably to make it more desirable and the more likely to be bought.
>
> (Berry 1994: 10)

What is undeniable is that luxury brands do indeed use the term 'luxury' to describe all manner of products and services from supermarket chocolate to a bespoke piece of jewellery, luggage, private jets, yachts and clothing.

Furthermore, the terminology used in an attempt to classify the goods and services is confusing and undermines the very clear definition of luxury as crafted and rare, where the finest materials are used, and the craftspeople have the skill to produce a product from concept, the initial sketch or idea to the realization of the finished product. They have the ability to, if need be, have full control of their output. Masstige (mass-produced goods sold as luxury), prestige, super premium, new luxury, old luxury and aspirational are all terms used by marketers to add value to products that otherwise have little else to distinguish them other than the designer labels they carry.

These illusory descriptions of luxury are a phenomenon of the market and continue to contribute to an ever changing and expanding 'space' where economics and profit dominate corporate strategies. Luxury brands are no more than designer labels whose *raison d'être* is a global retail presence and consumption. This is echoed in the physical and digital presence. The physical stores are marketed as experiential entities. Luxury stores focus on the shopping journey from the time the customer enters to the time they leave the store. This includes the attention they are given when inside the store and their post shopping experience. The offer differs according to the clientele; there may be a 'salon' where VIP customers are served in the privacy of a shop within a shop. They are treated differently. This experience is not unlike the top players in a Las Vegas casino. The high rollers are given hotel suites free of charge, as there is a guarantee of income generated through their gambling. Whatever the in-store experience is, it is there to make the customer feel special, but at its core it is designed to encourage the customer to part with their cash under the guise of a luxurious experience. Stores provide symbols of a luxury lifestyle that appeal to aspirational consumers whose relentless shopping is propelled by the fashion cycle.

The art of reinvention is critical to the continued success of a luxury brand. Unlike purveyors of luxury products, they introduce new collections multiple times a year, set fashion trends and aggressively market their products as seasonal offerings. These are not simply confined to the weather, i.e. spring, summer, fall and winter but also focus on critical shopping events around the holidays including Christmas, Easter and Valentine's Day.

Diversification is crucial to ensure a continuous flow of new products. Louis Vuitton at its inception in 1854, produced luggage. But after the merger with Moët Hennessey in 1987 to form the LVMH group, it has consistently moved away its core product to the production of fashion products. This shift is consistent with other contemporary luxury brands owned by conglomerates where in order to grow, expand their markets and increase their profit margins, the product offer increases. Louis Vuitton now produces clothing, jewellery, timepieces and perfume, as do all other global luxury brands. This extensive market reach is what distinguishes a luxury brand from a purveyor of luxury goods.

The luxury brands market must at least sustain its market share, but more importantly, grow to remain relevant to customers, and satisfy shareholders. The constant change they pursue is fundamentally in line with fashion where change defines the concept in opposition to what, at its core, luxury represents. This in itself is the generative function of capitalism where over consumption is encouraged. An expansive luxury brand, as previously stated, is committed to financial growth and defies the traditional approach to the production of luxury goods where the skill of the maker defines the process of making. The pursuit of financial growth is ultimately at the expense of the product and can only be achieved through mass production and consumption. London-based jeweller Theo Fennell suggests in an interview that one needs fame and global reach for craftspeople to expand their businesses.

It is important for people to say I have my shoes made by Fred. It's then very easy for Fred to start saying I am so famous now and I am charging so much for my shoes I can get Harry and John, my apprentices to do it instead of me and still put Fred on the shoes. In fact, I can get a hell of a lot of other people to make them because my name is now worth so much I can make 1000s of these things and people will assume the quality is there because it has my name on them. But it isn't really me doing it. Now that's what happened with branding and unfortunately what has happened is that the world has been duped into believing that Fred is still making the shoe but he is not. 1000s of people in Taiwan are making the shoes but they have the name on them. We have also been brainwashed into believing that just because it bears the name it is going to be good.

(Fennell 2020)

Products are no longer always produced in 'ateliers' in the country of origin – in most instances, France, Italy or England – but are produced all over the world. To ensure brand value is maintained the goods are shipped back to Europe to be completed in order to comply with European laws thus allowing them to have 'made in Europe' labels attached. All Louis Vuitton products sold in the United States, for example, are made there. This insight raises more questions relating to consistent quality control. In an interview, workers in one luxury brand factory in the United States gave anecdotal evidence that their products are produced under duress and are not of the same quality as those made in the country of the brand's origin.

The overriding question is how marketing methods articulate value to ensure the visual communication in whatever guise (print, social media and online) clearly expresses an illusory experience the customer buys into. These illusory and fantastical marketing ploys are what the customer buys into in part but ignore the actual product. They focus on the hype and visual narratives generated through communication channels perpetuated by celebrity endorsements and 'influencers'. This is problematic as it sets a precedent and creates a hierarchy through which value is added to a product with disregard for that product.

If one considers that luxury is founded on craftsmanship, mate-rials and exclusivity – all of which is reinforced through the significant contribution of the maker – this negates the luxury brand proposition as exclusivity is clearly almost always lacking. What is clear from many of the publications (Danziger 2019b; Okonkwo 2007; etc.) that consider luxury is that they fail to distinguish between luxury and luxury brands. The danger of this approach undermines and undervalues processes of manufacture in favour of economic gain founded on untruths.

Luxury brands therefore benefit from those whose skills define luxury – even when they do not follow those practices. There is also a lack of transparency around the manufacture of luxury branded prod-ucts, which is not evident in the production of luxury goods. Luxury branded goods are typically manufactured on a production line with machinists producing component parts. In some instances, they are separated from one another, creating 'departments' that focus on one component – such as, for example, inserting the lining, and adding a zip or a handle. It would be nonsensical for luxury brands to show how their products are actually made.

This is evident in the marketing and advertising strategies used to promote luxury brands. Evermore sophisticated marketing strategies are deployed to achieve maximum output and reach. Print advertising budgets have been reduced considerably over the past ten years to make way for a digital presence that is in itself diverse and constantly changing. All luxury brands, aside from having websites, have Facebook pages, Instagram, Twitter and TikTok accounts and YouTube channels. Their reach is extended exponentially through the use of influencers, who also promote the products on their own social media channels. The digital realm furthers its impact as new technologies emerge, enabling luxury brands to engage in numerous marketing platforms that extend their reach beyond print, television and film.

# Advertising and myth creation

Fashion at its heart is a system that through advertising, in whatever format, exaggerates the benefits of a product. Consider the Lindt 'Indulge in Excellence' chocolate advert of 2015. The chocolate is described as 'gourmet' and 'prepared by selecting the world's finest cocoa beans'. In another ad, Lindt features a 'master chocolatier' whisking melted chocolate in a setting that is obviously not a factory. The voiceover describes the chocolate truffle being made by a 'Lindt master chocolatier', played by the actor Leon van Waas. This method of advertising, where a set is constructed and actors and models used, is of course common as it creates a fictional environment that best embodies the story an advertiser wants to tell rather than the reality of production. In creating a myth around a product to ensure the customer buys into an aspirational lifestyle, the advertiser extends their visual interpretation through manifestations of the unreal and misrepresentation.

What is clearly omitted from these advertisements, and for obvious reasons, are the abhorrent working conditions suffered by the cocoa pickers. That is not to say that Lindt & Sprüngli engage in any untoward practices. Their website clearly states that they support their farmers and that their 'commitment to sustainability starts with a bean, a tree, and a farmer' (Lindt & Sprüngli 2020: n.pag.). What they do not say is how much the pickers get paid, nor are they completely transparent in describing the very complex supply chain – getting the bean to the customer and the complex web of pickers, consortiums, hedge funds, processing plants and factories. In the Netflix series *Rotten, Bitter Chocolate* the narration begins saying chocolate is a 'luxury item rooted in poverty' and 'the journey chocolate makes from bean to bar is rife with corruption, violence and exploitation' and that 'the supply chain keeps the profits away from those who need it most' (Harper 2019).

Louis Vuitton and other luxury brands do the same; they exaggerate the benefits of their products through advertising and are not fully transparent in where the products originate, or how the supply chain works. In 2010, Louis Vuitton commissioned advertising agency Ogilvy Mather to produce a series of adverts. The Savoir Faire campaign showed three different images of three models 'making' Louis Vuitton products; a man hand-painting a sole of a shoe, a woman making a wallet, and another hand-stitching a bag. One of the images features this caption:

> The seamstress with linen thread and beeswax. A needle, linen thread, beeswax and infinite patience protect each over-stitch from humidity and the passage of time. One could say that a Louis Vuitton bag is a collection of details. But with so much attention lavished on everyone, should we only call them details?
>
> (Yotka 2010: n.pag.)

The visual narrative proposes these 'craftspeople' make the products. The United Kingdom's Advertising Standards Authority took umbrage to the campaign and banned the adverts as they were 'deemed to mislead the public into believing the products were handmade' (Brownsell 2010: n.pag.).

In its appeal to the ASA, Louis Vuitton stated, 'the ads were a homage to the craftsmanship which was carried out every day by Louis Vuitton artisans' (Brownsell 2010: n.pag). They went on to say they had '200 employees working on different aspects of their products in each workshop' and they 'believed that the use of hand sewing machines and the associated tasks were part and parcel of what would be expected to amount to "handmade" in the 21st century' (Brownsell 2010: n.pag.). This confused response contradicts the advert, which clearly shows one person making a product. In addition, Vuitton's statement that '200 employees working on different aspects of their products in each workshop' may be construed as misleading as they do not say how many workshops they have, where they are, or how many 'aspects' there are in each of their products. In 2019, 4300 manufacturing staff worked in 16 manufacturing facilities in France with 1500 staff slated to be hired by 2022 (White et al. 2019; White 2019). In a correction to an article appearing in the *Wall Street Journal* in 2019, it states that there are 18 manufacturing facilities in France and 12 outside of France (Dalton 2019).

With no reference to a production line in any of their statements Louis Vuitton wants to preserve an air of mystery around how their products are made. Louis Vuitton also state 'it would not be against public expectation for a handmade product to be produced within an industrial setting' (Brownsell 2010: n.pag.). If this were the case, why then would they not show an industrial setting? In 2019, Louis Vuitton produced a short film titled *What is Savoir-Faire/The Art of Craftsmanship/Louis Vuitton*. This is the same title as the 2010 advertising campaign released and banned in the United Kingdom for misrepresentation. The difference now is the film was released on its own YouTube channel. This use of social media exemplifies the power it has over traditional paid advertising. It, in effect, removes any regulatory standards and frameworks to which the corporation must abide. They are free to make any statement they wish without having to justify and or substantiate the claims. This approach is questionable when the advertising strategies adopted by these corporations to promote products are founded on untruths. They can say what they say without regulation. The Vuitton film is much the same as the advert. It portrays 'craftsmen and women' in a studio setting making individual items in a workshop. Overlaid imagery of Vuitton-related heritage is used to emphasize craftsmanship.

Louis Vuitton and Lindt are not alone in their pursuits of misleading advertising. All luxury brands do much the same whether it is Louis Vuitton, Gucci, Chanel, Dior or Lindt. Furthermore, they all employ 'Savoir Faire' as part of their narrative. In Dior's Savoir Faire campaign to highlight their collaboration with luggage maker Rimowa (both owned by the LVMH Group) they too show a clinical environment in which their products are supposedly made. One could easily find images online that illustrate fantasy and reality. There is a stark contrast between the production line worker in the factory and the white gloved, white T-shirt wearing 'maker'. The answer to why luxury brands do not show the reality of the production process is simple. It is that the value of an image that does not show the true nature of production in favour of one that is fantastical, has more impact. The intention is to create desire that fuels the fire, leading to increased consumption of the products.

In these instances, it could be said that the Savoir-Faire campaigns are misleading. The same could be said for the Lindt advert referred to previously. There is no evidence to suggest either company undertook any consumer research to better understand how the customer would respond had they decided not to gloss over the reality of the production. There is also no evidence to suggest the customer does in fact accept that industrialised and or mechanised modes of production are used. In fact, the opposite could be said when analysing responses to the Dior film posted on Instagram. Of the nearly three million views and

1900+ comments, the responses are all positive. Most respondents comment specifically on the craftsmanship, apparently believing that what they see is the reality.

> **rescuevenuscow** What we imagine we create 😊 @ zotoral What a spectacle! 👏👏👏 @ kkmodelhipster Pure art 🔥 @ curvesisfashion true craftsmanship@_b_designs Gorgeous craftsmanship!
>
> (Dior 2020: n.pag.)

It is evident the customer or aspirational consumer is less interested in how the products are made. They are more inclined to consume the hype around the product and the narrative created by the company selling the goods. Protecting how their products are perceived is tantamount to maintaining perceptions of luxury and craftsmanship. Appearing to adopt traditional modes of craftsmanship adds value to the purchase, and the end product, and as such, luxury brands protect the perception of craftsmanship and the skill of the maker through the visual narratives they create. These narratives become increasingly important and relevant, specifically in the luxury brands market, as they add to the justification of the high price points of each of the products and the aspirational values attributed to them. In addition, as the luxury brands continue to extend their reach to attract more custom, and expand their product offers, the tightly controlled channels of communication must adhere to a clear narrative – regardless of the reality.

What is not shown in any of the images or the films, for obvious reasons, are the actual factories producing the products and the scale of the production needed to meet demand. The endless regulated and controlled production lines are conspicuously absent so as not to distract the viewer. Maintaining this myth around the brand is critical. And as technology continues to evolve, the brand has increased power over the portals their customers and potential customers are exposed to and ultimately use. Corporate reach expands, as does the speed at which content is changed, updated and released. Bypassing traditional and regulated advertising routes empowers the luxury brand to market its products in any way they choose. The stories they create are just that: fairy tales where the narrative is so far removed from reality and is seldom questioned by the consumer. The reality, however, is so very different.

# Mass production

To satisfy their global demand for their products, luxury brands employ manufacturing methods that are, as previously discussed, not what they show in their publicity material. Unless the client is purchasing something from the haute couture atelier or commissioning a bespoke product, all goods – clothing, shoes, accessories, jewellery, perfume and timepieces – are mass-produced in a factory. It goes without saying the more that is produced, the cheaper it is. And to lower costs even further, the luxury brand conglomerates – Louis Vuitton Moët Hennessey, Kering, Richemont, The Prada Group and privately-owned Chanel and Hermès – require nearly all their suppliers to implement a vertical integration model that ensures complete control of their supply chain and competitive advantage. From knitters to tanneries, most of the manufacturing is undertaken in factories they own.

Table 4.1 gives some idea of the extent to which the conglomerates have acquired as many of their suppliers as possible. This list is not extensive and provides just an example of the relationship between brands and their suppliers.

# Luxury brand corporate acquisition

In 2009, Hermès, due to an increase in demand for their crocodile Birkin and Kelly handbags, began breeding their own crocodiles on farms in Australia. It is reported that in 2012 they purchased Cairns Crocodile Farm (Dalton 2015). In 2013, they bought the leather tannery Tannerie d'Annonay and in 2015, Hermès Cuirs Précieux, the tannery division of Hermès International, acquired Tanneries du Puy (TFL 2015). In 2013, Kering the owner of among others Alexander McQueen, Bottega Veneta, Gucci, Balenciaga and Yves Saint Laurent, bought the French tannery France Coco (Crunchbase 2020). And in 2014, the Prada Group, owner of Prada, Miu Miu, Churches shoes and Car Shoe, acquired, in a joint venture with Conceria Superior, Tannerie Megisserie, who specialize in tanning lambskin (Za 2014). Chanel created Paraffection S.A. as a subsidiary in 1997, bringing all the couture specialist makers under one roof. The workshops are identified as 'independent' to allow them to produce goods for other companies. The acquisitions began in 1984 with the purchase of button makers Desrues, and have continued ever since. Parafection S.A. has continued to acquire Chanel's suppliers with the purchase of Lemarié, the feather, pleat and makers of flowers (1996); Maison Michel the milliners (1997); Massaro's shoes and Lesage, the

| TABLE 4.1: Table of luxury brand conglomerates of the supply chain. | | | |
|---|---|---|---|
| **Company** | **Acquired Company** | **Date** | **Specialist Offer** |
| Chanel | Desrues | 1984 | Buttons |
| | Lemarié | 1996 | Feather, pleat and makers of flowers |
| | Maison Michel | 1997 | Milliners |
| | Massaro | 2002 | Shoes |
| | Lesage | 2002 | Couture embroidery |
| | Goossens | 2005 | Costume jewellers |
| | Causse | 2012 | Glovemakers |
| | Barrie | 2012 | Knitwear |
| | Lognon | 2013 | Pleating |
| | Bodin-Joyeux | 2013 | Lambskin specialist tannery |
| | Renato Corti | 2019 | Leather producer |
| | Mabi International Spa | 2019 | Handbag producer |
| | Grandis | 2019 | Clothing manufacturer |
| Hermès | Tannerie d'Annonay | 2013 | Tannery |
| | Tanneries du Puy | 2015 | Tannery |
| | Cairns Crocodile Farm | 2012 | Crocodile farm |
| LVMH | Johnstone River Crocodile Farm | 2013 | Crocodile farm |
| | Heng Long | 2011 | Exotic skins supplier |

| Company | Acquired Company | Date | Specialist Offer |
|---|---|---|---|
|  | ArteCad SA, | 2011 | Manufacturers of Swiss watch dials |
| Kering | France Coco | 2013 | Tannery |
| Prada Group | Tannerie Megisserie | 2014 | Tannery |

couture embroidery company (2002); Goossens costume jewellers (2005); Causse glovemakers (2012); Barrie, the Scottish knitwear company based in Hawick in 2012; Lognon, the pleating specialist (2013) and Bodin-Joyeux the lambskin specialist tannery (2013). More recent acquisitions include Renato Corti, one of Italy's largest leather producers, handbag producer Mabi International Spa and the French clothing manufacturer, Grandis (2019) (AFP 2014).

LVMH and Kering have undertaken similar strategies. The former bought the Singapore-based crocodile tannery, Heng Long. What is important to note is as a result of the opacity of the information the LVMH group releases, it is virtually impossible to provide a clear and transparent account of how the acquisitions are made, where the companies are situated and the origins of their raw materials. In their press release of 7 October 2011, the LVMH Group stated, 'Heng Long is a valued and trusted supplier of fine quality crocodilian leather to luxury and high-end fashion product manufacturers globally, including LVMH. It is a family-run tannery in its fourth generation, based and listed in Singapore' (n.pag.). In contrast, and on the APLF website, APLF 'organise a number of international trade exhibitions for leather, material and fashion businesses' (2020: n.pag.) – a joint venture between Informa Markets and SIC Group Heng Long – is listed as Heng Long Leather (Guangzhou) Co. Ltd. and APLF, not the Singaporean based and listed company. They are listed as:

> Importer, exporter, manufacturer of fine quality exotic skins. Modern tannery based in Singapore specializing in producing top quality leather of American alligator from USA, crocodile from Africa, Australia, Papua New Guinea and southeast Asia and caiman skins from Central and South America. Agent of ostrich leather for KKLK, South Africa.
>
> (LVMH 2011: n.pag.)

This lack of transparency reveals awkward truths about the extremes to which all luxury brands go to preserve their image.

Not only do the luxury brand conglomerates acquire suppliers to enhance their supply chain but they also acquire companies outside of their traditional product offer. Their diversification strategies include vineyards, coffee shops and restaurants. In 2016, Prada bought Pasticceria Marchesi. Originally opened in 1884 in Milan, it is now set for expansion under the ownership of the Prada group. Since the purchase, two new stores have opened in Milan and one on Mount Street in London. In 2013, LVMH bought Caffe Cova, another Italian patisserie. Caffe Cova opened in Milan in 1817. They launched their first international store in Hong Kong in 1993. Since then, their international expansion extends to China, Taiwan, Monaco and Dubai. The LVMH Group also owns Moët Hennessy (Moët & Chandon, Veuve Clicquot, Dom Pérignon and Krug champagnes and Hennessy cognac) and vineyards including Clos des Lambrays, Château Cheval Blanc and Château d'Yquem.

Chanel own Châteaus Canon and Rauzan-Ségla, Château Berliquet in France and St. Supéry Estate Vineyards and Winery in the United States. Groupe Artémis is the French holding company owned by François-Henri Pinault (see Groupe Artémis n.d.), which owns the controlling share in Kering.

The examples above simply provide a snapshot of the extent to which global conglomerates go to diversify their portfolios for ultimate financial gain. They extend far beyond the fashion, food and beverage markets. That is another chapter in another book. The point is that each of the companies marketed as luxury brands all engage in mass production and product diversification in one way or the other.

# Mass production and the luxury conundrum

Luxury brands love to tell, or sell, a story of exclusivity, craftsmanship and innovation and in so doing, evoke a sense of mystery around their mass-produced, mass-consumed products. Brands use these stories for many purposes including to entice the aspirational consumer, encouraging them to part with their money on much of the same, but different, must-have fashion products, promoted by fashion, social media influencers and celebrities. This repetitive cycle is maintained in part by the luxury brand conglomerate creating and maintaining global presence, but just as important, by stocking their retail outlets with the goods for sale. What we have is a global fashion cycle that needs constant fuelling to generate mass consumption of mass-produced goods. That the products are mass-produced has little or no bearing on whether they are consumed or not.

Fashion production is invariably a wasteful activity as products must be produced each season to accommodate the seasonal cycle, which in turn encourages consumption. It is rare to find a product that sells out completely. What is not clear is what is done with the surplus. Some reports claim items are destroyed to avoid them being copied or appearing on the black market. These justifications are not credible. In 2018, Burberry, as reported by the BBC, 'destroyed unsold clothes, accessories and perfume worth £28.6 million to protect its brand. It takes the total value of goods it has destroyed over the past five years to more than £90m' (Anon. 2018: n.pag.). After considerable backlash, they released a statement – as reported in *The Guardian* newspaper – that it was to 'end its practice of burning unsold clothes, bags and perfume and will also stop using real fur after criticism from environ-mental campaigners' (Kollewe 2018: n.pag.). This wasteful activity is not confined to Burberry, although it is the only company to acknowledge it disposed of its unsold items.

Companies that do have sales – and that includes most of them apart from Louis Vuitton who do not – all have leftover stock but they do not fully disclose what they do with unsold items. This wastefulness is endemic not only in the fashion industry but also in the luxury brands industry as well. To counter this wastefulness the French government is to 'ban designer clothes and luxury goods companies from destroy-ing unsold or returned items under a wide-ranging anti-waste law' (Willsher 2020: n.pag.). France destroyed up to 20,000 tons of textile products each year. How the luxury brands will mitigate so much waste is unclear as there is no foolproof method of reducing production completely. There will always be excess stock to be disposed of. The luxury brand conglomerates are not alone in producing billions of dollars worth of merchandise each year, some of which will not sell. This raises further questions about the value of luxury brand products sold as luxury where the value is diminished purely, it could be argued, by the excessive amount of product produced. There are similarities in the digital and physical representations of a luxury brand. Both work in tandem to sell the product. The visual manifestation creates desire, which in turn creates need. The technologically led campaigns and significant reach sees to that. These systems, the social media jugger-naut and the production line, share remarkable similarities. They are both driven by the objective to reach as many people as possible.

Production lines generally operate in the same way regardless of what they are producing. Differences may be in materials, machinery or the ultimate destination of the product produced. They operate under the division of labour to ensure efficiency through the allocation of tasks assigned to individual workers to ensure maximum efficiency. Joseph Pine (1999), in his book *Mass Customisation*, describes mass production in great detail. He suggests, 'in mass production, companies increased output not only by adding inputs, but by increasing the throughput of machines and the productivity of the workers so that fewer workers were needed per unit produced' (Pine 1999: 16) He further states that this 'greatly increased fixed costs and the capital-to-labour (machine-to-worker) ratio, but also greatly lowered costs of each unit' (Pine 1999: 16). As previously stated, with an increase in production the companies' purchasing power is stronger, more raw materials are produced and the labour costs go down. Increased productivity results in a reduction of overall manufacturing costs. It is safe to say that despite reduced manufacturing costs, the savings are not passed on to the customer. The opposite is in fact the case. Since 2013 prices of Louis Vuitton bags have increased on average by 20 per cent. In 2013, the Louis Vuitton Mon Monogram Keepall 55 was £1190; in 2020, the same bag costs £1400. The small leather goods have increased on average by 15 per cent. A Louis Vuitton Multiple wallet was £275 in 2013 and, in 2020, the cost is £310.

As luxury brands continue to grow, LVMH is estimated to have over 4915 stores worldwide (O'Connell 2020) it not only controls but also owns. Its global network of retail outlets includes standalone branded stores, multi-brand department stores, online retailers and their own web shopping portals. In some instances and with some of its brands, as is common with its competitors, they have presence in discount shopping villages. This increases control and removes the middleman resulting in increased profit. The luxury brand conglomerate manages the entire supply chain.

One must also consider the introduction of lower cost, entry-level items that appeal to the aspirational consumer with limited spending power. These consumers typically buy an item such as a key ring, small leather goods or other types of accessories. These items are also mass-produced albeit at a much larger scale than the clothing, bags and luggage. In most cases, the smaller products are made by machine on an automated production line. Handwork is limited thus achieving a higher profit margin. These production and sales methods are of course not limited to LVMH; they apply to all manufacturers around the world. LVMH is used as an example as it is the largest and most prolific of all luxury brand manufacturers and retailers.

The overall power of these global corporations is significant. What we have is the ownership of the producers of raw products, the manufacturing facilities and controlled labour costs. They must, under all circumstances, achieve their margins to appease their share-holders, remain profitable and continually grow their business. To do this as Pine suggests, 'the product must be as standardized as possi-ble and the manufacturing process broken down into small speci-fied tasks. Workers and machinery must be highly specialized to drive down the time and expense of each individual task' (Pine 1999: 26). It is easy to get carried away with undermining the quality of the prod-uct through emphasizing the 'mechanics' of the supply chain without any reference to the makers, tanners, machinists, cutters, etc. One cannot deny there is an element of skill required to be able to under-take the manufacturing of mass-produced products. However, to place this argument in context, there is a difference in the process when comparing a craftsman or woman who makes an item from start to finish to a worker on a production line. The traditional handmaking techniques are not employed as the luxury brands promotional mate-rial suggests.

Uche Okonkwo, in her book *Luxury Fashion Branding*, suggests 'it is interesting to note that the majority of the successful luxury brands of today were started by skilled artisans and craft-speople who produced made-to-fit goods mainly by hand' and that this process is 'time consuming, expensive and labour inten-sive' (2007: 248). She goes on to say, 'luxury brands adopted the use of machines that produced more goods at less costs without compromising the product qualities and style'; she continues on a similar line explaining, 'this, however led to the standardization and uniformity of goods' (2007: 248). In addition, she states, 'companies that manufacture goods in other categories, including mass fash-ion brands, effectively use these techniques to optimize produc-tion and sales' (2007: 248). There is nothing unique about any of the processes to which Okonkwo refers.

Put simply, employing a division of labour ensures consistent and maximum outputs. In addition, her observations are the most basic principles of manufacture, the more you produce, the cheaper it is to make. Of course, the luxury brand would refute this suggestion and at the same time make claim to the skill of its workers, the working conditions (none of which are disclosed and is where the luxury brand conglomerates rank lowest on their performance in terms of ethical responsibility, transparency, etc.) and the quality of their products. In the 2018 KnowTheChain report, it is estimated that 60–75 million people are employed in the textile, clothing, and footwear sector around the world, more than two-thirds of whom are women. In the US it is a $3 trillion industry and the apparel and footwear sector is characterised by globally complex and opaque supply chains and competition for low prices and quick turnarounds.

(n.pag.)

The report attempts to hold companies to account through exposing bad practice and raising pertinent issues around labour and the workplace. What is telling is that 'six out of nine luxury companies score below 7/100 on recruitment (Kering, LVMH, Hugo Boss, Hermès, Salvatore Ferragamo, and Prada)' (KnowTheChain 2018: n.pag.) and what is most apparent in the report is the lack of transparency by and engagement from the luxury brands.

To admit to mass production would be extremely damaging to any brand purporting to sell luxury products. They would agree they do not compromise on style or quality but would never disclose processes, all of which are shrouded in secrecy. Okonkwo's attempt to justify her position by suggesting 'the use of machines that produced more goods at less cost without compromising the product qualities and styles' (2007: 248) appears to miss the point. Surely the foundation of producing a luxury product is that it is time consuming and labour intensive? It is this that justifies the cost of the product. To remain competitive and profitable, and meet global demand, work-intensive techniques must be employed, demands on manufacturing reduced, manufacturing costs lowered while outputs are increased. That is what makes mass production methods function at the appropriate level.

Okonkwo also fails to provide evidence that the quality of goods is not compromised. The issue here lies with quality control. All factories employ quality controllers to ensure the standard of a product passes the relevant checks and is suitable to be shipped for sale. It therefore goes without saying one would not normally be exposed to inferior quality products in-store. There is also no data released accounting for products that do not pass quality control. It is therefore virtually impossible to know if the quality of goods is compromised. Having conducted research into this, undisclosed sources state goods that do not pass quality control are either destroyed, sold on the 'grey market', in outlet stores or to the workers at reduced prices. This information is not released to the public and is a guarded secret thus maintaining the 'aura' of perfection of the luxury brand.

As previously mentioned, luxury brands are conspicuous in their opacity. They market their goods and services as exclusive luxury. They employ sophisticated marketing strategies to maintain that air of exclusivity. They do not disclose and/or promote the true nature of their manufacturing methods nor do they provide clear track and trace information.

# True craftsmanship

Defining true craftsmanship within the context of a luxury brand is challenging as luxury brands focus on myth creation. They persist in portraying their products in a way that bears no resemblance to reality. They adopt definitions of craftsmanship inherited from their founders with disregard. And they do all this despite their mass-produced products not possessing the same inherent qualities as those made in a workshop. In the long run, this only serves to undermine the skill of the craftsperson. Alison Lloyd,[2] who has worked in the industry for many years, acknowledges the skill of the maker but when it comes to manufacture of product for retail, she suggests:

> I think there's 100 per cent handmade where one person makes one thing from start to finish, but I think that's a very rare thing, it's almost a sample. I don't know whether some of these people who – you know, you can look at one of those films of them making a Dunhill bag which they have on their website. It looks gorgeous, it's a beautifully made film and whatnot, but I don't think they make them one by one, I'm not sure.
>
> (2020)

The skill of the maker is, and will always be, at the heart of defining luxury. Sennett, author of the seminal book, *The Craftsman*, makes two contentious arguments: 'first that skills, even the most abstract, begin as bodily practices; second, that technical understanding develops through the powers of imagination' (2008: 10). In a factory setting where the worker is assigned the arduous job of repeating a task over and over again, doing the same thing day in and day out, there is little requirement for them to undertake 'bodily practices', but more importantly, use the powers of the imagination. A craftsman or craftswoman is defined by their skill; 'the good craftsman, moreover, uses solutions to uncover new territories; problem solving and problem finding are intimately related in his or her mind' (Sennett 2008).

In this instance, it is worth considering the notion of tacit knowledge as described by Krogh, Nonaka and Kazuo in their book *Enabling*

*Knowledge Creation: How to Unlock the Mystery of Tacit Knowledge and Release the Power of Innovation* as this may be a more appropriate description of how the craftsmen and women hone their skills. Tacit knowledge, they say, is 'tied to the senses, skills in bodily movement, individual perception, physical experiences, rules of thumb, and intuition' and that, as such, tacit knowledge is often very difficult to describe to others (Krogh et al. 2000: 6). This kind of knowledge 'cannot be found in a manual or easily conveyed to a novice' (Krogh et al. 2000:6). The production line process does of course require the worker to employ some handwork. They may stitch, glue and assemble a product but the process is somewhat different from practices undertaken by craftspeople. Mass production could be described as a mechanical process as there is a requirement to fulfil the demands of the production line. The obvious intention of a production line is one that is defined by strict rules of engagement. It is imperative the manufacturing processes are clearly adhered to, ensuring the designated number of units is produced each hour as prescribed by the production manager to meet delivery schedules. There is no doubt the production line worker must acquire a certain level of skill to be able to produce the component parts required of them. However, there is no requirement to develop technical understanding through powers of imagination. In fact, the opposite could be said of a factory environment.

As Pine states, 'the product life cycle should be lengthened as much as possible, reducing per unit development costs as well as investments in product and process technology, allowing the experience curve to operate to its fullest' (1999: 26). This viable production process is most appropriate where products are produced as part of a continuous offer. Luxury brands have a history of incessant production of staple products, typically non-seasonal items, which are produced on a regular basis and form part of what are defined as core products. The non-seasonal merchandise is not considered part of the fashion, lifestyle or homeware collections that change multiple times per year. Examples include the monogrammed plasticized canvas bags and accessories produced by Louis Vuitton, the Chanel 2.55 handbag and Prada's tote bags. Included in this would be Hermès and other luxury brands whose production and sale of homeware is a prolific part of their product offer. The advantages to the company are numerous. It is able to pre-plan production, buying all materials in advance including trims and packaging resulting in an overall reduction in costs due to purchasing power. The production line is maintained, as the manufacturing processes are the same. There is no need to upskill the worker and the potential speed at which the products are produced increases as a result of the continuity of the production line. With the overall production costs reduced, the profit margins increase, and as seen, the retailer increases the retail price. Reduced manufacturing costs are never passed on to the end user.

Production methods vary considerably depending on the product. It is also clear luxury brands do not in the main manufacture their goods in the way they market them. There are no smoke-filled rooms with models in fitted T-shirts sitting at a bench with a needle and thread painstakingly sewing a bag together. The reality of production is far from what the consumer is shown. Saying that, we are under no illusion the luxury brands must protect the imaginary worlds they create where craftsmanship or perceptions thereof are pivotal to adding value to the product, in turn appealing to the aspirational consumer. And as luxury brands continue to expand, we have seen an increase in communication strategies placing the handmade concept at the centre of their social media campaigns.

Luxury products made by craftsmen such as milliner Stephen Jones,[3] on the other hand, are celebrated in their execution. There is no hiding behind elaborate advertisements and in some instances, the customer may be given full access to the maker and production process. In an interview, Jones says:

> The thing about true luxury therefore, and slightly in conclusion, is that it's halfway your thing and its halfway the person making it for you. And the interesting point is how far you go and how far they go. So it is a creative process, but with somebody in mind.
>
> (2010: n.pag.)

Access to the designer maker is a service luxury brands offer, specifically for a bespoke item. One of the often-neglected areas of discussion emerging from dissecting the meaning of luxury and its relationship to craftsmanship, is that of connection. The work environment, wherever it may be, is one that in practice should stimulate the workforce, encourage them to engage and promote wellbeing and of course produce good products. With luxury and indeed craftsmanship this connection is lost when the creativity, innovation and construction element of discovery is taken away in favour of a factory setting.

Often stories of how trade secrets are passed down from one generation to another enthuse and excite those fortunate enough to be able to share them. This tacit knowledge, as previously discussed, is not something written down in a book or manual; it is shared through conversation and the creation of a community. And again, this is another strikingly different approach taken by the craftspeople and the machine labourer. Craftsmen and women hone their skills over many years and pass them on to others, traditionally in an environment where an apprentice learns on the job, to preserve techniques that would otherwise be lost.

They are naturally inquisitive beings, looking for answers to complex solutions. They are problem solvers. The machinist is completely the opposite, specifically in the role they play on the production line. They do not have the authority to make suggestions and/or decisions, they are obliged to follow the construction manual to the letter, make no mistakes and not veer off script. The tasks are predictable and doing something that would disrupt the equilibrium of the production line could be catastrophic, resulting in a reduction in revenue or halting production as health and safety protocols are employed.

We apparently live in what is called a skills economy but this economy favours those who already have the skill, emergent skills that reflect the current needs defined by technological advances. Corporations are more inclined to replace one of their workers than upskill them. This is a manifestation of a complex supply chain founded on a basic principle defined by the need to continually increase market share and ultimately, profits. As the luxury brands market continues growing, definitions of luxury will continually change. This is potentially damaging to those makers whose product and or service is defined by craftsmanship. All modes of visual communication – be it advertising, moving image and or social media posts – disseminated by the luxury brands and their followers disregard the fundamental qualities of luxury in favour of promotion to encourage sales. They pay lip service to pertinent issues around the supply chain, sustainability and ethical issues and only time will tell whether, as a result of the demands of the consumer, they will adopt more transparent methodologies.

> It is also apposite to consider the differentiation between mass produced products, those that could be considered luxury brands, and goods that are made by highly skilled craftsmen in limited numbers. What may be needed is a clear market segregation to maintain differentiation between luxury and luxury brands. I suggest that craftsmanship is inextricably linked to luxury.
>
> (Borstrock 2014: 231)

# Luxury versus luxury brands

As the world of consumption changes so will manufacturing and distribution and the social and cultural issues underpinning global consumer industries. Most of the luxury brands – Louis Vuitton, Dior, Hermès, Chanel, Prada, Mercedes Benz, Audi, BMW, etc. – will continue to trade. It is how they trade that will change. Their customers may demand better quality products but less of them. They may not be so inclined to be led by the history of seasonal shopping. The distinction between luxury and a luxury brand will grow ever wider as luxury brands look to engage their customers in different ways. They will continue to mass-produce.

The offer of customization may increase as technology develops further and mass customization becomes the norm. If the process of customization is further streamlined it could be a cost-effective production method. 'Effective use of technology can lead to economies of integration, so that design and manufacturing flow seamlessly from one to the other, allowing rapid design changeovers' (Boradkar 2010: 124). Although written in 2010, Boradkar's views are as pertinent today as they were then. These mechanisms are already in use by luxury brands and will undoubtedly be further developed to maximize production. What we will be left with is more division and distinction that influences the way we assess products and services. The luxury brand product will continue to be the mass-produced homogenous product we have already come to know. This will serve the purveyors of luxury in good stead. The smaller designer makers will have the opportunity to reclaim the true definition of luxury as one defined by craftsmanship. This could be the hundreds of hours needed to hand-make a mattress, the treatment of the eight hides needed to upholster a Rolls Royce, the skill of the jeweller to craft a fine piece of jewellery and the horologist who crafts the cogs and springs in a handmade watch.

It is these skills and many more that come to define craftsmanship and truly distinguish their work from that produced on a production line. Luxury brands defined by history contributed to the global growth and access to better quality products and at the same time, reduced the value of both the craftsmen and women and their work. But there is an opportunity for them to reclaim luxury and redefine it once again.

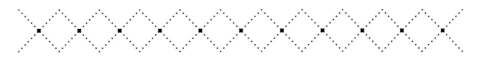

# 5

# Cultural Capital, Work and Production

*The focus of this chapter is on workers who make luxury products in large enterprises and in smaller ones and includes examples of those at the highest levels of the luxury trade. We discuss designers, artisans and couturiers who possess high levels of cultural capital, and work-ers who possess less cultural capital and by consequence, less agency and who may feel at the mercy of the companies for which they work.*

Working in the luxury industry could be compared to a feudal system. Those who hold higher status positions are rewarded financially and given status for the specialized skills and cultural capital they bring to the company. And those producing luxury items within global luxury companies would then be the serfs, who receive none of these bene-fits in exchange for their crucial work. Yet they are expected to show deference and loyalty to the company and its mission. The work of artisans and designers in large global companies differs from inde-pendents that can, to a large extent, forge their own paths within the broader luxury domain.

The critical exploration of the experiences of those engaged in luxury labour in this book is undertaken through interviews with those working in the sector. They present a focus on the different forms of cultural capital they possess, the degree of power this affords them, their experiences at work, their identification with the company, their professional role and identity, and their identification with the prod-ucts they make.

The leisure class consume luxury goods for many reasons. It is a means of securing their class position through the display of wealth and or good taste, or they may primarily do so for their own enjoyment. Those involved in the productive labour of making these goods largely belong to the working classes. As markets create new opportunities luxury brands capitalize on this to increase their revenue. As the market expands, products are sold to a wider segment of society and more people are required to work in the industry to meet growing demand. Those in elite circles or in the higher income brackets will always have the means to acquire luxury products and experiences. Further down the chain those with limited spending power are encouraged to spend via more accessible routes. Luxury brands are quick to service this opportunity and grow their market share. Luxury, particularly in its less diluted state, remains largely inaccessible to almost everyone while awareness, desire and demand for luxury products increases. This leads to established brands extending their product lines and more players entering the field and claiming a stake in the market. As we have seen, luxury is broadened beyond its requisite characteristics of rarity, exclusivity and the highest levels of quality to become something that includes characteristics associated with fashion.

With haute couture, luxury and fashion unite within the context of business. This association advances and eventually culminates in luxury fashion's full immersion in the world of marketing and an expansion into new domains for the purpose of greater profit. Once luxury takes on characteristics of novelty and ephemerality (versus a focus on a product with a long life and association with the eternal), coupled with a mandate of being more profitable, it may even be produced and distributed on a mass scale. There is a progression in modernity to a 'demoralized' concept of luxury, which serves the purpose of destigmatizing the pursuit of luxury in favour of promoting economic growth (Berry 1994: 102). In some cases, this reaches 'hypermodern' proportions. This notion of 'new luxury' sees luxury as not only accessible to those outside of elite circles but also accessible to all… at least from time to time.

In an interview, Jean-Nöel Kapferer gives the example of the Hollywood film *Titanic* where class segregation is depicted: 'Today that is finished. There are still people at the top and still people at the bottom, but they want, for maybe five minutes, ten minutes or half an hour, to go to the top of the boat and to enjoy luxury' (cited in Doran 2013: n.pag.). In Kapferer's example, luxury itself is not compromised but can be attained on occasion by a greater segment of the population. They consume voraciously – whether or not they can afford it. Events like product launches, sales and during other promotional activities both off and online are all designed to increase sales. Queues are a common sight outside luxury brand stores all over the world.

There are, however, inconsistencies and limitations dependent on defining factors restricting what customers can buy. In France, for example, this has to do with preventing entrepreneurs from buying in bulk and profiting by selling goods in China where pricing is higher. New brands arise with innovative approaches that capitalize on an expanding market. Chronext and eBay have entered what had once been the rather narrow field of luxury timepieces to become leaders in the secondary watch market (eBay 2020). These examples point towards a growing luxury brands market where new ways of selling through digital channels are taking precedence, and traditional retail methods working side by side with technological advances are introduced to adapt to changes in the marketplace.

Whether luxury workers can afford to purchase luxury items is not of course the most pressing question. It is, however, worth exploring as the workers themselves are not only alienated from the products they produce but those we interviewed expressed disappointment at not being able to afford the items they make – even with a company discount. Luxury workers are likely occupied with questions of day-to-day survival – making ends meet, holding on to one's job and navigating one's way in an often less than hospitable workplace. This inequity becomes increasingly apparent when one ventures out of more glamorous headquarters not only to back offices and factories owned by the brand but also further down the supply chain. The subcontractors providing and transforming raw materials, such as leather, are often found outside the brand's home country.

The luxury fashion sector encompasses many types of enterprises from the largest conglomerates to the small atelier of an independent designer maker. Its span reaches from the most exclusive flagship stores in fashion capitals to luxury outlet villages and resale shops – both brick and mortar and online. We consider the workers who make luxury products in large enterprises and in smaller ones, and include examples of those working at the top levels of the luxury trade. We discuss designers, artisans and couturiers who possess high levels of cultural capital and workers who possess less cultural capital and by consequence, less agency and who may feel at the mercy of the companies for which they work.

# How it all works

While we considered many sectors within the luxury domain, this chapter deals specifically with fashion. The luxury sector within the domain of fashion has various levels, which at first may be divided into 'haute couture' and 'ready-to-wear'. Companies with the haute couture designation often also design ready-to-wear fashion cloth-ing, and offer accessories, fragrance and perhaps beauty products to a much wider audience than those buying haute couture and ready-to-wear. The couture designation gives an added value or aura, which extends to all the brand's products. The more accessible items, such as fragrance and beauty products, may generate the majority of a luxury brand's revenue as anyone walking through duty free at an airport might surmise. These items, apart from their alluring packag-ing and symbolism, may have little in their ingredients and fabrications that make them scarce, high-quality products and which accord them 'excess value', as Veblen ([1899] 1953) points out when speaking of the essential features of luxury. These luxury branded items, as well as a large percentage of leather goods and fashion items, may have more in common with Karl Marx's ([1844] 2009) fetishized commodity where value is not connected to labour but to magical properties ascribed to the commodity by way of branding and marketing. The ability to make huge profits on items made inexpensively, quickly and in great numbers with relatively high-quality workmanship is what keeps this industry financially afloat, but it also challenges the authenticity of luxury brands and their products.

Haute couture companies such as Chanel, Christian Dior and Givenchy were granted their haute couture status by the Chambre Syndicale de la Haute Couture, a group whose membership is small, largely French and very difficult to attain. Other brands such as Hermès occupy a high status in the world of fashion and enjoy visibility but are not in the haute couture realm. Many well-known luxury brands such as Louis Vuitton, Prada, Gucci and Burberry are produced in large quantities to meet the demand of a growing consumer base. We can call many heritage luxury brands that have stepped up production or that fit more closely within the designation of a 'new', more accessible luxury, 'industrial luxury'. There is a contradiction inherent in the term 'luxury industry', a designation companies such as Hermès and Chanel refuse, opting rather to refer to themselves as 'maisons'.

The concept of luxury as an industry originated during the tenure of Bernard Arnault at LVMH (referred to by luxury expert Danziger as the 'reigning pope of luxury marketing' [2019b: n.pag.]). His insatiable appetite for acquisition and control of more brands created the world's largest luxury goods conglomerate, propelling him into the rarefied company of the wealthy founders of Amazon and Microsoft. At one point in 2019 and 2020, Arnault replaced Jeff Bezos and Bill Gates at the top of the world's richest list, but not for long.

At the other end of the scale of the industrial luxury conglom-erates are smaller and middle-sized brands producing one of a kind or small batches of handcrafted items. These include jewellery, a custom-made dress or suit, or items that are part of a line of clothing tailored to an individual. Most of these brands are not widely known and may be considered by an elite clientele to be 'true' luxury brands. There is no consensus on the scope of luxury and what brands are inside or outside of this framework. As the span of luxury stretches wide and far, some brands even avoid using the term 'luxury'. Wealthy consumers who know the codes and have the means to afford luxury do not need to be told that a condominium, hotel, car, chocolate or bag is a luxury commodity.

Can you have a 'luxury industry' within the realm of fashion or is 'industry' and 'fashion' antithetical to luxury? Brands such as Prada, Louis Vuitton and Gucci produce their leather goods within factory settings. Chanel claims to produce much less than these brands, take longer to do so and may sell some products at a higher price point, but do production methods resemble those of industrial manufacturing or are they closer to traditional processes used by artisans? Thomas in her condemnation of luxury's 'single-minded focus on profitability' (2007: 172) exempts Hermès from this category in her exposé, *Deluxe: How Luxury Lost its Luster*. She says it could have 'increased production to eliminate the waiting lists... It could have become a multibillion dollar company easily' (Thomas 2007: 172). She credits chairman Jean-Louis Dumas's integrity for preventing him from 'producing more goods faster and more efficiently like Louis Vuitton decided to do' (Thomas 2007: 194). Yet today on its website it clearly states that 'since 2011, the strong demand for leather goods has committed Hermès to increasing its production capacity' and there is mention of recruiting 200 artisans a year (Avvenice n.d.: n.pag.; see also Williams 2017, where the number mentioned is 250 new artisans per year). Considering leather goods, it is questionable whether the products produced by different brands are unique in terms of quality and design. Furthermore, Hermès was valued at close to US$18 billion as of January 2021.

The concept of luxury and its material ubiquity in the form of commercially available objects and experiences has a pervasive and highly visible presence in contemporary society. Its desirability has important social and economic ramifications. Luxury within the world of fashion has evolved from a craft with artistic dimensions available to a select clientele into a multi-sectoral global industry. Up to the nineteenth century, luxury followed an aristocratic, artisanal model. With haute couture, a commercial logic based on limited production emerges. This led to a ready-to-wear industry where fashion eventually became available to the masses. Mass marketed and the more extreme case of fast fashion is an example of how a steep increase in demand for product led to production being sent further offshore in what has been referred to as a race to the bottom (Bonacich and Appelbaum 2000). Luxury fashion is not entirely outside of this scope, particularly as well-known companies expand and the appetite for luxury fashion increases exponentially on the global stage of aspirational consumption.

Europe dominates the luxury fashion market, with a majority of design and product emanating from France, Italy and the United Kingdom. The world's most valuable luxury brands are in France (Louis Vuitton, Hermès and Chanel), Italy (Gucci, Prada) and the United Kingdom (Burberry). However, the manufacture of components and products is being outsourced further afield. Products manufactured in China but partly assembled in Europe can carry, as we have discussed, a Made In Europe label. This raises questions related to the current labour market and the inherent skills and 'ancestral savoir faire' found in luxury ateliers (Lembke 2017: n.pag.).

# Practicing one's craft

Sennett extols the 'craftsman' for his 'skill, commitment, and judgement' focused on 'the intimate connection between hand and head' (2008: 9). The creation of haute couture fashion clearly requires the presence of skilled artisans and cannot be entirely routinized. There are inherent differences between the work of a craftsperson and an 'unskilled' garment worker. Some goods presented as luxury have been produced under conditions, if not identical to then at least approximating those of mass marketed fashion. Luxury companies producing ready-to-wear fashion and accessories may do so in very large quantities and seek to reduce costs at the level of production. Nevertheless, there is a mystification around this process, which luxury brands leverage and extend to the narratives and representations they use to market products and build a brand identity. As mentioned in Chapter 4, this led to Britain's Advertising Standards Agency banning two Louis Vuitton advertisements from its Savoir Faire advertising campaign showing an artisan hand stitching a bag and noting the artisan's 'infinite attention' (Anon. [2010] 2017: n.pag.). We consider here what artisans themselves have to say about the processes undertaken to produce luxury branded bags similar to those made by Louis Vuitton.

The world of haute couture is one of avant-garde experimentation, fantasy and excess within the confines of a disciplined system. Look at two extremes within this system, taking into consideration the question of agency: While renowned couturier Jean-Paul Gaultier felt free to do what he wanted during his 50-year career, an artisan at Lesage describes the limitations under which she works. Her description is found on the website, Indeed, where employees can anonymously post reviews about the companies they work for. The reader will notice how active, confident and dynamic Gaultier is when he speaks of his winter 2019 haute couture collection in an interview on France 24. He defines the terms of the actions he undertakes. He makes a point of saying his creative vision is more important than whether or not these creations sell:

> It began with the desire to be a bit freer to do what I wanted to do, something closer to my desires. I wanted to create drawings that came straight out of my head. It could have started with some movement, some person that caught my eye. Say it was raining and someone flings a trench coat over their head like a sort of hood but it's actually the whole coat. I thought why not capes, quilted capes, capes that go down from the head like a sort of cocoon. And why not dresses too. There is a partly transparent black one that goes down from the head and that is what I wanted. It may not be something people want to buy but it is something I wanted to do.
>
> (Gaultier 2019)

In contrast to what Gaultier says about his creative expression, an employee at Lesage reveals on a career website that she is not in control of any aspect of the creative process surrounding her work. Lesage is an embroidery studio primarily serving haute couture establishments. Chanel purchased it in 2002. This employee must enact the script others present to her under largely predetermined conditions. She says of Lesage:

> A family enterprise (in all the areas there is a family member who leads). The age of the employee is of little importance; one is scolded like a child for even being the least bit contrary with the Management. Due to this fact the ambiance is morose. There is no communication between those who provide services and remain totally cloistered. Taking consideration of the human aspect: non-existent.
>
> (Indeed 2019a: n.pag., translated from French)

For Gaultier, the start and end point is his desire to be a self-conscious and self-determining agent. Even a fleeting moment captured by him in passing can become something significant if he deems it to be so and if he decides to invest it with his own creativity, transforming something he describes as totally banal into something fantastic. In other words, for Gaultier, the possibilities are limitless. We feel his excitement as he describes his process as a couturier. At Lesage, however, the 'ambiance is morose' to the point the employee finds herself 'cloistered'. Her words indicate she is suffocating. At Hermès an artisan titles her post as 'A very stressful job'. She goes on to say although this is thought of as a family-run enterprise, it is not a familial environment for the artisans. Note, also, that the artisan is decidedly less important than the product she produces:

> An employer who is in no case familial [...] as they say you are just a number that must never forget to be above the objectives and if not you won't exist anymore and certainly your bosses will end up on you and will finish by putting you down. A mother in the family must be quick not to lose footing because there will be no one to help you if you don't fit in their mould.
>
> (Indeed 2019b: n.pag., translated from French)

It may be surprising to hear that even at the highest levels of the luxury industry in France some artisans feel they are not treated with high regard and respect. The situation is worse when we consider factories outside of their home countries in Europe. Understandably, however, a person working in an organizational context will be subject to restrictions and limitations when the work is commissioned. It appears to be a common perception of many artisans that they do not feel appreciated or valued for their contributions.

# The practice of luxury

It is important to explore the world of the craftsmen and women who work at different levels of the luxury sector and who make a contribution through their craft. We present case studies of five people whose driving force is sustaining the traditional values of luxury. Two of the designer makers are based in London and have achieved international renown in their fields as a jeweller and milliner respectively. Another of the designer makers built a community around different craftspeople in New York. In San Francisco, we find a designer maker who established a school teaching craft leatherwork and finally, we interview a leatherworker who specializes in the renovation and restoration of luxury bags and shoes. These two designer makers and the leatherworker are representative of a larger proportion of entrepreneurs working in the luxury sector whose names may not be widely known but who have a great deal of importance to their clients. We also look at factory work, which tends to be a hidden and distributed operation of the luxury brands industry, and their suppliers. We consider four women who work as 'artisans' in a luxury brand factory. These workers represent the countless masses working behind the scenes. Through in-depth interviews with these people at such different points along the spectrum of luxury we discover that despite their differences, some commonality exists in that all participants are driven to be the best at what they do and wish to have this recognition by others.

We explore issues around cultural capital, its relevance in a luxury context and the impact craftsmanship has on our interviewees. We have purposefully selected a group of independent practitioners who in some cases can be seen as tastemakers in the luxury field. We've also selected factory workers whose experiences are distinctly different when it comes to the degree of power and influence they hold.

Cultural capital determines to a large extent one's position in society and is a means of reproducing privilege and inequality. Cultural capital is embodied in habits, skills and dispositions, a collection of concepts which comprise what Bourdieu terms a 'habitus'. Providing classificatory schemes provides one with strategies that can be adapted to a variety of situations. Bourdieu defines habitus as a 'system of lasting transposable dispositions, which integrating past experiences, functions at every moment as a matrix of perceptions, appreciations, and actions' (1977: 83). Norms of comportment and ways of expressing oneself, of feeling and thinking arise as 'second nature' (Bourdieu 1977: 83). Cultural capital can be passed down by families and acquired by individuals who seek it through education, networking, etc. It is also something one brings to and 'cashes in', if you will, within organizations such as the workplace.

Advantage is reproduced, most significantly in the educational sector where young people from privileged backgrounds meet the criteria of achievement and success set forth by the ruling classes. Bourdieu contends it is their values and interests that are adopted by educators and rewarded in the school system. Those who successfully negotiate this terrain achieve higher-level occupations. The occupational world is divided into various fields each with its own arbitrary beliefs, which reinforce power structures. The luxury field is a structured, symbolic space comprising various institutions and corporations. Actors possess unequal distributions of capital and thus will be subject to a variety of constraints based on their status within the luxury field. Some will attain distinction and fame and others will be subjugated within the established order.

# Independent luxury designer makers

## THEO FENNELL[4] – JEWELLER

Theo Fennell is a world-renowned jeweller who has been in business since 1982. He has a team of craftsmen and women working with him. Fennell works closely with clients on private commissions, and has a flagship gallery in London where all his jewellry is made.

Fennell is concerned the concepts of luxury and craftsmanship are being undermined by luxury brands that fail to meet the highest standards. The designers and cobbler we interview in this chapter share this opinion. Fennell believes luxury has been 'blurred into a blurred branded mish-mash that has cheapened and ruined the concept of craftsmanship and, if you like, genuine luxury'.

Fennell realizes that only when a craftsman or woman has 'got to the top of the game' can he or she have the opportunity to fully realize his or her potential:

> When they are at the top of their game then if you have the right sort of craftsman and the right sort of intent then you can have something that is absolutely exquisite, handmade with the best of materials. But obviously that craftsman needs a certain level of fame.

As has always been the case, Fennell says a craftsperson cannot spend '100 hours on one specific piece to make it absolutely perfect'. Rather he may be 'making 25 things to support his family'.

Fennell, who trained as a portrait artist, describes himself as an artist. He says:

> I think that great craftsmanship begets something that is very close to art. And if you can actually change the way you view things and change the way you feel about things, then it fulfils one of those golden criteria of being a work of art.

He compares the experience of acquiring something exceptional, something seen as a work of art, to the conspicuous consumption of branded luxury, and points to the 'hollow and jaded and ordinary lives' of these consumers:

If you want to see the most vapid faces in the world go to one of these places, watch people trying on those shoes, watch the people trying on jewellery, especially the stuff that doesn't have any resonance to it.

He contrasts this with the person who buys authentic luxury. 'I think where you find a real craftsman of shoes or a great tailor... you find people who understand just how lucky they are to be in that environment'. For him, branding is 'a terrible concept'.

Fennell enjoys working with clients on bespoke projects. His creations are always made in small quantities. On his website, he says he derives much pleasure from meeting a client 'abroad, on a beach or in a big city, wearing a piece of our jewellery'. He almost always has a conversation with them, and learns the significance that piece of jewellery has to the person (Theo Fennell n.d.).

He enjoys running his own business and the freedom this accords him:

I can make decisions... based purely on what I want to do, purely on what I am trying to make and if it's unpopular then it is my money. I need that freedom.

In an interview with *The Jewellery Editor* on 26 May 2020, Fennell speaks of having a 'blissful time' during his isolation in the country during the pandemic (Doulton 2020: n.pag.). He says he feels guilty saying that but then describes how well he has been able to use the time. It's clear how thoroughly engaged Fennell is in his craft and his dedication to building the talent of those who work with him. We see parallels to the example above of couturier Jean-Paul Gaultier. Like Gaultier, Fennell possesses charisma and is seen by others in the field as one who has exceptional ability. This allows him to see his own ideas and creations as important and worthy of attention.

## STEPHEN JONES[5] – MILLINER

Stephen Jones opened his first millinery salon in London's Covent Garden in 1980. On his website, he describes it as a 'place of pilgrimage and patronage, as everyone from rock stars to royalty, from Boy George to Diana, Princess of Wales, identified Jones as the milliner who would help them make arresting headlines' (Stephen Jones Millinery n.d.: n.pag.). Jones works with Christian Dior and Thom Browne; in addition to his Model Millinery collection he has a women's and men's diffusion line.

He recognizes each person's definition and experience of luxury is different and is quite open to various ways of seeing luxury. He says for some, a £100 handbag is 'complete luxury' while for others it's one of the Launer handbags Queen Elizabeth carries. Having himself worked in haute couture he finds it curious how everyone uses this word freely: 'But you know, couture is a word like bespoke or prestige or luxury. It's just become a general word of communication, like "Fascinator"'. He goes on to say the word is pervasive, whereas some years ago that was not the case. Jones believes luxury brands are the 'culprits':

> They have encouraged that use. I mean, certainly if you think Vuitton, Dior, Hermès, Gucci, maybe Prada and there are certain aspects of what they do which is luxurious, like if you have a Vuitton hatbox; it is made from thin wood and there is this little guy hammering the stuff all over the outside [...] it's like a little sort of magic container, and the mark-up for that must be phenomenal.

Jones purchased a Vuitton hatbox and uses it all the time but asks why a person would spend £1000 for a hat and then £2500 or £3000 for a Vuitton hatbox.

Asked about his own definition, he says he believes one has to spend time on something one was making for it to be luxury. The design has to be 'an evocation of the human condition [...] something beautiful and qualitative'. It is also crucial for Jones that a hat 'inspires the wearer'. He says:

> That's the sort of the luxury that is important to me. It's not so important whether it can be made of cashmere or crocodile or rhodium. It doesn't really need to be all that. The luxury is in the idea contained within the object.

There is 'real couture and luxury, and the sort of friendly couture and luxury. But the demarcation between the two [...] it's constantly shifting and a bit grey anyway'. Jones says for the Dior haute couture client, the attention accorded to her by the *vendeuse* with whom she works closely and by all those who are involved in fittings, is an important part of the experience. The *vendeuse* becomes her advisor. He says this luxury experience exists at all levels, for example, between a woman and her hairdresser. Jones says when he is making a hat for a client 'the amount of time and hard work that goes into this' makes it a luxury item. This does not depend on the material used because sometimes nylon, plastic or paper will be used if that is 'the best material for the job'. Jones is a person capable of taking ordinary materials and elevating them to a new level.

During the pandemic, Jones wanted to do something special. He designed a digital collection for the avatar and influencer, Noonoouri. He chose to collaborate with her creator, Joerg Zuber, as he felt that Noonoouri represented the best in digital fashion (Leitch 2020). His short film aired on 14 June 2020 during London Fashion Week (2020). He is clearly a leader, someone always innovating, building new networks and moving his craft into new domains.

## JUSSARA LEE[6] – DESIGNER AND MAKER

Fashion designer Jussara Lee has her own line of sustainable luxury clothing. She interacts and collaborates with designers and artisans whose products she sells. Lee has the luxury to determine her own path. Her experience is in stark contrast to the women who work in a luxury brand factory.

Lee is totally dedicated to supporting sustainability. She is concerned about the environmental costs of fashion production and the over-consumption contributing to the creation of landfill, as well as the pollution and destruction of resources such as the water supply. This vision extends to every facet of her business from where she buys the paper bags she uses for packaging to where she banks. After an order she'd had made in China was returned, Lee began making her own bags. The glue failed to stick properly and all the bags were returned and destroyed. To display her commitment to sustainability, she attaches a piece of leftover material as a decorative touch on each bag.

Lee no longer works with JP Morgan Chase because she objects to their 'bad business practices'. She moved to TD Bank. 'We support these practices if we do business with these entities', she says. Her commitment to sustainability is applied to her own designs and to the vendors with whom she works. Lee's work is totally focused on recycling products to create unique clothing and accessories. In doing so she believes she takes a stand in protecting the planet.

Lee is committed to supporting craftsmen and women, with a network including artisans, jewellers and tailors in Brooklyn, a shirt maker in Harlem and artisans from many locations. As Lee puts it: 'From Union Square [in New York City] to South Africa'. She is a fervent believer in the support of 'endangered' artisans and wants to give them voice. The Lesage employee discussed earlier in this chapter is a person Lee would value. The tailor in Greenpoint with whom she works has 40 years' experience in crafting suits. She sees his work as meaningful and worthy of support.

Those with whom she collaborates or whose products she sells must meet certain criteria in addition to being in sync with her design aesthetic. 'They need to use natural products or materials, they must use upcycled materials, be a social enterprise and they must be hand-made'. For example, shoes made by a professor at Parsons School of Design who runs a social enterprise in Pakistan. For each pair of shoes sold, he donates the proceeds, which pay for a child's schooling for three to six months.

Regarding her management style, she describes the artisans she works with as her 'bosses'. 'I defer to them', she stresses. She cultivates long-lasting relationships with them. She speaks of the fear the tailor she works with will eventually retire. She has three people working at different times in the store and she has had the same sample maker working for her for 28 years, and a woman who comes in three times a week to do embroidery.

She volunteers at a farm in Tarrytown, New York. She is inter-ested in hemp and other materials that could be made into fibres and used in her creations and she sees a possibility of linking her designs to farming. She is moving towards a zero commerce path by telling her clients not to buy excessively, instructing them on how to repair and recycle clothing and giving them examples of how to reduce their carbon footprint.

## BEATRICE AMBLARD[7] – CRAFTSWOMAN

Beatrice Amblard began working for Hermès in Paris as an artisan in the 1980s. She graduated from a vocational school in Paris when she was just 16 and was hired by the company. Six months after her training, she began working on the iconic Kelly bag as well as other designs made of exotic leathers such as ostrich and alliga-tor. She describes the workplace as 'a very friendly environment. The president was involved with everyone. He took the elevator with employees'.

There were 250 artisans in its Paris workshop. She says after the company went public in 1993, 'we became numbers, not humans. Managers were concerned with increasing production and selling' and those in high positions no longer communicated with the artisans. There are now 5000 artisans.

She explains the pride she took in her work and how the company seemed to value the skills and abilities of artisans:

> When I started working at Hermès I was making one piece at a time. It didn't matter how long it took. The most I made was four pieces at a time. I loved working for my bosses. It was hard work and we were expected to be perfect but it was rewarding. You did feel you were part of the bigger picture. You felt you were at the top. There was nowhere else to go. This was total luxury.

She says although she was appreciated, this did not mean artisans were not looked down upon: 'While we were appreciated by some this was not the case with everyone in the company. We were considered blue-collar workers'.

The culture at Hermès, at least in terms of how Amblard experienced it, is one of stratification. Her role was subordinate within this order, but she did not accept this as her self-concept was at odds with allowing herself to be dominated.

After working in the Paris workshop for four years, Amblard decided she wanted to study English in California. She was able to secure the company's permission for an unpaid leave of absence. 'The company agreed to give me six months. I received a letter saying I would be hired again once I returned'. After moving to the United States, she applied for and won a position as the company's brand ambassador there.

After assuming this role she gradually realized she could no longer in good conscience continue working for the brand. She felt it had changed too much and no longer reflected the standard of luxury it once upheld. She tells of her transition from artisan to ambassador to independent designer and artist:

> There was no creativity. I realized I was not made to be doing the same thing every day. Over the years I realized that luxury was not at all what it was said to be. There was a lot of lying and a lack of integrity.

She decided to start her own brand, called April in Paris. She has one person working with her making handbags in her workshop. Some clients buy models Amblard and her assistant make and are on display in the boutique. Others place orders online but many buy a custom handbag. Amblard works closely with these clients. She says they are an integral part of the process from start to finish. A handbag takes on average between 30 and 40 hours to make.

Amblard's clientele are not interested in the major luxury brands. The customer who buys a handbag from her would not necessarily buy a luxury brand bag, she says. This client recognizes quality and does not want something mass-produced, nor would she want to be seen carrying something readily identified by its logo or design:

> True luxury existed 30 or 40 years ago. Today people with money are not interested in luxury brands. They want something specific. They want to be involved in its creation. This is the true, new luxury.

Her customer enjoys knowing the maker of her handbag and that she had a role in its creation. It is something with a story she can tell to others. Amblard's quote about 'people with money' losing interest in luxury brands is something shared by several people working in the luxury industry. This new elite consumer, introduced in Chapter 3, is someone who can afford to buy luxury brands. Yet they are selective in what they buy and wish to be discreet, not conspicuous. Amblard's client takes pride in letting those in her social circle know her bag was made by a Hermès trained artisan who decided to strike out on her own. This client, as described by Amblard, could have put her name on the Hermès waiting list but decided against that route.

Amblard's skill as a craftswoman originated with the training she received at Hermès in the 1980s and early 1990s, and the pride she and others took in the work is no longer reflected at Hermès today. Yet she recognizes the formative role her training played and incorporates many of the techniques she learned in teaching others. Would her vocational training have been sufficient to help her establish herself as an independent artisan had she not been associated with Hermès? Would her clientele who reject Hermès have accepted her had she not worked for Hermès?

She goes on to say the focus of luxury today is on 'fast turnaround and demand'. She feels quality has declined and merchandise is not very innovative.

Amblard clearly has a keen interest in preserving the craft she has mastered not only through the products she makes, but also through the school she set up to train other aspiring artisans in the skill of leather making:

> What I am doing may not make me rich but I am much richer in spirit. I'm in a very privileged position. I try to keep all that is good and improve on it.

Amblard initiated the Amblard Leather Atelier, which has grown to about 50 students who study for one year and after finishing the programme, mostly work as independent artisans. In addition to this formal programme, she has several short courses, some as brief as one day. Her daughter joined her several years ago and also teaches at the school. Amblard says many of her clients attend the workshops and seminars offered at the school. She is proud she is passing on her knowledge to so many others. When she reflects on working at Hermès and considers her life today she feels extremely privileged to have become an artist and an educator and not to have remained someone who had to take direction and work under conditions where her voice was not heard.

## STEVE DOUDAKLIAN[8] – LEATHERSMITH AND COBBLER

Steve Doudaklian repairs and redesigns luxury handbags in his shop outside Washington, DC. His case is of particular interest in that he repairs and redesigns luxury branded products, primarily hand-bags and shoes. He has a deep understanding of how they are constructed.

Doudaklian describes himself as a leathersmith and also as a cobbler. He is the fourth generation in his family doing this work, taking over his father's shop, which had previously focused on shoe repair. He has expanded the business to focus on the repair and redesign of luxury handbags. Louis Vuitton bags represent the largest share of bags brought in for repair. He admires the quality of the work and craftsman-ship of this brand, which he says is consistent over time. After spend-ing years working with these bags and those of other brands such as Chanel, Gucci, Dior, etc., taking them apart and putting them together, he knows just what goes into their manufacture. And he even has ideas about how certain structural elements can be improved. He identifies an area on the strap of a model that often breaks and says, 'It's a minor detail. Just add a piece of nylon. To keep it strong. They don't do it. It gives structural support'.

His least expensive job probably costs $400 but these can go up to $4500. He is a perfectionist, like his father. His expertise allows him to identify counterfeit items even when they are very well made. He refuses to work on counterfeit bags because of ethical concerns but also because he never compromises his work and doesn't believe these bags merit his careful attention and skills. He videotapes many of his projects and posts them on YouTube and Facebook and also uses Instagram to publicize his work:

I do a lot of Louis Vuitton bags. There are a bunch of them here. There are tons of them here. And I think that the YouTube videos help a lot. Also throughout the years of doing them I belong to a bunch of social media groups where they know that I do Louis Vuitton.

How does Doudaklian define luxury? He says while for the 'layman' it is mostly visual and defined based on 'recognizability', he feels that the histories of the brands go a long way in giving them 'a presence'. There is an assumption that because of the name, the handbags are of the 'highest quality'. He says:

> If a consumer is going to be foolish enough to spend thousands of dollars for something like that, that is OK. You know that is their right.

Brands trade on this heritage and cut corners to save money:

> But the manufacturer says OK, it is a closed case. Where can we cut corners on this where no one can see? Everything on the inside, for example. The shape of it. The plastic forms that they use for the suitcase, stuff like that. If you are making how many thousands of pieces and if you save 5 cents on one of the cases and you multiply that that is what manufacturers look for, the bottom line, the figures, how much money can we save from this particular style by changing a small, minute detail that the consumer is not going to see.

Doudaklian, when speaking of the 'presence' and the 'history' of the bag, identifies the exact narrative used by the brands in representing their products to consumers. So what does he consider the essential features necessary to make a bag a luxury item?

> You know, it's unfortunate that most of the consumers [...] they just see a name. And they don't really know what goes into the bag at all because when I do some of my videos, you know I explain that OK I am going to take this $2,000 or $3,000 bag apart and all of the sudden there is paper inside [...] it's a fibre board stiffener to give it shape.

Asked if this was always the case and whether he finds this objection-able, he says:

Well, I think that it is just kind of misleading the consumer. Well, don't get me wrong, there is nothing wrong with it. That is how a majority of the bags are made. There is nothing wrong with that. I don't think they were made differently in the past. The majority are compressed fibreboard. They will take recycled paper and they will shred it and press it together. They have a bonded paper basically.

Doudaklian says this upsets many customers, as they believe it is 'cheaply made':

They don't want to invest the thousands of dollars in something like that. But they forgot that you are paying for the name, the majority of what you are paying for is the name. Take Louis Vuitton for example. It is basically fabric with a dye on it. So the major-ity of the bag is vinyl-coated fabric! And you've got leather trim.

Asked about the essential features of bags defined as 'luxury', he says:

Basically, overall the fixtures or the hardware are a little better quality metal. There are lots of fake ones with really cheap hardware. The leather, the leather trim itself. That's good leather. Quality. Top notch. No scars on it. It is not dirty, it is not stained. When you are putting edge dressing on the straps there is no overflow on the straps. All the little details like that. That is why I say you are paying for the name. But it is a good quality item. I mean I sit there when I go to the shops. I know we talk about Louis Vuitton because that is what I do a lot of. And sometimes I go to Prada, Gucci and Saint Laurent whatever and I look at it and it is just a beautiful job. It is flawless. There is no defect on it whatsoever. And doing something like that in a production line like that is not easy. No. Because even though it is machine made, human beings touch it and things happen. Obviously they have a good quality control department. You don't show the little defective bags to the consumers. For that price of course. You better not have defective items. So I just like to see when I look at it, it is a beautiful product. Quality. The leather is good. The hardware. The stitching. I tend to sit there and measure the stitches sometimes. If you have a pattern – there are magic patterns. If there are 15 stitches on the one side, there have to be 15 on the other side. Most people don't look at things like that. It is not their business. They shouldn't be there counting stitches.

He doesn't consider brands such as Michael Kors and Coach, on which he works from time to time, luxury brands based on the quality of their fabrication. He classifies them as 'base' or 'basic' items, even though he contends these two brands may have higher end lines.

Referring to a bag he picks up from a shelf, he says:

> This, for example, it is an older bag. It is a Burberry bag. Again vinyl coated fabric with leather trim. Now it is a good quality bag. It's probably a good ten years old. Maybe more. And it has lasted. The lining is in great shape. The leather trim as you see has kind of faded. That is normal for leather to do. We are going to add a little bit of colour. Change the binding on top. This is $365. She will use it for another ten years. Because if this is not dried and cracked, then you can continue to use the bag.

He classifies Burberry and Louis Vuitton as being on the same level of the luxury brand spectrum. 'They are a very similar style in terms of the types of bags they are making with the vinyl. And the leather trim'.

Asked to rank the luxury brands from top, middle and bottom, Doudaklian says:

> Hermès. Hermès is Hermès. There is no comparison. It is like a classic. Versace is good. Versace is more of, I say, like the crazy cousin business. Because they are off the charts when it comes to design. They are not like your basic traditional designs. Who else? Let's see. Prada is OK. Prada is very similar to Burberry. Yves Saint Laurent is not bad. But I just, I don't know, I am partial to Louis Vuitton. I don't know why. I do a lot of them. Maybe it's because I do a lot of them. I like Gucci also. Gucci is different. It has different styles. Artistic styles. I do a lot of older Guccis that come in. Again most of the stuff that comes in is not vintage vintage but it is old.

How closely does Doudaklian think price corresponds to the quality of the handbags he knows so well? The classic Chanel costs $5800. Do these bags warrant the prices?

> When a company has years of reputation and they spend so much money on public relations and commercials and advertising, you almost brainwash the consumer. You know. They are at a level where they can produce just about anything they want and there is a buyer for it. Whatever the cost is there are these people who will buy it. If they can get away with it, why not? To each his own.

Questioned about where the best quality handbags are manufactured, Doudaklian returns to an analysis of levels of quality among different brands. He compares the luxury brands to car manufacturers such as Ferrari, Bentley and Porsche, which only use top-grade leather with no imperfections. He describes the practices of the best farms producing top-notch leather. He speaks of ways of hiding imperfections:

> When you tan leather, there are lots of different ways of tanning it in which you can hide those imperfections. You can sand the surface, re-dye, stamp a pattern on there. But you want top grade leather with no imperfections.

He then speaks about how Longchamp takes shortcuts:

> I don't like some of the leathers they use. [Takes out a bag] So basically this is just a stamp. So not this particular one but what they will do with some of their styles is almost like split leather. They will take that top grade off and they will put a vinyl coat on the surface. It is leather underneath but there is a vinyl coating on the surface. What happens with that is when that starts bending it starts peeling the top. When it starts peeling there is nothing you can do. It is unfortunate that they do that. It bubbles up.

He goes on to explain they use cheap leathers with surface imperfections:

> They will sand that surface. They will coat it and now you have a hide that you can use on anything. But you can't repair that. Once the surface breaks like that, you are done. There is nothing you can do about it when it bubbles up. It is too bad because unfortunately the consumer finds out years later down the road after they use it. You can't do anything about it. So that is one company. I hate that they do that. Longchamp is known for that. I see a lot of it come in and it's unfortunate. We tell the consumers: 'Look, there is not anything we can do'. They are expensive brands; they are not very cheap.

Doudaklian sees his business as sustainable. His customers invest money in repairing their favourite bag. By and large they are not women who buy excessively. Rather, as he explains, they will use a bag for as long as they can, maybe for ten years or longer and then will bring it for repair.

He gives more detail on one of his more unique projects:

I've got tons of really good videos. The Chanel, Louis Vuitton and Gucci bags. We have one of them that generated a lot of views. It was a Chanel Boy Bag. It is like a messenger bag, flap over. It's got Chanel on the top, the word. She wanted to change it to crocodile. The flap. It was beige. It was a really light colour.

Despite thinking he would be unable to do anything with it, his work turned out so well that the client bought another $8000 bag in black and he charged her another $2000 to redesign it.

## EUROPEAN LUXURY BRAND FACTORY WORKERS

In an article in the *Wall Street Journal*, Matthew Dalton (2019) interviewed workers at Louis Vuitton's temporary factory in Alvarado, Texas, which was in operation two years before the brand completed its state of the art facility in Keene, Texas. Dalton speaks of how the brand 'pushed the boundaries of what separates the making of luxury goods from any other product' by having its employees work in 'sweltering heat without air conditioning' (2019: n.pag.). Amy Wynn, an employee who was fired, says: 'It was literally a sweatshop' and that it was 'brutally hot' (2019: n.pag.). One artisan who worked in a temporary facility in Burleson, Texas who titles his or her post on Indeed, 'Worst job I ever had' warns people to 'stay away' (2019c: n.pag.). Another says: 'Working for this company was a nightmare, the stress level you get from the supervisor is unbelievable. They don't see you as a human being, you are more like a machine' (2019d). Louis Vuitton is the LVMH group's most important brand, representing about 45 per cent of its operating profit (Abboud 2020), which totalled €53.7 billion in 2020 (LVMH 2019b) yet it seemingly did not invest in an interim facility with even moderately comfortable conditions for its workers.

For this book, we were fortunate enough to interview four women artisans who work for, or have worked in a luxury brand factory setting. To protect their confidentiality we will call them Woman 1, 2, 3 and 4[9]. Woman 1 no longer works at the factory and Women 2, 3 and 4 work at two different locations of the same luxury brand. Woman 1, who works in the factory of a European luxury brand outside of the brand's country of origin, describes an experience not dissimilar to the Louis Vuitton temporary factory described by Dalton (2019). She refers to her company as a 'slave sweatshop' and says this is the 'nickname' employees had for the factory in which she worked:

There was no AC, no relief from the heat. They barely had fans. In the summer there was one big fan pointed at one line. There were 19 stations with machines in a line. The fan only reached the first person on the line. It was hot, overheated, in a cage [and] felt like a slave or sweatshop worker.

Woman 2 has worked at this brand as an 'artisan' for nearly three years and says her factory 'went from worst, worse to decent'. The factory now has air conditioning and heat but the workers must use a restroom in an outside building.

Not surprisingly, the women were most troubled by their everyday work conditions, which were by any standard quite oppressive. The image portrayed of the brand and the lifestyle it conveys doesn't reflect the conditions within its factories.

Employees are selected for their dexterity and no prior experience is necessary. Woman 1 explains: 'On my interview we did a dexterity test and I thought it was like OK I am just going to type or something but no, we made wallets'. Asked how wallets are made and how many a person should make each day, she says they had to make 30 in a day but that the quantity has likely increased. They aren't hard to make: 'The wallets are double sided tape all the way and then they stitch around it'.

Unlike the mythology luxury brands create in their advertising, the training process at this company is rapid and not at all thorough. It comprised a two-week training where employees 'learn how to operate a sewing machine'. This is followed by line work. One has no choice and after training one works in 'sewing, inspection, painting, cutting' and receives specific instructions on how to carry out work. Woman 4 says of the training:

> It wasn't specific to one bag but it was specific to the X's [names company] bags, if that makes sense. We learned how to do jump stitches, back stitches, circles, monogram, how to manoeuvre the material, which machines were for what, changing needles, changing thread, different stuff like that.

In what Aldous Huxley (1958) would refer to as the 'nightmare of total organization', or Arendt (1958) as *animal laborans* (the triumph of labour over man) the 'task idea' in place in luxury brand factories such as this one allows for each movement carried out by the worker to be planned to the millisecond. Says Frederick Winslow Taylor: 'This furnishes the workman with a clear-cut standard, by which he can throughout the day measure his own progress, and the accomplishment of which affords him the greatest satisfaction' (1913: 120). Taylor explains that once management and work are elevated to a science

> each act of each workman is so great and amounts to so much that the workman who is best suited to actually doing the work is incapable of fully understanding this science, without the guidance and help of those who are working with him or over him, either through lack of education or through insufficient mental capacity.
>
> (1913: 25)

Describing 'the line' along which the work process occurs, Woman 3 states: 'You have to follow the instructions exactly. You can't make any decision on your own'. This statement could be interpreted as insurance, a way of ensuring all the products made in the factory are exactly the same. This is, in effect, brand control.

> You have to do ten bags in an hour. They get put in a box. I was the only one who could do three bags in two minutes. [...] I got to the point on a machine where I learned to do it automatically.

Woman 1 made a particular model selling for almost $1400. 'Supposedly when I first started we were only making nine a day because that was the hardest bag to make. And then slowly it kept going up on us and they said you have to make eleven' .

Taylor contends, without providing any means of assurance on how this might be enforced:

> It is absolutely necessary, then, when workmen are daily given a task which calls for a high rate of speed on their part, that they should also be insured the necessary high rate of pay whenever they are successful. This involves not only fixing for each man his daily task, but also paying him a large bonus, or premium, each time that he succeeds in doing his task in the given time.
>
> (1913: 121)

Relatively low salaries ($1150 before taxes and about $800 after taxes and health insurance are deducted) are coupled with being unable to live in close proximity to the factory, requiring a long commute. The calculation reveals Woman 1's take-home salary is $64 a day. Compare this to the $15,600 she makes for the company, and the imbalance is striking.

The three women still working in the factory reveal many ways in which they feel powerless. For example, they are unable to make suggestions for improvements in the work process. After performing the same tasks over and over, the women sometimes find ways to improve something but are told by their managers this is not their concern.

There is a sense of resignation and an acceptance that one's circumstances are not in one's control. A person with economic, cultural and or social capital sees other options and is more likely to feel offence and to take action to change his or her circumstances.

The mechanised worker is stripped of his or her humanity. This is something the designer artisans described above do not experience. Many of the acts of disregard towards the workers can be seen as what Bourdieu refers to as 'symbolic violence'. Not only does the dominant group impose a 'cultural arbitrary' – a standard it sets where its values and interests are taken to be correct – but it censures those who do not adhere to the standards imposed (Bourdieu and Wacquant 1992: 170).

David Swartz explores the influence Max Weber's notions of charisma and legitimacy had on Bourdieu's theory of culture as a 'power resource' (1996: 76). The luxury sector can be seen as a stratified 'field' that accords those who work within it with varying degrees of power and can also dispense cultural capital to some and strip it from others. By virtue of holding one or another position, one is accorded with privileges and enjoys the benefits of that office even if he or she does not possess certain qualifications normally associated with it. Factory workers occupy the lowest rung, which they share with others seen as peripheral to the core of a luxury enterprise. Drivers, forklift operators, those involved in packing and moving supplies in stockrooms are all providing important but invisible functions. Artisans are a paradox in that they are hidden and treated as peripheral in the ordinary life of the organization and yet are elevated by brands that gain value based on the work artisans perform.

The luxury factory quite literally has artisans in service to those at higher levels in the company who transform the goods they produce into symbolic goods: commodities imbued with the heritage of the brand. These artisans possess no power and no legitimacy in their own right and thus have little or no cultural capital in such settings. They are in many circumstances disembodied labourers. It is only at the highest levels of the organization that decisions are taken about the direction of the company, its culture, the design of its products, communications and marketing. Legitimacy is conferred from the top down. We have dominant and subordinate positions, those who possess agency and dignity within the confines of the brand's own definition and interests, and those stripped of basic forms of agency and dignity.

We can to a degree compare the experiences of Fennell and Jones. Both have achieved recognition in their fields and beyond, making them leaders in the luxury sector. Amblard or Lee inhabit a much smaller space within the luxury field but like Fennell and Jones, they are in control of their own creative process. Amblard and Lee can be described as empowered women who see themselves as privileged to be able to work outside of the industrial world of luxury brands. The four women who are called 'artisans' are in no way comparable to the designer artisans. They are artisans in name only.

Luxury labour exists along a continuum. In large luxury enterprises, the production mode is characterized by invisible 'material' labour in which workers may be described as 'disembodied'. Their working conditions are hidden not only from the public but also from almost all employees in the company not working in production. Immaterial and embodied labour is carried out by cultural intermediaries whose conceptual and technical skills, cultural capital, appearance and abilities to communicate place them in a visible position in corporate offices and within the larger context of the luxury industry where they may interact with others across divisions and companies and in some cases, with the public within the realm of consumption.

During production, costs may be cut, workers deskilled and labour subject to none of the safeguards or protections that should be advocated for the benefit of employees. Artisans and factory workers alike may in some companies be valued and fully integrated into the culture and philosophy of the company in a way that enriches their professional lives and self-concept. In Fennell and Jones' companies and in Lee's and Amblard's smaller ones, design and production are interconnected. In each case, the designer artisans take into account the concerns and convictions of those who work for them. They all fit the description of cultural intermediaries. As artists and or designers their 'self' is to a large extent implicated in the brand they represent and as such, the work each does can be described as embodied labour – which is also empowered labour. Some of the same characteristics are shown in Doudaklian's professional life.

The practices and experiences of these designer makers differ, as do their leadership styles and the types of organizational cultures they create. All work closely with the artisans they employ in their companies, who help them realize their creations. In the case of Fennell, Jones and Lee, they work with independent artisans and others on collaborative projects. Amblard teaches students in her leather school and Lee educates consumers in conversations she has with them and in formal workshops she runs. Doudaklian connects with his custom-ers, each of whom has a unique story related to their bag. Their small businesses allow them to make these connections. The creations of Fennell and Jones and of Amblard and Lee and the repairs and rede-signs of Doudaklian are unique and cannot be compared to the work of those who produce branded merchandise in large quantities in facto-ries across the globe. This is the antithesis of luxury.

# 6

# Social Responsibility, Eco-Design and the Circular Economy

*In a world dominated by fashion and consumption, consumers are continuously encouraged to consume products whose raw materials are extracted from the earth's valuable natural resources. The impact of this behaviour on all aspects of the supply chain, waste management and human wellbeing is becoming apparent, and needs to be addressed urgently.*

## Luxury and waste

The foundation of luxury has come to rest on unnecessary excess, creating a range of interesting challenges when considering social responsibility, eco-design and the circular economy.

    Georges Bataille ([1949] 1988) poses an interesting question concerning the organization of society. To understand how a given society is organized, we must look at how it expends its energy, something every society has in excess. For some societies, excess energy, which he equates with 'wealth', may be expended on war and for others on religious ritual. This use of energy will determine how production and consumption are structured and help decide a given society's position with respect to its natural resources. Variations in culture – and culture itself – are a result of the way excess energy, or 'surplus', is expended. It can be invested in an egalitarian manner, in the arts or sacrificed in a potlatch. The surplus can be reinvested in economic activities in a strict Protestant society, or it can be wasted:

> The living organism, in a situation determined by the play of energy on the surface of the globe, ordinarily receives more energy than is necessary for maintaining life; the excess energy (wealth) can be used for the growth of a system (e.g., an organism); if the system can no longer grow, or if the excess cannot be completely absorbed in its growth, it must necessarily be lost without profit; it must be spent, willingly or not, gloriously or catastrophically.
>
> (Bataille [1949] 1988: 21)

Bataille describes human sacrifice in Aztec civilization as a means of restoring a sacred order. In the potlatch, the person with a surplus is made rich by the act of ostentatiously sacrificing his wealth in the form of luxurious items: 'What is appropriated in the squander is the prestige it gives to the squanderer (whether an individual or a group), which is acquired by him as a possession and which determines his rank' ([1949] 1988: 72). 'Beyond the archaic forms', says Bataille 'luxury has actually retained the functional value of potlatch, creative of rank. Luxury still determines the rank of the one who displays it, and there is no exalted rank that does not require a display' ([1949] 1988: 76).

Can luxury exist without waste if, as Bataille says, its very essence is waste? It is essentially a display of excess in which very few can indulge. One is not, of course, sacrificing luxury products by throwing them in a bonfire. But parallels can be drawn in the actions of many luxury brands discarding surplus products to protect their IP. The contemporary luxury consumer is no doubt consuming rank but is also consuming selfishly, so much so that he or she wants to guard these possessions. In a hyper-consumption society, driven by fashion, there will be more luxury products on the market to consume and some of them will require less of a financial sacrifice to acquire. Waste, in this case, takes on another dimension. Natural resources are being expended in the mass manufacture of luxury products on one end of the spectrum. On the other hand, an effort is made to increase the desire for more rarefied forms of luxury.

# Social responsibility

Companies, if they have not already done so, are being pressured to imbed corporate social responsibility frameworks in their strategic

plans and to comply with increasingly complex territory specific legislation governed by border control, factory audits and end-to-end
paper trails.

Blockchain and track and trace are being implemented as more
companies seek not only to manage their supply chains but also to
give customers the option of obtaining details about the origins of
their products. This includes the raw materials, the origins of the seed,
propagation, where the seed was germinated, how much water was
used in the yield, who picked the bud, where it went for processing.
This powerful information is becoming increasingly important to the
consumer.

However, few companies are completely transparent. For
many, this technology is not implemented in a meaningful way and
may only reveal a small part of the story. Despite this, provenance
is now becoming normal practice and embedding it at the start of
the process through technology creates a future proof system for
information retrieval. However, there are still questions to be asked
about authenticity and transparency relating to the types of information provided when luxury brands are inherently opaque about the
details they release.

After Stella McCartney left Kering in 2018, she joined LVMH
less than one year later (the brand owns a 50 per cent stake in her
company). Lauren Sherman explains, 'Arnault certainly didn't need
McCartney to grow his business' (2020: n.pag.). What she believes
was most attractive about McCartney to Arnault was her visibility as
a leader in sustainability. Says Sherman: 'He could benefit from her
know-how and authority when it came to the sustainability conversation, a burgeoning battleground in which Kering was seen to be ahead
of the curve' (2020: n.pag.). McCartney has been hailed by the press for
her leather and fur-free fashion and has partnered with animal activist
NPO, People for the Ethical Treatment of Animals (PETA), on several
occasions to the extent of being a spokesperson for the organization.
Still, she has been called out for a variety of actions, which contradict
her image as a champion of sustainability and corporate social responsibility. The most notable example was in an article in the *Observer*
newspaper when it was revealed factory workers endured physical
abuse at the hands of their supervisors while making clothing for the
Olympics for Adidas designed by Stella McCartney (Chamberlain 2012).

This increased implementation of vertical integration into the
entire supply chain has also seen an exponential growth in supplier
acquisitions by luxury brand conglomerates. This ensures control and
could also arguably be interpreted as closing the gap on transparency
where materials and production are sourced. As previously discussed,

the range of acquisitions includes tanneries, weavers, knitwear factories, textile mills, shoemakers, clothing manufacturers and trims (zips, buttons and hardware). It is accepted that as a result of global reach, the luxury brands no longer rely entirely on home production, or production in the country of origin – the place where the luxury brand originated. Take Dior and Louis Vuitton in France and Prada or Gucci in Italy, for example. This approach raises many questions around the social responsibility charters released each year. The conglomerates identify their moral obligations around issues such as equality, fairness, employment and labour and clearly articulate their global strategies in their annual reports. But as one would expect, the companies' focus is solely on what they are doing as opposed to what they are not. This is a selective process of addressing social responsibility. More questions are raised than are answered.

> In today's socially conscious environment, employees and customers place a premium on working for and spending their money with businesses that prioritize corporate social responsibility (CSR). CSR is an evolving business practice that incorporates sustainable development into a company's business model. It has a positive impact on social, economic and environmental factors.
> (Schooley 2021: n.pag.)

If one were to take Schooley's quote at face value, every company in the world engaging in social responsibility would appear to be, well, responsible. However, in reality, the business world does not by and large operate in a manner that meets socially conscious criteria. Luxury brands are as guilty as any other corporation when it comes to saying one thing and doing another. In the end it is profit that matters, and far too many companies prioritize this above all else. Thomas at the time of writing *Deluxe: How Luxury Lost Its Luster* says for the last 30 years, a 'single-minded focus on profitability' characterized the luxury industry and to achieve this, it has 'sacrificed its integrity, undermined its products, tarnished its history and hoodwinked its consumers' (2007: 13, 41). This strong statement about the all-consuming drive for profitability raises serious issues around the values and practices of the major luxury brands and their commitment to changing practices for the better.

On 20 April 2021, a significant step was taken to form Aura Blockchain Consortium whose platform was built by Consensys and Microsoft. In September 2019, LVMH executives met with representatives from Prada and Richemont and a decision was taken on a collaborative governance and strategy based on blockchain. This tech platform enables customers to access information about production history, provenance and authenticity of products by matching a client ID to a product ID. Marjorie Hernandez, co-founder of the Lukso Blockchain platform, says this indicates a 'change of mentality within the industry' (McDowell 2021: n.pag.). LVMH joining forces with, as it puts it, 'competitors' Prada and Cartier, calls the move 'unprecedented' (LVMH 2021b: n.pag.). It remains to be seen how this consortium will operate and whether a significant level of transparency will result, or if it will merely provide the appearance of transparency.

# Luxury contradictions

If one were to look at, for example, Gucci, Dior, Hermès, Chanel and Prada it is evident they all continue to grow through an increasingly diverse product offer. The most striking difference between Prada and the others is that Prada started as a gift store in Milan in 1913 since then it has changed substantially to become what is now a global fashion brand.

Miuccia Prada inherited her grandfather's small family business and transformed it into an empire with Patrizio Bertelli, a leather goods manufacturer who runs the financial side of the business. Prada, who holds a doctorate in political science, explains that on a personal level working in luxury is a 'big conflict' for her. 'It's all an illusion that you look better because you have a symbol of luxury. Really it doesn't bring you anything, it's so banal' (Thomas 2007: 67). Prada, in speaking of her views on sustainability and her fall 2020 men's collection, which she says was 'almost zero impact', cautioned against cutting consumption because this leads to unemployment (Zargani 2020a: n.pag.). In a climate where luxury brands were being particularly hard hit by the global pandemic, more emphasis was placed on selling product and job stability despite the need to be more aware of being sustainable and environmentally responsible.

In 2015, PETA made a documentary exposing the conditions at Hermès' crocodile farms in Zimbabwe and in Texas. They showed how crocodiles are farmed in crowded pens and at the Lone Star Alligator Farms in Texas, in 'dank, dark pits' where they were immersed in water that was polluted by 'putrid and rancid excrement' (PETA 2019). At three years old they are viciously slaughtered and sometimes skinned alive, cutting short a life span that in the wild could reach 80 years. Workers themselves were sometimes bitten and injured. Jane Birkin, the actress and singer for whom the famous Birkin bags are named, was so disturbed by this that she asked her name be removed from the bag. Birkin says:

Having been alerted to the cruel practices reserved for croco-diles during their slaughter to make Hermès handbags carrying my name... I have asked Hermès to debaptise the Birkin Croco until better practices in line with international norms can be put in place

(Anon. 2015a: n.pag.)

The reverse baptism was short-lived. By September of the same year, Birkin was reported accepting Hermès' explanation of an 'isolated irregularity' occurring in Texas (Chrisafis 2015: n.pag.). In general, these scandals are quickly dismissed with companies issuing statements pointing to some misunderstanding and vowing to be more vigilant in the future. These practices are prevalent across the luxury industry and the only time brands admit to misdeeds is when they are caught red-handed. It is common to deny any wrongdoing and to promise to address these ongoing issues (see further Munro 2021).

# The luxury paradox

The luxury business was once niche and more sustainable due to the relatively small number of wealthy customers who could afford to indulge. The need for the luxury business to grow and expand exposed it to more lucrative and larger markets where the mass-market adop-tion of more affordable products created a more impactful sustain-ability conundrum. This creates a paradox. The problem lies in what the customer can afford. At the very top end, of course, the private jet, purpose-built yacht, handmade timepiece or supercar is still the preserve of those with great wealth. Not many of these items are produced. But perfume, a wallet, a keychain and many leather goods are affordable and widely available under the luxury designation. Due to the mass-market appeal of entry-level products, the environmental impact is exacerbated. Despite corporate social responsibility (CSR) guidelines being followed by the company, this does not necessarily address the sheer volume of goods consumed.

Such tensions are normal and customers are used to it. When a brand promotes its products by presenting social responsibility as one of the factors, consumers feel relieved, as they do not have to deal with these tensions in their choice to buy the product. While such tensions can be diminished, they can never be removed from the buying expe-rience. Tensions also tend to be buried in detail and the complexity involved in understanding issues around social responsibility and the impact consumer choices have on this. Revealing the root cause and getting to the truth becomes an inconvenient operation the majority of customers do not feel they have time for. For example, a cosmetic brand may state they do not test on animals. However, the ingredient suppliers for those cosmetics may do so. Furthermore some countries, including China, require products to be tested on animals prior to sale (PETA n.d.). Nearly all the luxury brands test either the finished product and/or the ingredients on animals. They include Chanel, Dior and Prada. But even those time-rich individuals who inquire about a product's origin, composition and heritage are not necessarily given insight into the working conditions and wellbeing of those who make them. CSR also creates a platform that encourages all in the supply chain, retail, fulfilment and wider society to care, something the luxury goods industry has always successfully achieved when holding up their actions and products as aspirational. Taking that duty of care further, so that it successfully tackles the environmental and social impact of their actions, would be a natural next step. Making their actions transparent and easily accessible would encourage customers to support them on their quest.

As the wealth gap continues to increase, those people at the top end have the means to indulge in all of life's luxuries. This creates a paradox where the needs of those at the bottom of the financial divide are simply met with the prospect or opportunity of factory work to make the products for those at the top of the pyramid. In most circumstances, the items being produced for luxury brands by the factory workers cost more, even at wholesale, than they earn in a week. As with all producers and retailers of products, whether it is fast fashion or luxury labelled items, the aim is to acquire something as cheaply as possible to ensure a healthy mark-up and significant profit. Leveraging the varying costs associated with labour markets around the world to maintain a competitive edge is something the majority of manufacturers consider to bring their products to market. The luxury goods industry is just as guilty as those involved in fast fashion and cheap consumer goods when it comes to sourcing materials, production and low-cost distribution.

The need to sell mass-produced items means the majority of luxury companies implement a sales model to clear and discount unsold stock at the end of each selling season. This creates a secondary market, where highly priced items become accessible to a wider customer base. Without the discount they could otherwise not necessarily afford to make these purchases. An entire sub-industry of luxury has emerged through the expansive need to move discounted merchandise. Luxury outlet villages have sprung up all over the world to address this need. The larger of these is Value Retail, which operates eleven such villages in China and Europe and offers merchandise at discounts of up to 80 per cent. In addition online platforms, including for example Brand Alley, offer current and past season merchandise at up to 80 per cent off the original price. The model is one that relies on the supplier to cover the costs, as they do not buy the goods outright, but rather pay once the product is sold.

The 'artisans' who worked in the luxury brand factory discussed in Chapter 5 were hopeful they would be able to purchase the items they made at substantially discounted prices. They were disappointed not to be able to acquire these coveted goods. These examples illustrate the chasm that exists between those who can and cannot afford luxury brand products, and points to a lack of recognition by the brands of their factory workforce. What we have is a fragmented fashion market that adopts luxury terminology to describe and define their products. This increasingly exposes a growing division of wealth, while at the same time uses their market position to sell an aspirational lifestyle to encourage consumption and selectively make it accessible to an ever-wider audience.

# Activities and products

There is also an interesting use of the terminology to distinguish tasks and positions within a luxury organization used when marketing the companies' activities and products. The luxury goods companies tend to promote themselves as the 'house of' or atelier and think of the manufacturing workforce as craftsman or artisans. But the reality is they still utilize mass production techniques and workflow to bring their products to market at a mass scale – just like the majority of financially successful businesses. The wellbeing and consideration of the workforce and the companies' environmental impact are equally important, regardless of company type or area of activity. To a certain extent, the CSR framework is the same for luxury businesses as the rather more mundane but equally important other areas of industry.

LVMH, Kering, the Prada Group and Richemont, whose controlling interests account for 90 per cent of the worlds' luxury brands, all promote social responsibility agendas, targets and ethical and environmental impact. But there is a need to better understand how this translates in practice. These four conglomerates' social responsibility agendas are alike. They use similar language to describe their commitments to their workforces, the environment, their suppliers and communities.

| Social responsibility agendas of the four global conglomerates | | | |
|---|---|---|---|
| **LVMH** | **Kering** | **Richemont** | **Prada Group** |
| This commitment concretely addresses the ethical responsibility of businesses in general, along with the distinctive role in society played by a group such as LVMH, both in France and around the world (LVMH 2021a). | Care, collaborate, create. Three pillars to develop more sustainable and more responsible luxury. Three pillars that shape Kering's 2025 sustainability strategy in a world where reducing resource consumption and respecting people are absolute necessities. Three pillars that embody and drive our ambition: to craft tomorrow's luxury (Kering n.d.). | It demonstrates how we are meeting our commitments and describes how we manage our social, ethical and environmental impacts. As a responsible luxury goods company, we seek to improve lives across all points in the luxury value chain (Richemont n.d.). | The Prada Group believes that it is part of its corporate social responsibility to be involved in issues such as respect for people, environment, communities and artistic heritage.

These principles, which have always been part of the Group's activities, find expression in corporate culture, relations with institutions and industry associations, with supply chain partners and in cultural projects supporting the communities in the areas where it is present (Prada Group 2018) |

Words are one thing, but their actions are a completely different matter. One could, if taken on face value, attribute their social responsibility 'mission statements' to an utopian existence where the corporation only does good for their communities of employers, suppliers, manufacturers and of course customers.

In its strategic plan, The LVMH group focus on women, staff development and opportunity and the environment. This is an excerpt of their corporate strategy focused on the environment in 2019:

Bernard Arnault gathered today at LVMH's headquarters top executives of the Group and its Maisons around its LIFE program

(LVMH Initiatives For the Environment), spotlighting pioneering initiatives in biodiversity and providing tangible elements about its environmental performance as well as ambitions in products' eco-design, circular economy and energy consumption. The Group also presented new commitments including its brand-new Animal-based Raw Materials Sourcing Charter, which is based on a sound scientific approach and addresses the environmental, social and ethical issues faced by the fur, leather, wool and feather industries by providing a new and clear frame of reference and sourcing rules.

(LVMH 2019: n.pag.)

LVMH also promotes its commitment to talent saying:

Our decentralized organization enables us to remain close to our customers, to rapidly make effective and appropriate decisions, and to continually motivate our teams, inspiring them to show entrepreneurial spirit. This environment encourages risk-taking and perseverance. It requires pragmatic thinking and an ability to motivate teams to achieve excellence.

(LVMH n.d.: n.pag.)

But what has the group actually done to address the issues they have brought to our attention? It is incredibly difficult to find the results of any action taken to address environmental concerns other than generic information on the social responsibility pages on their website. Mention of any resounding successes or significant accomplishments is scarce.

The questions that need answering relate to each and every statement of intent and the findings of their 'scientific approach' to addressing environmental concerns. Do they continue to manufacture their plasticized canvas that is used in the majority of their bags, accessories and luggage? The LVMH group is extremely successful in selling their positive credentials relating to their actions in addressing climate change and the environment. On the[10] website they stated:

The Maison is constantly innovating in order to sustainably reduce their environmental impact. The importance of improving a product's environmental performance is just as crucial as the customer's product experience. For example, the Horizon luggage includes a new, lighter weight that reduces $CO_2$ impact by 20 per cent per kilometre travelled. In order to minimise their impact on climate change, they are committed to reducing their carbon emissions, particularly product transportation and energy consumption in their buildings. This is aligned with LVMH's Carbon Fund that helps the Maison invest in a variety of initiatives to reduce their energy footprint'. They go on to say, 'In 2013, the LVMH group and 32 of its Houses signed the United Nations' global agreement on Women's Empowerment Principles (WEP). As a result, the Group is committed to making every possible effort to offer women and men the same opportunities to achieve their full potential by ensuring equitable treatment of both women and men and is demonstrated through financial compensation and benefits. The development of talent and equal opportunities has been well established throughout the business. This development includes L'Ecole des Savoir-faire Maroquinerie, a programme which was created in early 2010, with the objective of gathering all the Maison's leather goods know-how to teach and inspire the next generation of craftsmen.

(LVMH 2020: n.pag.)

These sweeping statements are not limited to LVMH; they are applied in various iterations to Kering, Richemont and the Prada Group. The statements and stats, generated by the companies themselves with no external auditing, are a result of a complete lack of transparency and undermine the entire process of self-justification. Back to the plasticized canvas that has become the most recognizable brand feature of Louis Vuitton. The monogram products are made from polyvinylchloride, which is a PVC derivative and is a widely used synthetic plastic, and the most damaging to the environment as reported in a widely cited Greenpeace article titled 'PVC: Poison or plastic'. There is little information available clearly stating how much of the plastic is used, where it comes from and what environmental impact it has in landfill, in the oceans or what its carbon footprint may be. These fundamental flaws in transparency are common throughout the luxury brands industry. And it is not limited to materials. Labour and manufacturing methods are also contentious issues.

Again, using LVMH as an example. It fervently promotes its equality credentials, and particular reference is made to the Elles LVMH initiative. On their website they claim:

In 2013 the LVMH Group and 32 of its Maisons signed the United Nations Women's Empowerment Principles (WEP). In fall 2014 the heads of LVMH Maisons based in the United States also signed the charter, bringing the total number of LVMH signatories to 41.

(LVMH 2020: n.pag.)

> Between 2007 and 2018 the percentage of women in key posi-
> tions at LVMH rose from 23 per cent to 42 per cent. This puts
> LVMH on track to achieve its new goal of 50 per cent women in
> top management positions by 2020.
>
> (LVMH 2020: n.pag.)

The focus here is clearly on the support given to management or those in positions of responsibility and not factory workers. What the company fails to address are the thousands of workers in their factories around the world who endure extreme hardship as a result of their working conditions. Not only do they have to bear physical discomfort, exclusion and poor working conditions but also their salaries do not in any way reflect the work they do.

The wealth gap creates a significant divide between those who have the means to indulge in a luxury branded product and those who do not. The workers, cutters, machinists and finishers in the United States are paid, at the time of writing, $13.50 an hour. The product they produce costs at the lower end on average $300 for a wallet. Through our own research, particularly interviews conducted with factory workers, we discovered the reality of the working conditions are, as one would expect, far from the advertising imagery of the workshops or ateliers and sumptuous retail environments Louis Vuitton promotes.

The luxury industry, however, faces an ethical dilemma when considering the aspirational framework it promotes. Luxury marketing continues to call into question the quality of life of millions of individuals by suggesting that their lifestyle could be better through the purchase of the high-priced products it promotes. The idea one needs to do better and earn more in order to be part of the luxurious existence the brands offer inextricably links luxury products to success.

This would seem to be a compelling argument for luxury, to better one's own existence through aspiration, to want the goods, services and lifestyle they promote. However, it is a message that is out of alignment within contemporary culture, where individuality is now becoming normalized. The individual is increasingly aware of how his or her purchasing habits impact the environment and is being encouraged to ask more questions and shop ethically through the development of their own ethical framework. But these ethics begin to unravel when a significant part of that luxury brand's market share is built from entry-level goods, perfume, for example. The perfume market alone was worth around $31.4 billion in 2018 and is expected to grow to $52.4 billion by 2025. It contributes significantly to the luxury brand's turnover but more importantly, the profits, as the mark-up on perfume can be as high as 90 per cent. The luxury brand may appear to be at the top of the food chain, but it is reliant on the 'bottom feeders' whose appetite for accessible luxury keeps it there. By throwing them some crumbs in the form of affordable mass-market products, the simple message the brands underscore is that people's lives will be better if they buy them.

Another interesting twist in this story is how the aspirational imagery often used includes travel references. Some of the luxury brands started with luggage, after all. The frequency of flights around the world is seen as a major contributor to $CO_2$ emissions. Now the industry faces a dilemma: do they continue to promote and grow the market of high net worth individuals that buy 'luxury' at the cost of the planet we're being encouraged to explore?

The market and the economy grow by intention. Each company has its own targets and these are generally defined through financial gain. Companies extend their market share, increase profits and return more value to shareholders. Successful growth through the implementation of targets means more is consumed, at a faster rate and then ultimately discarded. The burden on our natural resources is amplified through this growth and companies that convince customers to buy more and more do so without ever questioning the mechanism of exchange. Indeed, in most cases, companies will actively conceal the negative results of growth. But it is these capitalist mechanics that enable the economic system in the first place and it is a system continuously endorsed and celebrated by companies that continue to be successful regardless of how they operate.

As the luxury brands tend to focus on aspirational marketing, one that promotes success as a prerequisite to be part of what they do, and by pitching their products at a higher price point, they are in effect fuelling their own growth through encouraging the market. Population growth and the rise of the middle classes in some emergent nations are creating more customers able to indulge in luxury goods and services. If social responsibility is a duty every individual has to perform in order to maintain a balance between the economy and the ecosystem, then companies should do the same. As discussed earlier, companies are being held accountable for their actions through CSR frameworks and legislation. But these frameworks do not yet extend to including forms of psychological influence evident in marketing and advertising. The aspirational lifestyles, founded on excess, promoted by the luxury companies may just be the root cause of our social responsibility concerns.

The CSR agenda requires continuous effort to implement and to a certain extent, is easier for younger companies to follow and make part of their ethical framework. Older more established operations, such as those with a luxury heritage, take longer and find it more difficult to change behaviour. In order to increase pressure and force these companies to change, society is increasingly being made aware of the negative impact of their purchasing decisions and buying habits. The current drive to raise awareness around plastic, for example, is having a marked effect on how end consumers begin to assess their own impact on the environment.

# Eco thinking

Eco-design is generally integrated as a learning module within university design courses and school children around the world have been taking strike action initiated by the Swedish environmental activist, Greta Thunberg. Raising awareness for environmentally sustainable design practice and the philosophy of designing physical objects, the built environment, and services to comply with the principles of ecological sustainability is becoming common practice and is an increasingly important concern for consumers. Complete end-to-end and circular life cycle assessments of products are becoming normalized and the supporting services considered. Recyclable plastic bags used by one supermarket in the United Kingdom, for example, are not available through stores where the council local to those stores is not able to process the plastic. Many of the plastics used in luxury bags are made to imitate the look of leather, which only confuses the consumer and recycling centres. These bags tend to be made from a variety of materials including metal, plastic, other synthetics and internal cardboard stiffeners. Multiple materials need to be separated in order to be successfully recycled.

Luxury goods tend to be sold as heritage items you'll use again and again and pass down to your grandchildren. This pseudo heirloom reference enforces the notion of value customers are buying into. The whole idea of recycling just doesn't enter into the minds of those selling luxury goods for that reason. Who would throw their luxury bag away? They may not, but they are encouraged to buy another through fashion's seasonal marketing machine. Victoria Beckham is reported to have a handbag collection worth millions of pounds. And she is not alone. At some point, this volume of product will need to go somewhere, perhaps sold through the second-hand market, gifted or discarded.

The life cycle of a product is usually divided into procurement, manufacture, use, and disposal. Companies are being encouraged to pay more attention to how their products are disposed of, and by encouraging a circular economy, how that material can be effectively reused. Labelling of the product's material composition is the first step. Each has to be sorted by type to aid the recycling process. As this is becoming paramount to enabling a successful recycling ecosystem, the ease with which products can be separated into their material component parts is the latest design and manufacturing challenge.

High-value goods and services benefit from an increase in margin, which could contribute to a more thorough investigation and assessment to understand companies' impact on the environment. But often this uplift in revenue and profit is allocated to other aspects of the business. Shareholders frequently have little interest in understanding the product's environmental impact or the companies' eco credentials. When a product is introduced to the market, its value is established based on the companies' needs. If there is no allocation to eco-design, it is difficult to act on this retrospectively as the increase in costs is either passed on to the customer or eats into the companies' profit margin.

The shift to thinking more ecologically tends to be a result of external pressure from governments, legislation and media investigations into environmental issues surrounding mass manufacturing. Customers respond to this insight and are becoming more educated about the impact the products they buy have on the natural world. The new insightful customer is coincidentally forcing companies to pay more attention to eco-design and the impact their products have, particularly as they sell more items and the issues are multiplied exponentially.

Burberry suffered a massive public relations scandal after it burned £28.6 million worth of excess stock in 2018 to stop it being resold by discounters. This is a timely example of the quantities of waste products involved. The press drew attention to this destructive practice, which is common practice to protect their brand(s). In 2019, the French government intervened by introducing legislation that will ban this practice. By 2023, the destruction of non-food goods will be outlawed. But the ban includes a concession for luxury goods companies in order to protect their intellectual property, which appears to be a back door scheme to enable them to continue the practice. Often goods are manufactured in volume in order to achieve a more competitive unit cost. But if the order volume doesn't sell through, then destroying the excess stock is a currently accepted business practice, justified as being necessary to protect the brand. As if to justify their actions, Burberry was quick to point out they captured some of the energy generated through the burning and used it to power new production. The company mentions nothing of the initial energy, effort and materials used to complete the original production of products destroyed.

This retrospective damage limitation initiated the passing of new laws. As the French government moves to ban the disposal of excess goods, other countries will hopefully follow.

This presents a challenge to the luxury goods companies as they follow similar economies of scale models when manufacturing. If the goods do not sell through at full price then companies have the option of marking them down in a sale to clear the stock. Again, luxury goods companies justify limiting this practice, as they need to protect their brand. This, in effect, is about maintaining the illusion of exclusivity even though they are overproducing to achieve a more favourable price.

But marking down and sales change the behaviour of customers who become more inclined to wait for the sale to pay a lower price. Thus, luxury companies tend to resist the sales strategy, Hermès, for example, reports their products are never marked-down. But others often participate in the outlet village model and even make products specifically for those outlets so as to protect the full-price items within their exclusive stores.

All businesses are being encouraged to look closely at their manufacturing processes in order to understand the impact the products they sell are having on natural resources and explore other ways of servicing customers beginning to change their habits. The take, make, use, dispose and pollute or linear economic model is endemic to the historical way products have been sold. If resources used are not sold through, then what can be done with them? Changing this process is difficult. Why would a company selling products suddenly switch to a rental or a made-to-order model, even if these models do less damage to the environment?

Some companies are implementing new models of operation. H&M, the Swedish fast-fashion chain, has had some success with renting, rather than selling. Renting goes some way to keeping the materials used to make the products in the loop. And the vendor of these products should be best placed to maintain, repair, reuse and recycle their products. It remains to be seen if the same kind of revenues can be made through alternative models, but the automotive industry has been developing these tactics for a number of years and is now predominantly a leasing industry.

## All things circular

One catch-all area of eco-design generating traction is the circular economy. A circular economy (often referred to simply as 'circularity') is an economic system aimed at eliminating waste and the continual use of resources. The Ellen MacArthur Foundation defines the circular economy as:

> Looking beyond the current take-make-waste extractive industrial model, a circular economy aims to redefine growth, focusing on positive society-wide benefits. It entails gradually decoupling economic activity from the consumption of finite resources, and designing waste out of the system. Underpinned by a transition to renewable energy sources, the circular model builds economic, natural, and social capital. It is based on three principles; design out waste and pollution, keep products and materials in use and regenerate natural systems.
>
> (2020: n.pag.)

Currently, the linear economic model is based on a process of take, make, use, dispose and inadvertently pollute. This is strongly tied into financial economics where products are produced to be sold – which finalizes the process. After sales support services are typically a low priority. Generally, it doesn't make economic sense to prioritize this service as the sale comes first. Without the sale there is no business. But rethinking this established process is becoming absolutely necessary as the number of potential customers continues to expand. The volume of waste is increasing in parallel and all this waste material is already crippling and damaging huge areas of the world, its people, wildlife and natural resources.

Without exploring other options and implementing alternatives, the linear process of consumption to waste will never change. Make, use, reuse, remake, recycle and keep products in use for longer and service the customer to enable them to be part of the solution.

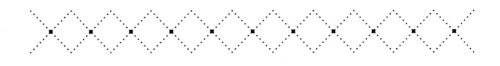

# 7

# Decoding Luxury

*As discussed earlier, the link between luxury and technology is defined through the relationship between material, tool and craftsmanship. But to get the most out of this triangle of tangible assets, there needs to be another, less understood factor driving the undertaking of work that delivers an outcome that surpasses expectations. This could be classified or understood as desire, which in most cases is driven by individuals with an obsession for discovery. These explorers are driven to push the limits of their existence, expanding their skills and under-standing to gain new knowledge. This may be the means through which they make sense of the world around them. Their renditions communicate this to others who subconsciously adopt the messages as an explanation or aspiration that resonates. Enter advertising, and its impact on the minds of consumers.*

Technologies have played a key part in the reimagining of luxury in the 21st Century. Machine processes are used to differentiate a product's make-up, highlighting the techniques used to achieve results, which set this version apart from others. These go hand in hand with the enhanced emotional connection and benefits attained through making an indulgent purchase. The focus is shifted from that of a first-hand inspection and experience to one that is more ethereal. The story behind the product, enhanced through aspirational endorsement and believable but saturated advertising methods, creates a very different impression of the things on offer.

This psychological insight is something that lends weight to the brand's offer and even acceptance that this ethereal quality is worth paying excessively for, even though it is not evident in the product we may buy. It is simply carried in the consumer's mind and is triggered when they encounter the messenger brand's physical renditions.

All this value is created from what could be argued as nothing. The idea of spending $7000 on a handbag becomes a feasible exchange when based partly on a trust in the technical skill and the technology used to manipulate the materials, but the emphasis is undoubtedly on how that handbag makes you feel. The technical considerations are downplayed as they tend to be taken for granted, unless the customer takes an interest and asks about them. The function of the product is in essence less important than the emotion felt towards it.

For the luxury goods company, its longstanding heritage justifies the price point. A heritage that has shown an enduring obsession with materials, the tools to manipulate those materials and the investment in and refinement of the skills required to maximize the effect of this manipulation. All these points and actions justify the price. And factors such as exclusivity and lifestyle proposition will further endow the product with value. A transaction not only takes into account the cost of the materials, the processes and individuals involved but also a profit margin that varies widely from company to company and often accounts for the majority of the value in any transaction.

The transaction now includes an accepted marketing spend, one that has become integral and used to paint the picture of the product that encourages its consumption. This aspect of the product is also technologically enabled through advertising. It reveals a proposed pinnacle of existence to create a complete picture of what could be. Often the exclusive quality is built solely around the high price point reflected in the accompanying visuals. A large proportion of the population are encouraged to aspire to luxury purchases but do not have the disposable income to support such purchases.

But those that do, have either come from money amassed through the use of early technologies, or have used modern-day technologies to attract investors who want to be part of the next big thing or have simply used these contemporary technologies to great effect. The idea of luxury as something that is not necessary is perpetuated through disposable wealth where its real value becomes meaningless to those with the resources to purchase high-priced luxury goods and services. Luxury's only lasting impact is to divide and separate which further promotes the industry's growth, as this fracturing is labelled 'aspirational'.

The link between technology and luxury has enabled the industry's unprecedented growth, just as the idea of discovery was linked to the ruling factions and nobility of the seventeenth century. Those affluent individuals and families sought novelty, possibly to enrich their lives through experiences, which relieved their relatively tedious and repetitive existence. As these new things filtered down to be enjoyed by the mass market, then the technologies for processing, manufacturing and distributing took hold. This was based primarily on realizing the product's value at scale, which would keep those who first enjoyed the product at the pinnacle of the hierarchy.

Sugar cane, for example, was thought to have first been used by man in Polynesia around 3500 years ago. As this sweet substance was refined in India around the first century CE it spread and found its way to the Mediterranean in the thirteenth century. During the Middle Ages, it was considered a rare and expensive spice. As it moved through the region, the island of Madeira in the Atlantic was the first place to cultivate sugar cane for large-scale refinement and trade during the late fifteenth century. The Portuguese then located sugar production in Brazil. Due to its favourable conditions a slave-based plantation system was established. Sugar cane then spread to the Caribbean around 1647 and led to the growth of an industry that fulfilled and fed the needs of western Europeans who were now craving sugar.

Realizing sugar's value on a mass scale became the technological task of the day. Sugar refinement and its distribution were essentially enabled through technology. A raw material, sugar cane, was manipulated initially by hand and then through tools and then machines to unlock its potential which was fully realized through a technology-enabled supply chain and distribution network.

Nonetheless, even though it lacked the refinement of modern sugar, it was coveted as a precious commodity and used sparingly and at great cost. But activity around this new substance changed the behaviour of those who participated in its sweet elixir. Sugar transitioned from a hard to come by luxury product to one that is predicted to be worth in excess of $89 billion worldwide by 2024. It continues to grow and fuel technological development in other industries. Health care and the treatment of sugar-related conditions are just one example. Diabetic treatments alone are valued at more than £6 billion per annum in the United Kingdom. It is estimated diabetes and related health complications cost the United Kingdom's National Health Service (NHS) more than £6 billion every year (DRWF 2018).

# Excess and exclusivity

Sugar has become a luxury of excess where once it was a luxury of exclusivity, all because of technology and the action and the effect it had on making people's lives more comfortable, enhancing the existence by making food and drink taste better. Early adopters were mimicking the nobility at the time, feeling a sense of achievement as they adapted their lifestyle to make it comparable to those they aspired to. But this appetite also came at a great human cost, particularly through the creation of the slave network that made it all possible (Bentley et al. 2015).

The link between luxury and technology goes even deeper when considering the wealth of experiences and products available today. As we have discussed, historically a company would become established through the refinement of a single activity. Indeed, most of today's luxury companies started out tackling very different problems than those they may service today. Gucci, a leather company, made saddles and equestrian products. Louis Vuitton made luggage. They made them very well.

What happened to cause Gucci's transition into other product and service areas while maintaining a luxury focus? When looking to expand, a company will first examine its core competencies. If it had a history of working with leather for equestrian purposes, then it had the skill, knowledge and associated technologies to work that material into successful outcomes. It would then determine it could also make leather bags for customers, thereby increasing its customer base and reducing its dependency on the equestrian market. As these leather bags became fashionable and aspirational – probably due to customers aspiring to the image of the leisure classes and their activities at polo matches (the game of kings) for example – then the leather bag became attached to a narrative others wanted to be part of. The fashion then changed and the market expanded. The narrative painted a fashionable image and the company then realized it could produce other items such as clothing and accessories to complete the Gucci look. By doing so, a company like Gucci increased its market share and spread its risk across a number of product types, price points and markets. As it expanded its areas of activity, it naturally transitioned from equestrian to consumer goods with a focus on luxury fashion as this area proved successful. Gucci was recently praised for its use of technology to attract the millennials through social media and targeted advertising campaigns. This made it accessible to a new generation of customers, thereby extending the reach of the company's products, which in turn promoted its values to a completely new audience.

But has Gucci's expansion into other areas diluted its luxurious sheen? The company has always used its core values to direct its growth and its popular image of disenfranchised/disconnected youth has allowed it to explore many product categories. These categories have become necessary to sustain and support growth. Most of these luxury companies' revenue is generated through perfume, cosmetics, small leather goods and accessories. The adoption and sale of these items are dependent on the company's projected narrative, which creates the means for it to command high price points and profit margins. These categories also enable the luxury business to explore and implement other technologies. In turn they contribute to its overall changing business practice and allow it to investigate new technologies within other areas of its business, such as different stock management systems across categories and new material expertise in glass bottles.

Luxury's focus shifted to one of indulgence and excess probably around the time of Louis XIV. Was it luxury's wealth creation that became increasingly evident as it matured, resulting in those that pushed its uptake benefiting from the wealth it created to display the signs of conspicuous consumption and indulgence?

# The advertising illusion

As discussed in Chapter 3, luxury's popularity grew from the aspirational experiences of the nobility during the seventeenth century. The novelty of their existence was distributed discreetly through the travel and leisure classes, those that had the means to instigate and embark on voyages of discovery around the world. Knowledge, experience, products and technology are spread through those undertaking such journeys.

The early discovery of other continents and the establishment of trade routes meant the lives of indigenous people were affected by these visits and vice versa. A word of mouth network began to emerge, particularly as language barriers were broken down through the understanding of local dialects. This activity became the advertising of the day, telling stories and sharing experiences allowed all involved to experience new things. The wealthy could supply those who wanted something they had discovered on one of their many trips. Trade routes formed as a result of the technology that enabled travel, and value networks were created in the process.

These connecting endeavours created the foundation for an aspirational system. Those who had things and those who wanted them, set in motion a mechanism for trade where things were seen to better the lives of those who had them, by those who suddenly needed them, based simply on aspirational betterment. This psychological procurement could arise through the need to discover and experience the new, enabling citizens to better understand their position in the world. It was those explorers and adventurers that took those first steps into the unknown. Individuals who had the know-how to develop the technology made their travels possible. The fact that a wealthy bene-factor would fund such endeavours meant they could still embark on a voyage of discovery but without the risk that their employees had to endure. The message of the leisure classes would transform the globe as they traversed its surface, discovering new things along the way while introducing those discoveries to those they met, albeit at a cost.

These messengers created an early communication network that would grow as the technology for transmitting messages developed to the point we are at now in contemporary society. Anyone can visit anywhere at any time, first virtually through a small and portable mobile phone, a device that has become intelligent enough to know what the user is looking for based on an accumulated digital search profile used to push polished advertising messages. Discovering these destinations for real is as easy as pushing a button and booking a flight. The flights themselves are achieved through aerospace technologies.

The advertising and the price of these adventures are becoming increasingly fluid. The message adapts as the user's historical profile gives insights into what they will most likely to respond to, substitut-ing imagery and fluctuating costs to suit their apparent preferences. As technology is used to drive consumption through targeted advertis-ing, the messages are becoming distorted as they adapt to fulfil a task. The luxury hotel sells excess rooms at a discounted price and a luxury car becomes affordable due to payment plans that suit an aspirational pocket. Consumers know full-price luxury garments will soon be avail-able on discounted websites at prices they can afford. The advertising creates the need, and the company is happy to get whatever it can for fulfilling that need. Advertising has become much more than simply the means to get a message out there. With the growth of online advertis-ing and network-connected digital billboards, companies can target specific groups of people at specific times using appealing methods to get their attention, all with the intention of encouraging them to make a purchase.

# The reality of experience

Promotional methods are becoming increasingly sophisticated as new technologies such as augmented reality (AR) emerge to further blur the line between reality and technology.

Luxury brands are beginning to use AR to add another dimen-sion to their marketing campaigns. The pages of a brochure come to life when viewed through a smartphone. Animated elements move around a shop window display and products can be tried on without walking into a store. It is early days for the technology but it will soon be available through a simple pair of glasses making the experience accessible, more convenient and transparent. This will make it easy for those who want to live in a luxurious world provided by one of the big luxury brands simply by putting on a pair of AR glasses and subscribing to the experience. This new method of augmenting the field of view with content provided by companies potentially rewrites the process of advertising. Imagine if the technology becomes advanced enough to superimpose catwalk collection garments onto everyone walking down the street. Suddenly, the world through AR-enabled glasses looks very different, and simply activating a menu with a flick or blink of an eye can change it.

One of the proposed applications is an advert blocker through a technology called 'diminished reality'. All advertising in the real world is replaced with images of the customer's choice in his or her augmented version of the world. How would the advertisers respond? This may be a feature paid for through advertising, or it could be a subscription application bypassing the advertising industry altogether.

There is an increasingly noisy reality ahead as marketing and advertising activity reaches a deafening point and becomes ubiquitous across all touch points. Screens, billboards, audio applications and sponsored events are all sought after real estate used to promote products and services – including those of luxury brands. If advertising blockers become available and technologies such as AR allows us to shape our view of the world then the conglomerates will have to find new ways to tempt consumers to consume. AR applications could become the new luxury, as they are the only option for truly changing the world for the better, at least from an individual's perspective. Objects, advertising, even people could be changed or even erased to create an easier, more comfortable existence where the world could really be paved with gold, albeit virtually.

This rose-tinted alternative could shape a new beginning, one where the old methods no longer work and the technology enables change on a scale never seen before. Hyper-reality researcher Keiichi Matsuda (Matsuda 2020), on his website hyper-reality.co, paints a dystopian version of this where participants longing for a new life are in conflict with the acquired currency, that is, 'points' of their current AR existence, while the threat of being 'hacked' means the loss of everything connecting them to the world.

Author and AR specialist Dr Helen Papagiannis from AR Stories, playfully introduces Louis Vuitton to the possibility of extending its brand and engagement through animated window displays and printed brochures. These appear static in the real world but come to life when viewed through an AR device. Dior has an Instagram AR makeup filter and Chanel recently jumped on the AR bandwagon with a snow globe Christmas campaign. These examples all indicate different uses of the technology but focus on introducing a new dimension to existing reality. These examples sit in an area being explored by artists, companies and technology providers around the world. Accessing reality-bending content is currently not that convenient, as it requires the user to view the world through a cumbersome headset or by looking through a smartphone screen. Smaller, usable and convenient devices are in development by a range of companies, including Apple and Facebook, who announced that their discreet AR glasses would be available by 2023.

Once the content works seamlessly and is viewed through glasses appearing to be normal, then these new virtual worlds will become compelling. The technology will conveniently augment reality through a range of different methods, making the user's life easier, more relevant, convenient and helpful through prompts that react to the wearer's context. You will never forget someone's name again as facial recognition through the glasses will be able to tell you everything about the people you meet. If it is a cloudy day, digital filters could brighten it up with a simple flick of an eye. And logos on T-shirts of brands whose business practice you do not agree with can be removed, replaced or anonymized. This technology potentially reintroduces the idea of discovery. Nintendo has successfully engaged millions of explorers through its successful Pokémon Go series of games.

As the world becomes increasingly connected, our experience of it does the same. Armchair surfing is becoming the norm: simply swipe the screen on your phone to discover and press a button to experience it. The ease of this process is so convenient and rewarding it could be argued there is no need to go anywhere anymore. It is the beginning of the much-hyped gamification of services. For example, the popular game *Fortnite* allows players to purchase in-game clothing, accessories and weapons to enhance their gaming alter-ego avatar. The players can also take that avatar to a movie theatre and watch the latest films as a seamless experience. This digital form of social activity is growing and successfully holds onto participants. Some players regularly spend hundreds of hours in game. Gaming companies are initiating and investing in games as a spectator sport with million dollar payouts for successful players. The market for virtual game assets – clothing, weapons, accessories, vehicles, real estate and currency – is growing. Digital asset marketplace, Wax, estimates the in-game asset market is worth more than $50 billion. Some traditional real-world fashion companies have begun exploring this emerging market and newcomers The Fabricant and Carlings sell digital-only garments. Gucci introduced its first pair of digital sneakers in March 2021.

AR reintroduces discovery at a level that has never been seen before. Familiar items in the home suddenly reveal new facts and insight about themselves. The embedded provenance discussed earlier now comes alive and shows when and where the product was made, who made it, any updates, service records, other options, other customers that have the same product, etc. This gives users the opportunity to discover new things about their clothing and products they never knew. Rediscovering details that may have been concealed will undoubtedly arise through the way things are becoming increasingly and transparently connected.

Probably one of the most informative technologies currently being developed and tested by companies is the ability to track and trace all aspects of a product's lifecycle. Blockchain technology can describe a list of connected metadata that becomes an integral part of any product. Its entire history can be interrogated and can include data such as where the materials came from, who designed it, who made it, any ethical concerns, how they were addressed, how many were made, over what period, who bought it and its location are just a sample of how companies will be able to query the products they make. It is touted as a complete end-to-end system and is being developed to address stock control, ethics and environmental impact, among other things. This information will be made available to the end consumer, who is becoming increasingly concerned about the origins of the things they consume. AR then provides the opportunity to discover hidden and personally relevant information about a product by simply looking at it.

The product is slowly becoming more than just its physical manifestation. Associated content – such as celebrity endorsements, video reviews, film placement, animated renditions, event sponsorship, its theme tune, history, heritage, what was said or mentioned in a novel or scientific journal – are all used to describe the product in ways that extend its existence beyond its physical rendition and to connect that product, and the company, to an increasingly diverse customer base.

We have discussed the Kelly and Birkin bags with reference to craftsmanship, availability and mythology and continue this discussion in relation to experience. Both bags still carry an association and connection to a golden age of film, stardom and fame. This connects the product with a shared experience that humanizes it and makes it more desirable. This may happen through an observation that allows an experience to be understood, shared and (if needed, or encouraged) adopted. This then extends one's personal reality experience into new territory: living the dream. But even this association is dependent on technology. The idea of celebrity requires people to achieve stardom and become famous. The platform of film elevates these stars and communicates their performance to wider audiences through technologies such as cameras, projectors and even the printing press.

# Material world

It is not just celebrity that elevates the value of a product; materials can also increase this value. The use of precious materials immediately elevates the perception of a product's value and therefore its luxury status simply because it is a diamond or made using gold. Both are relatively affordable and prohibitively expensive. Mixing them with other metals to produce an alloy can dilute a raw material such as gold, symbolized through the carat system; 9 ct (carat) gold, for example, only contains 375 parts of gold out of 1000 parts or 37.5 per cent, the remaining parts are a mix of other plentiful and affordable metals such as copper. Alloying metals together in this way also changes its properties, and the benefit of these new and improved material properties is used to sell the diluted but improved version. 9 ct gold is stronger and harder wearing but the colour or lustre could be considered substandard. The technology for transforming metals continues to be refined and new technical applications push creative boundaries. The German jewellery company Niessing, for example, develops performance-based alloys engineered to hold a diamond using contemporary tension settings.

The reputation of any material, precious or otherwise, is easily tarnished as concerns for the environment, human rights and other issues become increasingly important as the consuming public is made aware of the impact their choices have on the world. Competing companies, human rights groups, legislative organizations and non-profits actively investigate mining conditions to better understand the wellbeing of the workforce. This activity's primary function is to keep on top of malpractice but it also services the need of the customer who is being encouraged to ask questions and remain informed about all aspects of the materials processing, refinement and the companies involved.

Encouraging society to be more aware also inspires engagement by making customers aware of the impact their decisions have on the wider world, the ecosystem and people. Raising awareness for certified diamonds, and gold including fair trade, beach, ocean, recycled and Welsh are all becoming understood alternatives and highlight some of the malpractice that the industry has been guilty of. Brands of all types are seeking ways to engage more fully with their customers and governments are introducing new legislation and regulations forcing both brand and customer to consider these concerns and their impact by giving them a more sustainable choice. Product manufacturers are now being encouraged, and in some cases, forced to include all aspects of a material's life cycle. Where did the raw material come from? How was it processed? And, as discussed, blockchain technologies are being implemented to keep track of the material and the product's lifecycle.

Traditionally, giving customers reassurance when buying precious metals takes the form of Assay marks that guarantee the quality of precious metals in the United Kingdom along with the implementation of other quality guidelines. Diamonds, for example, use the '4Cs': Clarity, Colour, Cut and Carat (weight), a grading system devised by the Gemological Institute of America (GIA). De Beers created the tagline 'A diamond is forever' to give the customer confidence in their purchase and create an aura around diamonds. But the shifting fashion of opinion calls these certification methods into question. The colour of a perfect ruby is described as pigeon blood red. However, lighter shades are referred to as pink sapphires but both stones are corundum. Coloured diamonds have become increasingly popular and marketed for their rarity. The term 'chocolate diamonds', for example, links a desirable description to a substandard industrial grade stone. Fashion and marketing have a significant impact on how consumers interpret the world around them and can guide their decisions. Seasonal colour palettes define a fashion collection and bring certain hues to the forefront making them the season's 'must have'. This acceptance through fashion creates value for that season but due to fashion's constantly changing ideal, the value cycle is continually reinvigorated.

As these trends continue to change, technologies have been developed to alter the colour of a naturally occurring stone to make it more desirable. This is usually a heat treatment process that can shift the intensity of a hue.

If we consider the idea of value being attributed to something because it is rare and that rarity formed the basis of its worth, then when mining and sourcing such stones, the desired colour makes a contribution to that evaluation. When stones do not exhibit that preferred colour, the idea that it can be adjusted in order to gain a greater market value and return is just one example of how materials can be manipulated to become more valuable. Conflict arises as its original value was based on a naturally formed and found object; the idea that substandard material is then processed to achieve the same value as its naturally occurring counterpart could be seen as deceptive or considered counterintuitive.

# Introducing synthetics

Cultured pearls opened up the market for pearls as many more were produced to meet demand. It takes time for an oyster to produce a naturally occurring pearl and a top specimen is not found every time an oyster is shucked. The natural irritant, usually a grain of sand of various sizes and shapes, is what starts the pearl-making process. But there's no guarantee that it will be, what the industry may term, perfect. Many oysters have to be shucked to find the perfect pearl.

Through understanding the natural process of pearl making, the industry has been able to manufacture pearls on demand. Inserting a man-made irritant into an opened oyster or clam, pearls of any size and shape (within reason) can be made. One aspect that makes large, natural pearls expensive is the time it takes to produce and their rarity. If a large, spherical irritant is artificially inserted, then a large cultured pearl becomes a certainty in a fraction of the time.

The same is happening with diamonds, which are being formed from a diamond wafer using technology developed by Russian and American companies (Davis 2016). The results are astounding and initially had the industry in turmoil. If flawless diamonds can be manufactured, would there still be a market for the natural stones? As these traditionally accepted icons of the luxury world are replaced with cultured alternatives, the balance of supply shifts as customers begin to question the ethics of those traditions. Some of the companies controlling the diamond market do not have a particularly good human rights record and have been accused of operating as cartels. Cultured diamonds are now readily available and being incorporated into jewellery and other industrial applications as a more considered and ethical decision due to historical natural mining malpractice. Even diamond industry stalwart De Beers now sells synthetic diamonds.

# Modern manufacturing

As these alternatives are manufactured, the technology making them will undoubtedly improve and be refined to the point where luxury is manufactured on demand and is available to all. The only way to stall the demand curve is if the supplier or company chooses to apply a foot to the brake. But even this activity can have beneficial results by restricting access to a product or material and elevating its price. Consumers interpret this as validation the product is even more desirable, and consequently more valuable, as the product becomes rarefied through design and marketing. The Kelly and Birkin bags are good examples of this where customers have to, supposedly, join a waiting list. If this were the case, as discussed previously, the waiting game could easily be overcome through the employment of additional craftspeople or technologies to increase the rate of production. But many of the luxury manufacturers prefer not to do this or say they are not doing this, to position time as an important consideration when it comes to luxury.

Including a reference to the extended time taken to make something as part of the product's story increases its perceived value. But when this barrier can be overcome through technological know-how, choosing to not follow this path creates conflict as there's still uncertainty about the production methods luxury companies use to manufacture enough products to meet ever-increasing demand.

The accumulation of knowledge and understanding needed to manipulate material into creating something is great. The challenge often requires determination and failure is part of the process as the individual or team of makers continually try to achieve their objectives. This iterative process feeds back to the maker, giving them insight into the material and the tools they use. The way in which material reacts can spark an unexpected journey of discovery not evident or even conceived of when the material was first discovered.

Diamonds, for example, require enormous effort to locate, extract and then work up into the coveted object held in such great esteem. This process is continuously refined in order to maximize the raw material's capability, thus increasing the value of an ideal sample or specimen. The placement of diamonds within jewellery are then used to further enhance its properties through engineering a complex support structure generally comprising precious metals. In a ring, for example, the setting or mount supports the diamond, elevating it off the finger so it can be appreciated, recognized and admired for its purity, clarity, cut and size. A well-cut stone takes into consideration the angles of each facet so light can be captured and refracted for maximum effect. This understanding of the material goes beyond the qualities a raw diamond may exhibit when dug up in the mine. It is only through the determined activity and the development of technology that it is possible to realize the potential of the material.

Once this investigation and investment into the materials' potential reach a minimum viable conclusion, the value in that activity is hopefully appreciated and results in increased demand, and expansion of the market for diamonds. As the techniques and technologies are refined, the way in which a raw mineral can be transformed into something of value is passed on to others to help meet the demand for the new commodity. As more individuals become equipped with the know-how and necessary skills through training and sharing of the techniques used, an industry emerges. This refinement process – as used in a number of industries from oil and leather to foods – becomes subject to efficiencies whereby the process is scrutinized, usually with a commercial agenda. But the constant refinement process takes into account a variety of concerns and agendas.

You could liken this process to an action plan, where the refinement ideology is split up into parts and compartmentalized, even departmentalized. A connected hive of activity emerges through the task, rather like bees and honey. But unlike bees, whose manufacturing process has evolved and refined over millennia, modern manufacturing processes are comparatively infantile. Communication techniques are prone to fail or be misinterpreted as instruction is passed through the resulting but fragile hierarchy. Each company may have its queen but that CEO has a difficult job ensuring everyone is doing as instructed, particularly as societal structures encourage individual thought, action and realization. The binding rules and ideologies of corporate mantras are subject to change or reinterpretation as new perspectives come to light.

Because of the constant change, fluidity is now the norm; the idea of a fixed and systematic approach does not capture enough customers, particularly as the number of players (businesses) increases. As these organizations focus on market share, they need to diversify in order to succeed. This is an age of acquisitions; if a company is not active in a particular area then it can buy a company that is. Even if the company's focus was initially on media, it expands its potential customer base through other areas of activity, sometimes related, sometimes not.

As the market becomes increasingly fractured with competitors, businesses attempt to retain customers and market position through acquisitions or by simply establishing a company within the area they feel to be a lucrative opportunity. This complex ownership structure changes the market as few end consumers can ever hope to gain a full and complete picture of the companies' interests. Indeed, in some instances, a company will go to great lengths to conceal its other business concerns or become active in a market not so heavily promoted.

De Beers, for example, also has a division specifically focusing on the industrial applications of diamonds.

Another misleading aspect of the supply chain comes into play when specialization is required. As an example, spectacle and sunglass frames are complex and often fall outside of the luxury brands' area of core competencies. A single company may be responsible for making the frames of 80 per cent of these products. Luxottica, for example, manufacture under licence for a range of brands, including Chanel, Prada, Versace, Burberry and Tiffany & Co. It also owns RayBan and Oakley. The global cosmetic manufacturers also service the big brands. American company Coty makes cosmetics for Marc Jacobs, Calvin Klein, Chloé, Gucci, Hugo Boss and Tiffany & Co among others. Coty was established in 1904 and Luxottica in 1962. Both companies are skilled in their respective areas of expertise and have spent years developing technology and know-how to enable them to become world leading in their respective fields. But the impression from a consumer point of view is that the logo on the pair of glasses or perfume denotes that that brand is responsible for it and is the reason why they are buying into it. Few realize the product they are buying is not made by the brand and that the manufacturer is also making products for what could be considered competing brands. It also becomes difficult to extrapolate individual brand intellectual property. In this instance, hinges on spectacle frames and lipstick carrier tubes may be identical across the brands, and the only defining feature in some cases is the logo.

# Trust, transparency and ethics

Most companies want to be more transparent, particularly with customers becoming increasingly aware of their actions and activities through independent investigations and exposés. Ethics statements are playing an important role in that transparent future as more businesses begin to lay out their ethical ideals. Banks use ethical statements focusing on their agenda with the aim of giving customers an insight into their business practices. e-Bank Starling in the United Kingdom, for example, states, among other points, that it practices ethical banking:

> We do not provide banking services to organisations that use excessive power to systemically promote public behaviour that is harmful to individuals, groups or to the whole of society in order to maximise their own profits. This may include, for example,

arms manufacturers and tobacco companies. We do not invest in such organisations or take investment from them

(Starling n.d.: n.pag.)

Ethics statements are a positive start but even they do not provide the transparency or trust most consumers want these days. Statements are prone to missing interpretation where the links between companies are complex. Chanel, for example, does not say whether it tests products on animals, but it does sell products in mainland China. A condition to sell cosmetics in this territory is that they have to be tested on animals. Focus, as mentioned previously, can also be diverted away from the brand by saying they do not test on animals but the ingredient suppliers do!

Proprietary technology development and invention creates a perplexing situation where different companies partner, collaborate and compete to bring branded products to market. Some focus on their specialism, others buy companies to expand their area of specialization and others licence or partner with companies to give them the required area of specialization through collaborative practice.

The complexity of these arrangements leads to complexity across the supply chain. It also makes it difficult to be innovative when corporate structures and processes are fixed to their needs, usually tied to commercial gain and meeting the requirements of an organization at scale. A cosmetic brand that makes for multiple brands may be able to offer a more compelling financial deal on a lipstick shade if it is the same as one they are making for another brand. They simply change the packaging and logo; this clearly puts commercial gain over and above innovation.

# Technological impact

Innovation has become a buzzword in recent years; the word's popularity has been on the increase since the early 1960s (Green 2013). Innovation could be considered one aspect that fuelled the growth of the luxury goods companies as their founders sought to investigate and be inventive. Individuals, companies, even countries are continuously encouraged to innovate to enable new economic growth. We hear about disruption, being agile, about changing the world and making it a better place. It is primarily technology driving and shaping this new world. Communicating an agenda to the world's population is now relatively straightforward through communications networks and the internet, now used by 59 per cent of the world's population. Sophisti-cated ways of delivering innovative messages have been created and can pitch solutions to a huge audience. By recognizing shortcom-ings in existing solutions, they can be improved through technological innovation to become more agile in order to accommodate the world as it rapidly changes. Technology enables understanding all aspects of current solutions and business practices, giving an informed perspec-tive that is global in scale.

Negative spin is forming as discussions around businesses' environmental impact come to light and travel the world with the click of a button. Consumers are now more informed about how current consumption behaviour affects everything from our individ-ual well-being, the environmental crisis, global warming and plas-tic waste as well as human rights, privacy and the ever-increasing wealth divide. This dissemination of information, coupled with ease of access, has become one of the greatest technological achievements in the modern age. Through this evolving digital resource, many of the world's historical hierarchies established as luxury spread around the world are being broken down and reconfigured to meet the demands and aspirations of a new kind of customer.

The hierarchical structures that emerged through the discovery of new lands and the exploitation of its indigenous resources helped shape the world's economic format. But in contemporary society, they are being reconsidered, complemented and, in some cases, replaced with new ideas centred on the individual, society and refined ethical considerations. An increasing number of people are establishing their own businesses or enjoying the opportunities, freedom and choice offered by the gig economy and moving away from the corporate workforce configuration. This growing trend is linked to technology as working can now take place remotely via personal computers and smartphones. Wi-Fi connections enable anyone to seek and undertake work anywhere (Jones 2018).

A distributed workforce comprising many individuals operating across boundaries and disciplines as well as being flexible and agile has begun to shift the traditions that defined the previous genera-tions. Contemporary luxury advertising is beginning to look out of date when related to the emerging techno-savvy, eco-aware generation. Particularly so when the ecosystem is under increasing stress. Luxury, fuelled by the overindulgence of those at the pinnacle of their exist-ence, seems increasingly out of touch.

The technological redistribution also creates uncertainty where existing methods of social hierarchy are questioned, and in some cases can be seen as divisive. As individuals are encouraged to have a point of view, they distribute their ideas, thoughts, personal perspectives and grievances through clever use of the digital network. The messages are becoming more powerful as stories that have been buried for years rise to the surface to create social unrest, protests and ultimately, change.

Obviously, this can create contention as individuals find their voices and broadcast to the world. Everyone has an opinion. Generally, this behaviour results in conflict amplified through social media and even enhanced or purposefully directed through cleverly orchestrated campaigns using psychological profiling, the likes of which were witnessed as part of the 2016 presidential campaign in the United States and Brexit in the United Kingdom. This shift is gaining momentum and we are only just beginning to realize what is to come, but essentially it all hinges on the technologies we've implemented and come to rely on.

The uncertainty extends beyond the corporate framework and into the consumer market. Our appetite for information and the emergence of fake news is only emphasizing what print advertising has been doing for years through the creation of compelling, desirable and believable campaigns whose task it is to persuade us to make decisions. As social media transforms the world around us, new technologies manage these increasingly complex relationships. On the one hand, the technologies are effective, enabling us to interact and achieve, but, on the other hand, they increase the physical distance between people, businesses, customers and even the organizational structure of the workforce itself. Employees no longer talk or discuss, even when in the same office, as e-mail and digital office applications have become the means to increase productivity, to prove accountability and to manage complexity. Technology enables the flexible arrangements the working world now demands, and on which we rely more and more.

There is much discussion and implementation around engagement, where the technology allows and encourages customers to connect with the company. However, this is also achieved at arm's length through technological applications that essentially allow customers to interact and do the tasks a company employee would normally do through a call centre or face-to-face in a retail environment. Engagement can also involve how a customer uses a company's website. This activity is captured and recorded and produces pages of website stats informing the development team about things such as retention or orders. All of this talk of engagement is primarily focused on the customer: to draw in and retain customers. The company services this through automated, and relatively more affordable digital processes. But the customer is given a feeling of being more in control and informed so is generally happy to accept this newfound method of interaction, albeit with machines rather than people.

When considering luxury against the backdrop of digital automation, these high-end goods and services should be about connecting the customer to the experience in a meaningful way, sharing the insights the luxury brand has amassed over the years and encouraging its customers to discover something about themselves, the brand and the reality in which they exist. But it is also taking the digital route, automating where it can, distancing its workforce from its customers – except in special circumstances generally defined through spend.

Some companies are now taking a different route, investigating how to define and establish an ecosystem other companies, and ultimately the customer, becomes part of. The opportunity to define a new ecosystem generally comes with the introduction of a new technology. The internet changed working practices almost overnight and the resulting ecosystem has had an impact around the globe, touching all aspects of our lives. Everything is now different and any reluctance to deal with change is only met with further encouragement as technology continues to disrupt every aspect of a life we thought we understood. But when much of the world's economic function is built on traditional systems, change, although inevitable, will never be easy.

# Just-in-time manufacturing

3D printing or additive manufacturing (AM) is one area of technology development that is beginning to disrupt physical supply chains, manufacturing centres and of course the actual physical products and our relationship to them. AM is the technology allowing 3D objects to be printed in a range of different materials. The term encompasses many different types of technologies that build objects additively, rather than subtractively. Subtractive is easy to imagine if you think of a sculptor with a block of marble and a chisel; the sculptor chips away at the marble block to reveal the form. This process is wasteful because of all the discarded material. AM requires a 3D digital file to start the process and that file can be very simple, or it can be extremely complex. The technology doesn't mind and can reproduce all manner of complicated geometries that in some cases would be difficult to achieve through traditional methods. The machine is also quite happy to produce one item, or thousands of the same item or thousands of items in which each is slightly different. When AM first became available it was heralded as the beginning of the era of mass customization. The process allows items to be produced and customized to the needs of the end customer.

Luxury has a heritage of offering bespoke goods and services. AM has the ability to take this further and engage with a greater number of customers interested in bespoke services. AM is one part of a range of digital machines including scanning, cutting, printing and assembly.

Some companies' brands have already started to offer web-based configurators, where the customer is presented with a range of customization and personalization options through a web browser. They could be simple details such as monogramming small leather goods to multiple options for shoes where each component part can be tailored within a controlled range of options and colours. The automotive industry has been using these systems for some time, allowing customers to visualize colour, trim and other details of the car they are interested in buying. These configurators benefit the customer in that they feel they have a choice and can see a photo-real representation of their decisions before they buy. The system benefits the company by encouraging the customer to engage in the process, retaining them until the purchase is made, and the digitization of the customer's requirements directs the company's internal processes from manufacturing and fulfilment to shipping routines. However, as the customer has ordered a bespoke product, they have to forfeit some of their consumer rights to return those goods as new legal policy dictates the item ordered is only suitable for them. Customization services focus the customer on the choices they made.

AM also decentralizes the factory; this means products can be made locally at the customers' point of origin, potentially cutting down shipping costs and associated $CO_2$ emissions. One recent success story was during the 2020 pandemic where personal protective equipment was in short supply. Digital CAD files describing items such as face shields were distributed around the world and downloaded by anyone with a 3D printer. Collectively, they manufactured thousands of units for their local hospitals.

As the number of AM machines increases, and their use becomes more widespread, they need to be making things rather than standing idle. As each machine in the network reaches capacity, costs fall, making the proposition even more attractive to companies and customers, resulting in a win-win situation where the ecosystem becomes highly effective, efficient, economical and more environmentally conscious.

Additive manufacturing is not industry-specific and can be used across a range of different product types, from automotive to aerospace, to medical and consumer goods. The technology offers a range of different materials from plastics to metals and organics, and the machines themselves can also handle complex geometries with negligible cost increases. This so-called 'design freedom' allows engineers and designers to make decorative and/or functional objects that have become prohibitively expensive, or not economically viable to make using traditional manufacturing methods. This backdrop potentially allows for objects to exhibit complexity but without the assumed costs that define many luxury products.

# Informed insight

These new techniques for interrogating the world extend to understanding it in ways that once seemed unimaginable. Despite already feeling immersed in the real world, the immersion experience is taken to a new level once understanding is reached as to what is conveniently made accessible through comfortable technologies. With heightened understanding comes a new chapter of discovery, one that potentially gives a tailored, complete picture of all we touch and experience. It also provides the opportunity for meaningful change, as any aspect of an indulgent, unnecessary or excessive lifestyle that potentially affects existence can be managed in a variety of ways. Companies abusing their fortunes can be held more directly accountable as this can be highlighted to the customer at the point of purchase, or even before. Our psychological state could be influenced to change our behaviour away from those whose practices we deem unsuitable within our own ethical framework. If the industry is squeezing a supplier in a developing part of the world, then we can act from an informed position and influence that industry's course of action. Advertising can take on the role of political activist as was recently uncovered in the Cambridge Analytica scandal that influenced the 2016 United States presidential elections and Brexit.

As people become increasingly aware of how they can be manipulated through technologies, hopefully they will want to exert more control over the touch points where they gather this information and AR could do that for them. This gives the people all of the power, but only if these technologies are open and not controlled through a small number of technology super companies. One area of AR being developed is that of Diminished Reality. Software can be trained to recognize objects in your field of view through a pair of glasses, and if required, these objects can be made to disappear from your field of view and replaced with other objects as desired. Fayteq, the German computer vision startup, has been developing technology to do just that and in 2017, Facebook acquired Fayteq for an undisclosed sum. This technique essentially enables companies and their users to rewrite reality (Etherington 2017).

As our world views continue to alter through technology, it seems reasonable to assume the big players want to control what we see. Any company is essentially an entity whose intention is to provide goods and/or services and for that provision to grow so it can sustain itself. This means acquiring more customers through means that successfully bring them on board and ideally, retains them. Sustainability continues to be a growing concern, developing in tandem with companies that have grown to such an extent that their drain on the world's resources is measurable. In most cases, there is evidence to show their actions are having a detrimental effect on natural resources. But consumers must also take responsibility, as without customers, the companies wouldn't be stripping the planet's resources to fuel the demand.

We've become used to the spoils of a contemporary existence and demand more without even realizing the impact of our choices. The developed western world is even seen as an aspirational condition and technology is distributing and making it accessible. Everyone is being encouraged to experience it and be part of its supposed success. This is a step change from the early days of luxury with its discrete, limited and exclusive reach.

# Service realities

If luxury is founded on excess, then its primary objective could be the one thing fuelling all the world's problems. An increasing population and the expansion of the middle class means there are more potential customers for luxury goods and services. But the market for luxury, although expanding, is beginning to experience a bit of a backlash as its founding principles become increasingly out of sync with a more considered world view whose focus is steering towards sustainability, the environment and well-being.

As technology becomes ubiquitous across all touch points, the opportunity for it to inform us about our daily actions becomes inevitable. A simple application for personal budgeting could inform us about how much we can spend and when. Companies can incentivize potential customers through promotions triggered when browsing a website or entering a store. Financial applications can tailor a payment plan for goods and services according to a personal budget. A company's ethical standpoint and the ethical decision needed to make prior to purchasing can also be made available to inform actions. An impact statement or infographic that makes these complex relationships easier to understand can be tailored to a standpoint on issues we believe in.

This new level of service is becoming a reality due to customers wanting to know more about the things they buy. Their questions can be far-reaching and in order for a sales associate to have all the answers, they must be able to reference information about the qualities, associated industries, individual expertise, material composition and origin, environmental impact and a vast network of other links and connections that make that product possible. Companies have to not only respond to this heightened sense of inquiry from customers but they also have to comply with the introduction of more complex legislation concerning corporate social responsibility or being able to analyse, understand and report factors concerning their environmental impact. Both consumer-generated and corporate information contributes to an ever-increasing volume of data.

The growth of data is unprecedented. As more data is created it becomes increasingly complicated for an individual to fully understand the bigger picture. Also, the management and use of captured data present challenges in order to realize the opportunities data mining big data sets can offer. But data generated as an ongoing concern can be equally beneficial and give insight into how corporate processes can be further refined and optimized. Product development is a complex process that requires efficient and effective management to ensure it is delivered on time. This is particularly important in increasingly competitive markets. Managing all the considerations surrounding product development and having a more transparent agenda is driving the use of technological systems, spreadsheets, databases, team management systems and proprietary software in order to make information concerning the product development process relevant and accessible with the click of a button. The need to meaningfully analyse or mine data, particularly in real time so issues and opportunities can be acted on instantly, is becoming of paramount importance. It is fuelling the development of other technological processes based on machine learning and artificial intelligence. Through these processes, companies are able to interrogate their datasets, revealing new patterns and insights to give a competitive advantage. Prior to these analytical techniques, the value in the data would have been overlooked and not realized.

Another area benefiting from data analysis technology is customer service, which increasingly focuses on individual needs.

Servicing arrangements become more complex as companies begin to relate to specific individual profiles – but on a mass scale. Machine learning and artificial intelligence are already becoming more adept at servicing very specific customer needs and inquiries. This will only become more accurate as the volume of data collected increases along with the number of unique inquiries able to be serviced by the customer service agent. Then more quality data can be collected and analysed. This continuous cycle where data are collected, analysed and offered back to the customer in the form of targeted and relevant services in order for more data to be collected ultimately improves the customer experience. Demand grows, fulfilling the company's main objective – which is growth. Servicing increased demand will be met with efficiencies of scale that bypass knowledgeable staff in favour of more effective digital systems that can hold the company line regardless of the situation. These trained bots will be able to draw on a wealth of situations that feed their insight and inform them of the most effective course of action while taking into account a centralized mantra/dogma/policy that suits the requirements of the company. These so-called 'intelligent agents' potentially become the automated face of any of the businesses' concerns, from customer service to even sitting on the board. One company, Deep Knowledge Ventures, already has an artificial intelligence board member (Burridge 2017).

The product as a service business model is an area linked to the development of new technologies. As companies further incentivize customers to remain loyal, they are rethinking how the products they sell can be servitized. The pervasive Internet of Things (IoT) is one enabler of this emerging model where sensors and 'always on' devices connected to the internet report back to the manufacturer or supplier. Usage data is then analysed and used to provide the customer with a customized arrangement. As technologies become adept at analysing a product's use, and then understanding the needs of the user through their activity, the companies supplying them with products can address them. If the car purchased through a credit agreement turns out not to be the most suitable based on how it is being used, then the car company can suggest a more appropriate version. Data from modern vehicles can be collected to gain insight into how customers use them. This feeds back into the manufacturer's product development process allowing them to refine future generations and models based on user activity. And the customer is probably not even aware of the types of information being collected and profiled.

The advice from artificial intelligence that sits on the board of the car company would come from a unique perspective, one focused on the success and reputation of the manufacturer. It could then advise excluding specific customer profiles from its sales targets. The service becomes linked to a system continuously evaluating and adjusting its priorities; as long as the customer fits the required profile, then all is well. But what happens if the customer falls outside that preferred customer profile? Is it possible to change consumer behaviour to fit a desired profile?

Personal profiles and credit scores (another commonly used metric) can be used to inform a company on the suitability of new customers. The company can then make an informed decision about whether to sell them something or not. If a customer's profile does not meet the company's expectations, they would be deemed unsuitable. However, the company has sales targets to meet in order to grow and expand, how then can it begin to attract customers that meet its profiling benchmarks? Advertising could be considered a process of indoctrination. Advertising messages are broadcast by companies competing for market share, which they hope to increase by encouraging change in consumer behaviour. Anyone's lifestyle is based on the illusion or myth that the company as a broadcaster represents. Presenting these ideals as a visual story creates aspiration, linking the narrative to the products and services the company is selling. Indulge in this product and live this life, and if you live this life, then you can be a customer, and as a customer, your activity generates more demand as you promote the values of the product and accompanying lifestyle, encouraging others to participate. This may sound absurd but it happens every day, particularly through celebrity endorsements, as these seem to be the most successful application of this psychology. Aspirational imagery changes consumer behaviour by projecting a vision of what their lifestyle could be – if they buy a particular product.

# Selling and sales

The mechanization of the sales process continues to be refined. Uber, for example, allows consumers to take a taxi ride without them taking their wallet out of their pockets. Since the introduction of the credit card by Diners Club in 1950, the idea of living on credit has become widely accepted, readily available and expected financial practice due to how it projects an economy and society into the future.

> Credit enables us to build the present at the expense of the future. It is founded on the assumption that our future resources are sure to be far more abundant than our present resources.

> A host of new and wonderful opportunities open up if we can
> build things in the present using future income.
>
> (Harari 2015: 344)

Credit enables anyone that has access to it to live a life of luxury. When you combine the ease of access to money with a luxury industry founded on excess and aspiration, then luxury becomes a very powerful and sought-after indulgence perfectly aligned with a capitalist agenda; in a sense, it is a self-fulfilling prophecy.

As data creation through digital technology continues to increase, more novel uses of the information collected is discovered and developed. Applications go beyond establishing an individual's credit rating and include targeted advertising, purchasing advice, comparative service analysis, among many others. Stories covering social and political events, art, science and technology unfold daily and are distributed widely with relative ease as a result of how efficiently connected we are to the world via the internet and our precious smartphones. Packets of data have become highly transferable, accessible across a wide range of devices and can be translated into any language. In 2017, *The Economist* declared that data was the most valuable resource on the planet – even more valuable than oil (Anon. 2017).

Data, artificial intelligence and machine learning deliver relevant news stories and product suggestions based on a digital profile, but it can also help drivers avoid traffic via GPS navigation or build an insurance package that includes a bank and a fitness regime that is tracked and confirmed via a wearable monitor such as Fitbit. These applications on an individual level can be beneficial, convenient and allow us to discover something about ourselves through the patterns that emerge when our behaviour, habits and lifestyle are analysed. The data we each generate can be used to tailor our experience in more meaningful and relevant ways. Historically, the traditional bespoke luxury offer of made-to-measure and made-to-order were areas only available to those who could afford such services. As seen in Chapters 2, 4, 6 and 8, technology heralds an era of mass customization and bespoke services for everyone. The more individual data collected and analysed, the more accurate the proposed goods and services can be. This shift is also touted as having sustainable benefits as society shifts from mass production to mass customization. 'A shift to an on-demand, made-to-order economy could force people to more directly confront the consequences of each of their purchasing decisions' (Toussaint 2019: n.pag.).

But user data is generally locked into the providers of free services, e-mail or social media platforms, for example. The more their usage becomes popular, the more data they amass from millions of users. Tech companies controlling the data pool can analyse and glean insight into a range of different scenarios. Those insights can be used to leverage change on a much bigger scale. City planning is suddenly subject to the analysis of large data sets describing the movement of people and vehicles. Patterns become obvious, showing, for example, activities on deliveries that can then be made at certain times of the day. Cars can be re-routed to avoid congestion or even cause congestion to create delays if needed. With the rise of the tech companies, and their unprecedented wealth with the top four breaking through the trillion dollar barrier, data has become the new definition not only of value but also power.

Now a new story is emerging that seeks to redefine our view of reality yet again. This time it is Dataism that encapsulates the idea data is fundamental and permeates throughout the known universe giving it form. Some are even seeing Dataism as a new form of religion. With Dataism comes the realization that algorithmic processes are responsible for everything; complex codes enable us to exist along with everything else. As technologies become increasingly sophisticated, they too permeate our lives by making the complexity we face on a daily basis relevant by conveniently solving the problems that challenge us and offering solutions we actually want to use.

# A data-driven reality

Dataism benefits situations that accelerate the flow of data. This is best understood by looking at the growth of organizations whose primary activity lies within the field of data collection and analysis. We are all encouraged to log activities, events and occasions on social media. We freely give up our locations, disclose how we're feeling, what we're looking for and what we value. Data analysis then uncovers how we compare to others, how we rank against what companies are looking for and what kind of inferences an artificial intelligence or machine learning routine could glean from that data. All to make our lives better or make recommendations that align our lives with the ethical standpoint or strategy of the companies doing the analysis.

Our view of the world tends to be defined by others as few of us can hope to accumulate the knowledge and experience needed to accomplish an independent worldview. Brands, companies, governments, organizations and individuals project their opinions of what they feel is right, wrong, appropriate or desirable with increasing sophistication, particularly through the use of technology and digital media.

These stories enable us to connect with reality in a meaningful way. Religions do the same, giving us hope and guidance, something to help make sense of reality. When you think about it, nobody really knows what reality is as the scientists, academics, philosophers and everyone else with an idea will testify. The voyages of discovery that gave rise to luxury in the first place went some way to enabling and enhancing our experience and understanding of the world, but once all corners of the globe had been discovered, the established luxury purveyors could only push their own, reinforced story of heritage and entitlement with increasing success to promote and sell what they do.

These stories continue to successfully connect us; they have become the backbone of our social structures and reinforce the need to construct meaning from experience. Our emotional response is wide and is continually challenged through the changes happening around us, and the discoveries we make experiencing that change.

Understanding of what is happening is being nudged into a realm where technology has all the answers but also raises new questions – some not yet considered. The appetite to discover the unfolding data-driven reality is both fed and interrogated via a small device that has become to some, more valuable than anything. As the human relationship with smartphones matures and transforms as the technology develops, the connection to everything will change forever.

The increasingly data-rich reality is also becoming a concern. The value of data, how it is used and who actually owns it in order to realize that value is a debate resonating around the world. Currently, we sign up to free services and confirm cookie usage to gain access, signing away rights to the data generated as we browse, share and navigate. This raises the question as to who should rightly own it. Privacy, human rights and the intent of those companies with access to personal data and the ability to mine rich data sets for value is linked to the ethical debate. The process is also used to expose and open up psychological doorways that are then manipulated to achieve desired results with elections, sales, stock prices and legislation. Some individuals are campaigning for data ownership to reside with the person generating the data point in the first place. If data really is valuable to the companies collecting it, then it is probably safe to assume they are realising this value in anyway they can, including selling or sharing data sets to other partners or companies.

Brittany Kaiser was part of Cambridge Analytica, the data analysis company that weaponized users' Facebook data for political gain. As the activity of the company was made known, suddenly the world realized what could be achieved with access to large data sets, psychological profiling and tailored algorithmic operations to nudge particular users. Judging by the results of the Cambridge Analytica campaigns, data proved to be extremely valuable to those that have it and are able to analyse it. Its value was realized through political gain where users were manipulated towards a preferred outcome without really realizing it. Kaiser now campaigns via #Ownyourdata, demanding that data be owned by the users who generate it, rather than the tech companies collecting and using it for economic and political gain.

Data and its true value are only now coming to the fore, but it is worth considering that if user data is valuable, then why shouldn't users be able to sell it to companies that want it? Flipping data owner-ship on its head would be difficult to achieve due to the ambiguous methods by which data is generated and captured. Digital intelligent agents could be the answer here as they could negotiate on a user's behalf and retain an element of bias set to what the user wants, rather than that of the organizations it interacted with.

As digital systems become ubiquitous, reliable and integrated, essentially enabling big businesses to operate, then dependency on these systems becomes paramount. Indeed, system failure, cyber attacks and even power outages can easily bring a company to a grind-ing halt. The more sophisticated these digital systems become, the more dependency on them is increased. And as they begin to connect and are more finely integrated across a range of different facets of indi-vidual lives and corporate idealism, Dataism is only going to increase.

At the beginning of this chapter, we spoke about how luxury is linked to discovery, something that made our lives better through directly observing and responding to the world around us. This is becoming increasingly difficult as our means of observing and sens-ing in general are becoming redundant because we are increasingly dependent on technology to interpret that world. Data is out there, in the cloud, but without the means to interpret that data, we are miss-ing out on an important facet to life, particularly as the data and life become intertwined. As few of us understand how data is generated and used, we then become dependent on those who do know. We hope they hold our best interests at heart but we don't know for sure as this area of discovery through technology is complex and possibly only able to be fully understood via autonomous digital agents or arti-ficial intelligence. As digital discovery unfolds, we will become more reliant on artificial intelligence to make sense of the new world emerg-ing around us, an intelligence that will hopefully ensure our lives are comfortable, better and valued.

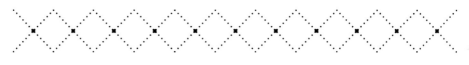

# 8

# Luxury and the Retail Environment

*The fast pace of change, underpinned by technological advancements, poses a new set of questions for the entire world of design and architecture. New roles will need to be established for designers and every other actor involved in the design, construction and presentation of the retail environment. If, in fact, the environment will increasingly be a hybrid of physical and virtual, and characterized by the continuity of experience between on- and off-line, the experience will be very different. This as much for customers as it will be for designers. The space of luxury to which we refer in the context of this work is the dimension where new relationships occur between customers and brands.*

Through a series of case studies, this chapter discusses the growing relevance technology has on the retail environment. The impact of new technologies becomes significantly evident in the context of luxury stores. This chapter is divided into four sections. The first contextualizes the use of new technologies in the luxury retail market. This includes the use of standard gadgets such as beacons, radio-frequency identification (RFID) and magic mirrors, the idea of ubiquitous computing, the Internet of Things (IoT) and smart tracking. In addition, we discuss more advanced and experimental technology such as hybrids of virtual reality (VR) and augmented reality (AR), use of machine learning (ML) and artificial intelligence (AI) and the use of complex algorithms to determine customers' social profiles.

    In the second section, we present and analyse a series of case studies where all these technologies are used. The aim is to evaluate the extent to which the projects are successful in engaging existing and new customers.

The third section is a reflection and assessment of the impacts, positive and negative, on the implementation of such technologies for the retail environment. The section presents a tripartite view that combines the designers and technologists that developed the project, on the one hand, and the customers' experience and feedback, on the other hand. These facets are then considered in conjunction with the luxury brand that underpins the projects.

The final section of the chapter is a generalized reflection on the future of the retail environment and the ways in which its physical and spatial characteristics, as well as the nature and the demands of its users, are evolving as new technologies are developed.

# Technology, shopping and the urban environment

Since the 1990s, architects, geographers, urban designers and interior designers have increased their focus on the notion of shopping and the importance of the retail environment, paying special attention to luxury brands. There are a number of key points that help understand the development of this trend.

The first is the globalization that characterized the second half of the twentieth century and, with it, global consumerism. People have gradually become used to finding information about products while browsing and purchasing without necessarily needing to go to a physical store. With the wide distribution of the internet, customers have become global shoppers, able to compare the same product as offered in different markets across the world.

This point has gradually led to the second aspect, the generalization of the physical store (intended as a unique place, part of the purchase experience) and the gradual idea of genericness and ubiquitous shopping. This aspect is explored in-depth by Rem Koolhaas, who began a number of projects and studies with *The Harvard Design School Guide to Shopping* (2002), made by his office OMA and the Harvard Graduate School of Design. In an 800-page book, this work explores 'the spaces, people, techniques, ideologies, and inventions by which shopping has so dramatically refashioned the city at the turn of the century' (OMA 2002: n.pag.). Koolhaas holds that shopping as a social and cultural practice has 'infiltrated, colonized, and even replaced, almost every aspect of urban life' (Goldberger 2002: n.pag.). The study contains a number of projects and thought-provoking statements, including:

town centers, suburbs, streets, and now airports, train stations, museums, hospitals, schools, the internet, and the military are shaped by the mechanisms and spaces of shopping. The voracity by which shopping pursues the public has, in effect, made it one of the principal – if only – modes by which we experience the city. Perhaps the beginning of the 21st century will be remembered as the point where the urban could no longer be understood without shopping.

(OMA 2002: 1)

The idea of pervasive shopping that changes the very fabric of cities and public space is elaborated in Koolhaas' essay 'Generic city', contained in *SMLXL* (1995). It explores the idea of generic and sameness permeating all aspects of human life.

The Generic City is the city liberated from the captivity of centre, from the straitjacket of identity. The Generic City [...] is nothing but a reflection of present need and present ability. [...] it is easy. [...]. If it gets too small, it expands. [...] It is equally exciting or unexciting everywhere.

(Koolhaas 1995: 1249–50)

Reading Koolhaas' interpretation of the generic city, Maarten Hajer suggests the genericness of place in the twenty-first century city is due to the increased presence of technology (Hajer 1999: 142–143), where technological advancements erode the ideas of physical presence and proximity (Hajer 1999: 142).

The third point hinges on the idea that technology is the main trigger of the increasing detachment of people from space and place. This idea can be traced back to the work of David Harvey (1989), where, for example, he discusses the 'revolutionary properties of a capitalistic mode of production' (1990: 418) in relation to technological innovation. In this instance, capitalism is 'always restlessly searching out new organizational forms, new technologies, new lifestyles, and new modalities of production and exploitation' (Harvey 1990: 424). Driven by capitalism, technology is a force of 'social definitions of time and space' (Harvey 1990: 424) and 'radical reorganizations of space, relations and of spatial representations' (Harvey 1990: 424–25).

The final point consists in the extension of the latter, whereby technology is distributed to potentially every aspect of urban life, becoming the informational infrastructure that characterizes the city of the twenty-first century. Among many others, Steve Graham and Simon Marvin have extensively observed this phenomenon. Their book

*Telecommunications and the City: Electronic Spaces, Urban Places* (2002) proposed a new framework to understand how boundaries between the digital and physical cities are gradually blurring, whereby the idea of ubiquity and displacement are gradually important. They explain that, 'telecommunications simply displace, substitute and lead to the eventual dissolution of the physical city' (Graham and Marvin 2002: 243).

The importance of the immaterial part of the city (intended as data and information) has been expanded, among others, by Paul Dourish in his work *The Stuff of Bits: An Essay on the Materialities of Information* (2017), where he examines the materiality and immateriality of physical spaces and information. In particular, Dourish holds that material realities are starting to be considered by many scholars in the social sciences together with social phenomena between the physical and the digital worlds (2017: 3). Moreover, Dourish explains that 'the shift to an information society is, often, a shift from material objects to digital equivalents on computer screens (as in online shopping, online movie rentals, digital libraries, electronic newspapers, and digital health records, for example' (Dourish and Mazmanian 2011: 2–3).

# An updated notion of space

As a consequence of this new immateriality increasingly permeating all aspects of our physical space, we suggest the idea that space should be considered through the lens of an updated notion. The definition of space in general terms is gradually changing from the traditional binary view of physical versus digital space to a more hybridized version, whereby the physical and the digital elements of our everyday lives are increasingly intertwined. Among the many recent studies in architecture, urban studies and human and urban geography, the work on the notions of transduction (MacKenzie 2002) and code/space (Kitchin and Dodge 2011) are perhaps the most relevant in the context of this book.

The first notion, articulated into transduction and transductive spaces, was elaborated by MacKenzie at the beginning of the 2000s and was defined as a 'kind of operation […] in which a particular domain undergoes a certain kind of ontogenetic modulation. […] Through transduction, a domain structures itself as a partial, always incomplete solution to a relational problem' (MacKenzie 2003:10). In other words, a transductive space indicates a relational space developed as it unfolds. Unlike a traditional Euclidean space, where space is determined in terms of measurable relationship between elements, and where there exist binary relationships of void/empty or inside/outside, a transduction space is an entity in a continuous relational mutation.

The second idea is code/space, defined as

> the relationship between code and space is dyadic code and space are mutually constituted, wherein how the space is used and produced is predominantly mediated by code, and the code and its data exist in order to produce the space and its attendant spatiality.
>
> (Kitchin and Dodge 2011: 198)

Code/space is an example of an inseparable combination of space (intended here as the physical space) and the software mediating it.

One way of understanding the changing nature of space, which encompasses the ideas of transduction and code/space, can be found in the notion of digital assemblages (Carta 2019). This can be defined as the combination of three elements: software, representing a ubiquitous infrastructure that allows all the relationships to occur; individuals, who navigate the environment modifying it as they move into it; and the built environment, intended as the combination of the physical elements of the world (from buildings to communication infrastructure [Carta 2019]).

Taking these new descriptors for a changing nature of space and spatiality, we argue that luxury can no longer be considered within the context of binary spatial notions (luxury/no luxury, digital shop versus bricks and mortar, inside an exclusive shop versus being outside, etc.). The space of luxury needs to be projected into an updated notion of space. As seen, this space is hybrid and in continuous evolution, increasingly distant from the traditional idea of Euclidean spatiality, which was characterized by elements such as physical location of the store (e.g. city centre, prime location, etc.), size (think of the whole notion of diamond carats or cuts) and proportions.

Space, and more specifically the space of luxury, should be considered as an evolving and mutating element where luxury occurs increasingly as an experience dissociated from physical elements. We explore this hybrid dimension while looking at new forms of publicness, where

> since our environment and daily routines are being mixed in with smart technologies and big data, ultimately creating smart cities, we as individuals become a product of that space. [...] The interaction between the digital presence of individuals and the physical space [...] occurs through various forms of interfaces, intended as mediating systems that connect physical and digital facets of the individual human practices.
>
> (Carta et al. 2019: 227)

Luxury will very soon take place in a new dimension where customers will be seamlessly immersed into a new environment where tangible elements will be combined with computer-generated parts of our reality.

It is important to note that space should no longer be understood as volumes, distances or capacity. Space is now relational and, more specifically, it is described by informational relationships. Relationships are no longer direct (as a customer who enters a store), but mediated by technology, and more specifically, by software. Many researchers and designers have been observing the mediation of space through software, including Kitchin et al. (2017), and Manovich (2013), as well as the work of Graham Cairns' Mediated City Programme and the Architecture, Media, Politics and Society (AMPS) think-tank. For Cairns, the mediated space is,

> for some, [...] little more than the inevitable evolution of urban space in the digital age. For others, it represents the city's liberation from the condition of stasis. For scaremongers, it's a nightmare scenario in which the difference between the virtual and the real, the electronic and the material, the recorded and the lived, becomes impossible to identify. In every case, corporeal engagement is placed at one remove from the physical world.
> (n.d.: n.pag.)

If space is the dimension of new relationships between customers and brands mediated by software, how do these relationships look? How do customers behave in this new spatiality? What are customers seeking in luxury brands? What is the luxury industry offering to its customers? What is the role and responsibility of software in all this? Is the software in control (as suggested by Manovich)? Or are customers embracing new technologies and taking advantage of them in order to find new ways to approach and experience luxury? As detailed in the following section, a new notion of space should address all these questions in different ways and from different angles in an attempt to provide new insights on the emergent relationships between individuals and brands.

# The luxury retail environment

In his account of the wirelessness world, Adrian Mackenzie (2010) commented on the sheer number of wireless devices gradually permeating all aspects of social life:

> At the end of 2007, one billion IEEE 802.11 or Wi-Fi chipsets were in the world. One billion such chipsets will be produced each year

by 2012 [...] [of which] two-thirds will find their way into electronic devices, especially consumers electronics and telephones, and many will percolate into wireless network infrastructures in cities, in industrial and institutional facilities, and in environmental sensor networks.

(Mackenzie 2010: 59)

In 2019, the number of Wi-Fi chipsets was estimated to be around nine billion (ABI Research 2014). A majority of these chipsets power mobile devices, providing people with instant and ubiquitous access to the internet, and therefore to information. Mobile devices, in turn, generate a huge number of data, both automatically (like logging GPS position, timestamps, etc.) and as the result of any action of the user (searches, sharing on social media, messages or bank transactions).

The fashion business and, in particular, the section pertaining to luxury brands, is increasingly including new digital technologies and (big) data in its agenda. 'The use of rich data and granular customer insights to inform decisions offers business opportunities across the fashion value chain, in areas ranging from dynamic pricing to optimized product replenishment' (McKinsey and Company 2017: 18). Since the appearance of what Kitchin (2013) defined as the 'data deluge', whereby the amount of data available on every person in the world is exponentially growing, data are becoming increasingly important in practically all fields of human activity. Several aspects of social life have been gradually datafied, translated into a data format and transposed (or extended) to cyberspace. This includes aspects that have 'never been quantified before – friendships, interests, casual conversations, information searches, expressions of tastes, emotional responses, and so on' (Van Dijck 2014: 198). This phenomenon is particularly interesting in the fashion industry and retail environment in general. Data is a prime asset for fashion brands, managers and retailers, and for any company generally interested in using digital technologies to better understand the preferences and spending patterns of their clients. 'Access to consumer data is the holy grail for platform businesses because exclusive ownership of data allows them to exert control over the rest of the ecosystem and makes it attractive for third parties to come on board the platform' (McKinsey and Company 2017: 49).

The growing interest in customer data is partially due to the availability of information that characterizes the industry of the last two decades but also to the growing demand from the consumer. Younger clients in general, as well as those interested in luxury markets, are increasingly in search of a tailored shopping experience as they 'demand a customer-centric shopping experience – one tailored to their wants and needs as valued customers' (Donnelly and Scaff 2013: 3).

This combination of data and technological availability, and customers' demand for personalization, is one of the main triggers for the extensive and expanding use of AI in the fashion industry.

In particular, AI has been identified as an element of growing importance in the luxury market. 'AI enhancements will go beyond the traditional areas of machine tasks into creative and customer interaction processes, blurring the line between technology and creativity' (McKinsey and Company 2017: 27).

One of the first applications of AI in the fashion industry was the delivery of personalized offers to customers. The idea is to, 'provide cutting-edge individualized curation and tailoring for consumers that take into account purchase journeys and customer feedback; to increase relevance of their storytelling and contextual channels; and to refocus on creating products that are distinctive' (McKinsey and Company 2017: 45). This seems to be a crucial point in the business strategy of companies investing in the use of AI and machine learning as a part of their branding:

> Powered by artificial intelligence and big data, the world's biggest e-commerce platforms can make an impersonal environment seem highly personal. With tailored products, personalized recommendations, and smarter supply chains, will fashion brands find working with these giants an increasingly persuasive proposition?
> (Kati Chitrakorn cited in McKinsey and Company 2017: 48)

Many companies are investing in AI as a way to improve their supply chain and forecast the demand for products. 'What artificial intelligence (AI) can do is help turn large and diverse data sets into enriched information that can be used to improve the entire supply chain, from design and manufacturing to sales, marketing and customer service' (McKinsey and Company 2017: 49). The idea of predicting with accuracy the number of products that may be requested by customers in a specific store at a particular time, so as to minimize the unsold pieces, movements of goods etc. is appealing to many large-scale brands. This results in more control of the entire movement of products globally, price and resources optimization and a more accurate trend forecast: 'most early adopters in the fashion industry have focused their AI efforts on a few elements of the value chain, the most significant being demand forecasting, operations automation, and customer experience enhancement (in particular in personalization)' (McKinsey and Company 2017: 60). Examples are Kering and LVMH websites, and Bain and Co.

AI is also used to emulate the creativity of designers. 'Leading fashion companies will use it to enhance the creative process, design and product development; they will, for example, use algorithms to sift vast amounts of data to predict which product features customers are most likely to prefer' (McKinsey and Company 2017: 58). In addition it is used to determine the profitability of certain styles that can then be ordered on repeat, increasing profits and further reducing excess, unsold stock.

When AI is combined with other digital technologies, the customer experience in and off store becomes enhanced. A case in point is offered by the Farfetch's 'Store of the Future' where

> [a]utomatic customer recognition at the store's entrance, RFID-enabled clothing racks and digital mirrors that allow customers to choose sizes, colours and directly check out, all demonstrate how AI can be employed to excite customers in-store while seamlessly integrating the online and offline experiences.
>
> (McKinsey and Company 2017: 59)

Another example is Neiman Marcus' Fort Worth (Texas) store, where the Digital Memory Mirror has been installed. Developed by MemoMi, this platform/mirror 'provides a realistic and personalized augmented reality experience [...] using a physics and pixel-based algorithm' (Memomi n.d.: n.pag.). This smart mirror combines artificial intelligence, gesture recognition, sensors and augmented reality to superimpose the selected clothing onto the mirrored image of the customer in real time. The selected dress follows the movements of the customer in front of the mirror without the need to undress. This technology lets the customer quickly try out all the products in the collection. It also allows the customer to save images of themselves with a particular item of clothing and share it through social media.

If AI is the mechanism behind such an augmented customer experience, it is with VR and AR that the retail environment appears to be really booming. The use of these technologies is, in fact, growing rapidly: the global retail market for VR and AR is forecast to reach US$1.6 billion by 2025 (Goldman Sachs 2016).

In 2017, Burberry collaborated with Apple to create a new AR-based app allowing customers to take photos and augment them with illustrations designed by Danny Sangra. The enhanced pictures encompass comments and symbols, and can be shared on social media. This strategy has a triple effect: it increases users' engagement, it improves the customer's experience and finally, it creates attention towards the brand on social media that will eventually convert into revenue (Rawal 2017).

The retail environment becomes entirely virtual in Swarovski's experiment with VR. Customers interested in the Atelier Swarovski home decor line can wear a VR headset and experience the crystal home accessories collection as a part of a number of rooms and domestic environments. The client can therefore visualize the selected product directly onsite, along with other domestic objects, and understand the object in context. The pieces are linked to information about the manufacturing process, origin of materials, price and delivery. The tech company Ripe.io takes this approach to a more extreme extent, where clients can access in real-time information about the entire supply chain of the product. This works with aggregate data fed into a dashboard where clients can access predictive consumer analytics (Ripe.io 2020).

In 2018, Gucci unveiled its Hallucination campaign. A combination of AR and VR, this project shows a screen within the windows of the Milan Montenapoleone store, projecting videos and illustrations created by artist Ignasi Monreal. The videos could only be activated with a QR code the client received after buying in store.

If we consider the virtual space of social media as an extension of the physical shopping environment, we can then appreciate the investments and strategies companies are deploying to engage with customers. A good example of this is Louis Vuitton's chatbot system in which an AI-driven software replies on Facebook to about 23 million followers in real time. Such chatbots use Natural Language Processing, automation and cognitive technologies to incrementally customize answers based on the ongoing conversation, with the aim of providing to the customer the feeling of talking to a real person. Conversation with chatbots can be sophisticated and surprisingly believable.

According to Naveen Joshi (2019), AR and VR could bring a number of positive aspects to the retail environment in the long run. He highlights five main points where the retail environment will improve: the increase of the customer's engagement (as they will feel an active part of the shopping experience), the accuracy of the personalized customer experience (as data will be characteristic of the individual, so the experience offered), the customer satisfaction will increase (as the service will be more tailored and personal), more marketing methods will be enabled (new ways of shopping, browsing, trying out, delivery etc. will be available) and employee training will be facilitated (using AR and VR not only with customers but also with staff in training to simulate real-life scenarios) (Joshi 2019).

## Some case studies

The first category of projects includes designs where technology is used in an explicit manner and as a main strategic element to appeal to the customers. For example, UNStudio (n.d.b) has designed a complex system of curved glass for P.C. Hooftstraat 138 in Amsterdam (2017–19) where the store window mimics 'both in form and function […] billowing transparent cloths' (UNStudio n.d.b). Albeit the final effect appears simple, the technological effort to realize such a construction detail is remarkable. The openings are realized with large laminated annealed low iron glass panels, both curved and straight. They are then framed using structural silicone with stainless steel edge mullions. In addition, a hidden steel frame holds the glass boxes to ensure safety and protection.

The same architects designed a luxury shopping plaza in Wuhan, China, Hanjie Wanda Square (2011–13), where the façade is constructed of a combination of a large number of spheres made of polished stainless steel and patterned glass. Divided into nine types, these façade features occupy their mutual positions in such a way that 'recreate the effect of movement and reflection in the water, or the sensuous folds of silk fabric' (UNStudio n.d.a).

In the same street in Amsterdam where the UNStudio's glass façade is located, MVRDV designed the Crystal Houses, an interior and exterior project for Chanel in 2016 (the building was subsequently occupied by Hermès). Similar to UNStudio's, this project was particularly successful in establishing an elegant and sophisticated transition between the brickwork that characterizes the traditional appearance of P.C. Hooftstraat (one of Amsterdam's most popular luxury brand shopping streets) and a new and transparent look. The modular pattern of the original brickwork and window frames has been retained, and the original elements replaced with a complex and technologically advanced new glass façade. The façade consists of solid-glass bricks individually produced in a laboratory near Venice. Researchers from the Delft University of Technology, engineering firms and contractors developed a novel structural system and, with it, a related fabrication and assembly technique to construct the glass wall. The glass bricks were bonded together with a new type of transparent, high-strength and UV bonded adhesive developed for this project by a specialized German company. The construction phase of this project was as delicate as it was complex:

> […] six to ten experts worked every day for a whole year in a place that bore more resemblance to a laboratory than a construction site. Due to the sensitivity of the materials, an extremely high level of accuracy and craftsmanship was required and a technical development team was onsite throughout the process. Since this construction is the first of its kind, new construction methods

and tools had to be utilised: from high-tech lasers and laboratory
grade UV-lamps, to slightly lower-tech Dutch full-fat milk, which,
with its low transparency, proved to be an ideal liquid to function
as a reflective surface for the levelling of the first layer of bricks.

(MVRDV 2020: n.pag.)

In 2015, Christian de Portzamparc and Peter Marino completed the
design for the Dior flagship store in Gangnam-gu Seoul, Korea. This
is another example of a sophisticated use of technology employed to
realize a challenging design idea. In order to represent Dior's clothing,
the designers

wanted the surfaces to flow, like the couturier's soft, woven white
cotton fabric. These surfaces, which soar into the sky and undu-
late as if in motion, crossed by a few lines, are made from long
moulded fibreglass shells, fitted together with aircraft precision.

(De Portzamparc 2020: n.pag.)

The shape of both the inside and the outside creates an impressive
sculptural effect where hard construction materials behave like soft
draping. This illustrates quite well what we discussed earlier in this
chapter. Not only do luxury brands employ the most recognized architects in the world to design their stores and other significant spaces,
they also have the luxury to be as creative and innovative as the client
allows. This creativity extends beyond the space and environment in
which they work to encompass the materials they use and the location of the store.

The concept of construction technology applied to the luxury
retail environment is taken to an extreme in Thomas Heatherwick's
Pacific Place (2005), a Hong Kong luxury shopping centre for international and fashion brands. The level and quality of craft in this project is
remarkable. With more than 1.6 million man-hours spent in its realization (Frearson 2011), every detail of this one hundred thousand square
metre building has been meticulously designed, prototyped and built
by experienced craftspeople, carpenters and builders. This includes
anything from the push button panels in the lifts to the sophisticated
use of wooden panels in the lavatories.

Technology can also be applied to specific and localized parts
of larger buildings to attract people's attention. A clear example is the
pop-up store designed by Asylum Creative for the watch brand Hublot
in the Paragon Shopping Centre, Singapore. In order to generate an
'inviting sense of excitement and wonder' (Asylum n.d.: n.pag.), over
35,000 pieces of paper in the shape of black crystal were connected

to a series of suspended fishing wires. With this, the designers created a two-storey block-like pavilion in the middle of the shopping centre's atrium. It is described by the designers as 'an ephemeral, fleeting point in time, caught in a still image' and as 'an illusory space; magically solid yet porous and structurally monumental yet light' (Asylum n.d.: n.pag.). This project clearly illustrates how a combination of a relatively low-tech approach and highly sensorial and aesthetic design can generate an exclusive, luxurious experience.

One of the areas where new technologies are rapidly growing is the automotive industry. Increasingly, car manufacturers are experimenting in new luxury segments that combine high performances and standards with cutting-edge technology. Examples include BMW's Vision Future Luxury concept car (BMW 2014), the 2020 Mercedes-Benz GLE or the Tesla Model S, among a growing number of makes and models. This new generation of cars include a number of innovative features, among them an AR system whereby the driver can see in their sightline on the windscreen relevant information about traffic, speed and other indications on environmental data gathered by sensors on the outside of the car. They also offer the driver augmented services including Intelligent Terrain Mapping (with live information directly on the dashboard), Augmented Marketing (with ads and commercials linked to physical landmarks), Automated Parking Assistance (where AR is used to help with parking) and Intuitive Road Safety (where AI is used to predict pedestrian behaviour and possible obstacles) (Vanarama 2020).

# Designers and customers

In 2013, Sara Manuelli selected four projects in her book *Design for Shopping: New Retail Interiors* (Manuelli 2006) to represent the relationship between technology and shopping. They are OMA's Prada in Los Angeles (2004), oki-ni in London designed by 6a Architects (2001), Shoebaloo in Amsterdam by Meyer & Van Schooten Architecten (2003) and Y's in Tokyo by Ron Arad (2003). It is interesting to note the technological aspects characterizing these projects are related to new materials or their innovative use, unfamiliar objects (like in Shoebaloo) or spatial configurations (Prada and oki-ni) or moving sculptural elements (like in Y). In the Prada shop, there are a number of digital technologies, including LCD screens, sensors, Privalite glass panels in the changing areas and RFID technology.

Since the early 2000s, the technology available for the retail environment has changed significantly. Computers are increasingly disappearing in the environment, following the prediction of Weiser (1994), in which he foresaw the disappearance of physical computers (intended as physical objects in the room), calling this phenomenon ubiquitous computing (or ubicomp). In fact, as computing becomes increasingly more distributed across servers and clouds, the part that people, and customers in this particular case, are able to see are simply interfaces, screens and monitors. These are just the end section of a larger assemblage of parts where memory and databases are stored in different servers scattered around the world. In some cases, calculations occur directly on the cloud, which is located on other servers, probably somewhere other than the place where data are stored. Today, we are more likely to deal with interfaces and frontends than with computers in stores and public places. In this scenario, where computation and data are displaced, the computational power and connectivity that underpin digital technologies are growing and increasing. One of the effects of this is that stores have become smarter, more responsive and intelligent. Current technology allows stores to be simply the senses and the final output of something larger (simulations, data crunching, machine learning, AI-based processes, etc.) that takes place somewhere else. In a 2018 interview Hideki Hayashi, Security Product Group Product Manager at Hitachi Europe, explained, 'Hitachi's sensor can track the number of people entering and leaving shops and collate data on customer behaviour, including tracking aisles visited, time spent in particular locations, products viewed and touched and then selected for purchase' (cited in Waugh 2018: n.pag.).

These new technologies have a significant impact on designers, customers and the luxury brands behind these stores. First, designers have largely embraced new possibilities, not only including new devices and data-driven aspects in their design but, more significantly, some of them started their own concepts from the potential challenges of new technologies. This is a significant difference between interpreting technology as an add-on to a traditional design (e.g., including some more widgets) and using new technologies as a starting point for their own design concept. Designers choosing the latter option have tried to have a real understanding of the technology (e.g. VR, AR or AI), including in their design team computer scientists, data analysts and software engineers. These projects are no longer interior design or architectural projects, where the main elements were traditionally space, materials, symbols and atmospheres. Rather, the fundamental components of such projects are data, sensors, information, connectivity and experience. Designers have started generating their concepts using data as a connective element between space and people. This means customers experience the spatiality of the store through a ubiquitous interface made of data.

# Tailoring the customer experience

This brings us to the second aspect of the evolution of luxury stores: the customer experience. If we imagine data are ubiquitous and, as such, invisibly surrounds each customer, this means data precedes and, at the same time, succeeds customers. Before physically going into the store, it is quite likely the customer has already visited its digital twin (that is the online version of the store on its website). By doing this, the customer generated some data (e.g. by searching, clicking on links, zooming on items, etc.), as well as accessed (or consumed) some other data (by temporarily downloading on the browser of their device cookies and other similar data from the server). While in the store, the customer uses data, for example while interacting with a magic mirror and, inevitably, generates data as the sensors, cameras and other devices in the store log their information to describe their behaviour (which item they have looked at, what caught their attention, how long they stayed, etc.). After the physical visit, data crunching and analysis is mostly done by AI systems with the aim of interpreting the customer's behaviours in the attempt of making sense of it. AI systems infer valuable information from this data. For example, the reasons behind a certain action, what part of the products on display has the most successful results and why, as well as the spending patterns of each client.

Finally, with these types of data at hand, luxury brands can devise and then offer a truly tailored experience for each of their customers. Not only can they know more about their clients in terms of quantity of information, but more significantly, they are able to gain more precise information about their client from the data generated. In fact, what has changed with the most recent technological advancements, and especially with big data, is the granularity with which the data can be gathered and analysed. It can be collected and stored with very high precision and in large quantities (that is more data per each piece of information). More interestingly, it can be considered with previously collected data from the same individual to generate patterns. This can be compared with data coming from other individuals, so to establish generic patterns or find new information. Luxury brands now have powerful tools allowing them to understand and predict the preferences of their customers. They can then design their products, their stores and everything else around their brand in order to meet and exceed clients' expectations. But equally to surprise them, making them feel unique, taken care of and special. Laurence Barry and Eran Fisher (2019) observe this point in their work about digital audiences. They explain that new technologies have resulted in the shift from a generic audience, where one (say brands) can refer to imagined communities of undistinguished people (Barry and Fisher 2019: 212), to individual audiences, characterized by the transformation from averages to individuals (Barry and Fisher 2019: 215).

> With big data technologies and the datafication of the world, the arbitrary quantification of phenomena is now obsolete; essentialised categories are not necessary any more for the treatment of information. Furthermore, the accumulation of data at the individual level allows the application of statistical techniques, once focused on the collective, at this same individual level: statistical techniques are now applied to the individual. Big data technologies have thus rendered possible the treatment of populations without the need to rely on aggregate indicators such as averages.
>
> (Barry and Fisher 2019: 223)

# The future of the retail environment

In this book, we provide a number of analyses and discussions around the idea of luxury and, more importantly, we speculate on how luxury is changing. Luxury is always in a hybrid phase, transitioning from what was an old and well-established understanding of luxury as elitarian, unique and for a small and select group of people, to something completely different.

In the future, luxury will be more based on experience and access to knowledge and information, as well as focus on the uniqueness and the craft of a certain object or service. This has been explored in previous research, 'Reifying luxury, gold to golden: How the showroom became a digital showreel, from object (gold) to experience (golden) – experiencing luxury by abstracting the object' (Carta and De Kock 2019). In that, we traced the current transition between what we defined as the luxury of golden (made of materials, spatial qualities and tangible features) to the luxury of the gold (where luxury is intended primarily as the access to exclusive experience based on knowledge and information). We are currently in a transition where luxury is gradually assuming an increasingly intangible nature. We characterize this transition through eight main aspects:

> The extensive use of highly visible patterns and textures to identify a specific brand, is superseded by more anonymous surfaces and amorphous geometries (1). The use of large logos and recognisable texts almost disappear (2) in favour of a familiar feeling and overall atmosphere. [...] Direct experience is no longer the main goal (3). The understanding of luxury becomes subtle and customers are required to infer and make links by themselves in order to appreciate the experience. Often these links are informational and technological. Users are required to use a multiplicity of platforms to create the entire experience, for example, in moving from mobile devices to variations of in-store gadgets. The physical store and its location lose importance in the experience, while access to something more ethereal becomes key. The idea of access (4) from everywhere (5) is pivotal in understanding how the nature of luxury is changing. People want to perceive the power of doing, even if there is no action. The idea of potentiality and access is what is important in the experience. The Renault Symbioz Smart Home and related infrastructure is an epitome of this notion; where the user can access in-depth information related to this extended environment from any location, including the comfort of their own home. In many cases experience is no longer unique to or limited by the process of people having to travel to a specific location at a specific time to afford luxury. The experience is replicable (6), and fully accessible. Luxury is available on demand and whenever desired, through the infrastructural technology at people's disposal, and can be repeated and sustained after access has been granted. Finally, it can be argued that these days the emphasis of a new paradigm of luxury – from gold to golden – rests more heavily in perception than in direct and physical experience (8). The overriding concept of gradations of visibility (7) is a crucial factor in fully understanding and contextualising this last point, because we hold that luxury is no more evident than in the complex gradations of visibility found in visually sustainable constructs (8).
> (Carta and De Kock 2019: 204–05)

As the world becomes increasingly characterized by digital information and access to it, we agreed it was likely for the future of luxury to be intrinsically connected to information technologies and somehow driven by them. With this working hand in hand with the physical object – tech is not going to replace luxury, but contribute to redefining the luxury experience.

Among many speculative studies introducing visionary perspectives for the future, the one presented by Pedro Domingos in his *Master Algorithm* (2015) theory is perhaps the most appealing. In this work Domingos explains that different algorithms are used (and good for different tasks) and that

> [w]hat we really want is a single algorithm combining the key features of all of them: the Master Algorithm. [...] If it exists, the Master Algorithm can derive all knowledge in the world – past, present and future – from data [...] It would speed up the progress of knowledge across the board, and change the world in ways that we can barely begin to imagine. [...] (it would be) a unified theory that makes sense of everything we know to date, and lay the foundation for decades or centuries of future progress. The Master Algorithm is our gateway to solving some of the hardest problems we face, from building domestic robots to curing cancer.
>
> (Domingos 2015: 4–5)

Domingos expands this vision in a TED Talk titled 'The next hundred years of your life' (Domingos 2017). In the twelve-minute presentation, Domingos sketches out how the future could be with extraordinary technological advancement. The first stage of this would be a world where screens disappear, as well as any other source of information directly addressed to users. We will no longer need interfaces (as we know them now) in order to access information. We will be able to access information directly through our eyes, where LED chips will project directly into our retinas. The physical dimension of the work, as we currently understand, will be indistinguishably mixed with the digital dimension. Physical and digital will ultimately be the same reality and we will not be able to separate them. We will accept both of them as 'real', without distinction. This would be the ultimate concretization of Mark Weiser's idea of ubiquitous computing (Weiser et al. 1999) which we discuss in Chapter 9.

In this scenario, luxury will be free of any physical constraints that characterize the luxury industry today, including scarcity and availability of resources, sustainability, circular economy (cf. Chapter 5), but also logistics, storing and stocking of goods, transportation and geo-political boundaries. Luxury will be potentially seamless and limitless, where the main characteristic is the experience a brand or product can give the customer.

# Speculations: new spaces and new roles for designers

Technology now more than ever provides the customer with increasing ways to shop, to experience everything around the brand and, more significantly, to establish a new relationship with it. Customers are no longer confined to a physical environment. The emergence of online retailers focusing on the sale and resale of luxury products continues to make an impact, as previously discussed, with a focus on second season items, hiring, repurposing and recycling.

The fact that more outlets satisfy the market and the need to increase profits raises questions about the availability of goods and their status within the luxury realm. Technology plays a significant part in the way luxury products are not only made but how they are sold. As such, the market continues to evolve to ensure products are continually available to the consumer. Through new technologies, customers have now the chance to engage with the brand at a higher and deeper level. They can, for example, customize their own patterns, clothes or shoes, consume their own unique pieces through their phone app. People can now follow daily updates of their favourite brands, commenting on news and updates, sending their opinions, and reposting what they find interesting on to other social platforms. In turn, luxury brands can respond to their customers in almost real-time, adapting public relations strategies and refocusing on specific directions. Technology today can create an unprecedented rich interaction between customer and brand in a two-way relationship they can engage in freely and daily. The increasing adoption of new technologies as a part of marketing strategy is significantly transforming the shopping experience of luxury brands, providing customers with an augmented relationship with the brand. This experience exceeds the boundaries of the physical store and nowadays online shopping as well. Luxury brands are probably better defined as a cloud of services, where shopping is just one aspect, deeply intertwined with online presence, new forms of advertisement (think of influencers) and real-time access to the brand (mostly via a chatbot as discussed in Chapter 7).

In 2016, Jonathan Faiers analysed the state of disruptive luxury in the context of the relationship between luxury trades and new technologies, mostly focusing on 3D printing. For Faiers disruptive luxury is a 'semantic umbrella from which to consider the role new technology might play in destabilizing our entrenched notion of how luxury is produced, disseminated, and commissioned' (Faiers 2016: 83). At the end of this article, he concluded that the 'contemporary disruptive luxury has yet to fulfil its promise and, in the context of algorithmically produced luxury goods, will hopefully avoid the fate of its visually similar progenitor art nouveau' (Faiers 2016: 95).

The point we make in this chapter is that, if we consider the retail environment and the relationships customers have today with the spatiality around a luxury brand, technology is no longer disruptive, but the norm. Data, information and connectivity are increasingly distributed, pervasive and ubiquitous. Technology is progressively calm (Weiser and Brown 1997), that is in the periphery of one's attention, as opposed to being at the centre of focus in each case. As Mark Weiser and John Seely Brown predicted in 1997:

> It seems contradictory to say, in the face of frequent complaints about information overload, that more information could be encalming. It seems almost nonsensical to say that the way to become attuned to more information is to attend to it less. It is these apparently bizarre features that may account for why so few designs properly take into account centre and periphery to achieve an increased sense of locatedness. But such designs are crucial. Once we are located in a world, the door is opened to social interactions among shared things in that world. As we learn to design calm technology, we will enrich not only our space of artifacts, but also our opportunities for being with other people. Thus may design of calm technology come to play a central role in a more humanly empowered twenty-first century.
>
> (5)

Alexandru Tugui provides an acute reading of the development of calm technology gradually happening nowadays. He explains:

> The field of computer science tackles more and more types of data (text, sound, static images, dynamic images etc.). That is, it works with many different media with a minimum effort. This leads to a super-computer-assisted world where computers are ubiquitous in people's lives. Data processing technologies should calm down and induce calm, in other words be calm technologies. This is easily achieved if we take into account the multimedia aspect of data processing equipment and applications. We conclude with the conviction that in a super-computer-assisted world we feel better when special emphasis is placed on the visual side of the means of communication or information/knowledge transfer, which is a multi-media presentation of the world we relate to.

> Moreover, if this makes using technologies less tiresome, then
> we will have the satisfaction of a 'child playing at his work place'.
>
> (Tugui 2004: n.pag.)

Within this understanding of ubiquitous technological presence, and more specifically in the context of luxury brands' retail stores, we may argue that technologies are increasingly calm. Their presence is everywhere and with the customer who walks within the space. They take the form of data produced and consumed before, within and after the visit and the physical store. Technologies are also the infrastructure that invisibly underpins the informational experience of the customer. The technological advancements are also quietly present in the design, control and construction techniques employed to create spatial experiences for customers.

By the same token, the luxury retail environment is becoming a potentially exciting and surprising place, where customers are truly unique and special. It is their data that provides unique profiles with large datasets that give accuracy and granularity to their profiles. The infrastructure allowing all this is an increasingly omnipresent, invisible system comprising sensors, cameras, projections, LEDs, LiDARs, RFIDs, beacons, microphones and speakers and the like, automatically controlled and continuously improved by intelligent machines that learn from the behaviour of their customers by consensually observing and comparing them.

The speculative future of the retail environment will be more pleasant, tailored to the customer's preferences and surprising at the same time, albeit with some limitations at the moment. Conversely, technology will be increasingly dispersed, displaced and in the periphery of customers' attention. In a near future, we would like to think the physical and virtual experience will be utterly seamless, one in which people are continually immersed in a hybrid of the two. There will be no thresholds, no entrances or exits from the store. The shop will be continuous, as the experience of the brand will form part of customers' daily lives. The brand will probably always be present with immersive experiences appearing wherever one goes, sharing stories with others on social media, or simply carrying on with their own lives. Similarly, the retail environment will be as continuous and (possibly) as ubiquitous too as the data and information systems gradually representing it.

If the retail environment will become a continuum between the digital and the physical dimensions, designers will soon need to become experts in the design of this new spatiality. Their skillsets will need to adapt soon to include a wider variety of expertise, from website building to digital user experience, and from content management to data analysis. The dual dimension of physical/virtual will be crucial for the designers of tomorrow.

However, the interrelation between these two conditions will be significant too. In fact, users will soon move instinctively and, hopefully, seamlessly, from the online to the physical store. In this continuous transition between the two, the experience needs to be seamless and fluid as well. Designers will need to ensure the transition between the virtual and the brick and mortar store is as smooth as possible. This may involve contents (let us imagine an object, a dress, or a luxury time-piece, e.g.) to be duplicated (as doppelgängers), augmented, where the physical one is connected to the virtual one, and exclusive, where some products may be only available in the physical or digital store. Designers will need to master these new opportunities and reclaim their position in the design industry, which they currently share with colleagues with expertise in data science, web design, user experience (UX) and other technology-based roles. All of us in the design industry will soon need to adapt, as the retail environment is changing, and the demand from technology-savvy customers is evolving, following the constant offer of new technologies.

In this sense, the retail environment can be considered today as the result of the combination of a number of market and innovative forces. On the one hand, the technology industries issue new patents, design new technologies, propose new gadgets and devices that will enter the market. On the other hand, customers are increasingly inter-ested in testing the new technologies on offer to enhance their experi-ence. The retail environment is the background and the space where the encounter between new technologies (offer) and customers (demand) takes place. Quite often, such space, as it is hybrid and in continuous mutation, is not designed in its entirety, but it appears as the results of several actions that sellers and buyers take as a part of their transaction.

In all this, designers (of spaces and retail environments) have temporarily lost their leading role (as they had in the pre-digital era, where stores and flagships were identified with companies and brands). As with all times of change, there will be an adjustment period for designers across the world to fully engage with the new technologies and take a leadership position as innovators and interpreters of the retail environment. In order to do this, designers will need to change their understanding of technologies, in particular the relatively new fields of knowledge like data science, user experience, service design and digi-tal design in general. The new direction shows a plethora of possible applications for a design and a data-driven environment promoted by the Human–Computer Interaction (HCI). This is defined as a multidisciplinary field of study focusing on the design of computer technology and, in particular, the interaction between humans (the users) and computers. While initially concerned with computers, HCI has since expanded to cover almost all forms of information technology design.

(Interaction Design Foundation n.d.: n.pag.)

HCI illustrates a clear example of a new field of work where different roles, expertise, research and practice interests coalesce into new products and investigations. Although the ideas underpinning HCI have been around since the 1980s (when the first personal computers started to enter the domestic environment), this new way of collaborative working epitomizes what the future of design should or could look like: where humans (customers in our particular interest) are at the centre of design (human factors) and where engineering, computer science and data-driven design are all facets of the same interest: producing a better world.

A significant part in all this is played by the effort in understanding the cognitive science behind the human/machine relationship. In other words, the lens through which we look at the relationship between technology and people is inverted here. It is not technology that leads the way in which customers should experience the world. Rather, there is a common effort from people with a variety of different and combined skills to understand the impact of new technologies and their potentialities for all of us starting from the human perspective. In this, it is becoming increasingly relevant to appreciate how the cognition, perception and the overall understanding of how technology works for individuals as well as groups. This is substantiated by the fact that many sub-areas of HCI are directly invested in the human perception of technology, including user-centred design (UCD), user interface (UI) design and user experience (UX) design.

As technology is evolving at a fast pace, a new generation of designers, researchers, thinkers and practitioners are reorganizing themselves into fresh multidisciplinary groups, creating new areas of practice.

The future of the luxury industry in all its guises, in relation to the retail environment, is dependent on the ability to embrace new technologies and address the challenges. This means overcoming the passive position we find ourselves in as amazed observers (and testers) of new technologies when a new device or technology is invented. We should move to a proactive stance, really understanding the mechanisms behind new technologies. This will ensure designers return to a position of leadership as innovators that characterized designers so far. Only in this way designers, as a part of larger multi and interdisciplinary teams, will become pioneers again, as they always have been.

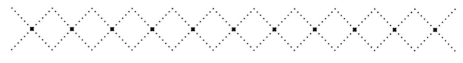

# 9

# Industry Perspectives and the Future of Luxury

*There is no doubt the luxury market has experienced exponential growth over the past twenty years which is not limited to fashion, accessories and beauty products. Ownership of private jets, super yachts, super cars, art and bespoke 'trinkets' has also increased. Is the success of luxury, and its future, going to be defined by longevity? Will true luxury items continue to appreciate in value, not only financial value, but value that has social and cultural significance? Does this create a forum and need for re-establishing what value is, or could be, and are environmental concerns, social responsibility and mass consumption issues promoting a more meaningful investigation to create more discerning customers? These are all questions we have explored in this book. Now we look into the future of luxury, and question how it might look and change.*

The world of luxury is constantly in a state of flux. Many factors influence and force change in the way luxury goods and services are created and managed. We question how they are consumed and how technology, the environment, working conditions, tradition, sustainability and social responsibility all impact on how luxury is perceived. This complex web is increasingly defined not by the products produced, but by the modes of communication delivering messages to the consumer through numerous portals.

Communication and messaging around luxury include traditional print advertising, product placement and digital, incorporating social media channels. The messages transmitted ensure the legacy and/or heritage of a brand is maintained through effective communication. Fashion, trends and social media define this methodology.

But is this luxury? Could it be that the product and the experience with which it is associated will once again define luxury? Will an enhanced shopping experience, enabled through traditional and technological advances, provide an alternative opportunity that is truly meaningful to customers? Will the marketing techniques employed by luxury brands continue to transform how customers relate to what is meaningful, important and change how they feel? Will a new concept of luxury replace the flippant adoption of mass-produced goods in favour of those that are rare, and truly crafted with skill by master craftsmen and women, thereby responding to a logic other than that of fashion? And will these shifts in consumption patterns, reassessment of value and renewed appreciation for the depth and breadth behind the wonderful things we make lead to a renaissance in the capitalist infrastructure that has delivered us to this point, but is struggling to progress unless things change? Finally, what will change look like?

The traditional aspect of luxury is addressed through the adoption and implementation of specialist skills. Talent is identified and encouraged to take up crafts that are in decline to ensure their longevity. These will be taught by master craftsmen and women and novices trained to hone their skills through practice and repetition. It is important to note the repetition of tasks by a craftsperson in a studio or workshop is not the same as a factory environment where production line techniques are used. The craftsperson practices all tasks needed to design and assemble an entire product whereas a factory worker focuses, purely, on a section of a product. 'As a person develops skill, the contents of what he or she repeats change' (Sennett 2008: 37).

> The capacity to continually improve one's work expands and is done so through repetition where through observation one might discover a better or different way of doing something. The open relation between problem solving and problem finding [...] builds and expands skills, but this can't be a one-off event. Skill opens up in this way only because the rhythm of solving and opening up occurs again and again.
>
> (Sennett 2008: 38)

This refers to the traditional way of making and one that thrives in the hands of the maker. There are also emerging reports concerning the benefits making and craft practice has on individual wellbeing. Participation in physical and online practical short courses is on the rise, allowing participants to recognize and practice skill, discipline and the importance of having patience. This, in turn, gives rise to an informed customer, one that is mindful and understands the processes involved in making and is more equipped to ask questions about the production of luxury goods. In contrast, the technological advances in design and manufacture must be considered as they too have an important part to play in the future of luxury and its definitions. Industry continues to innovate, to find better, and sometimes cheaper and more efficient ways to produce products. Industry 4.0 plays a significant role in influencing the production of products, primarily due to the digitization of manufacturing. This provides the luxury conglomerates with more advantages as the acquisition of their entire supply chain can effectively result in an automated system controlled by a single entity. This would reduce the need for human intervention as the smart factory is realized:

> A combination of cyber-physical systems, the Internet of Things and the Internet of Systems make Industry 4.0 possible and the smart factory a reality. As a result of the support of smart machines that keep getting smarter as they get access to more data, our factories will become more efficient and productive and less wasteful.
>
> (Marr 2018: n.pag.)

Automated factories will also further the capacity for the manufacturer to make more customized products on demand. And it is evident that,

> increasingly luxury brands have introduced options to customize and personalize their products to enhance their offer and thereby creating the perception that the customer is purchasing something individual. However, these options within the realms of the luxury brand do nothing more than offer variations on a theme. Component pieces within an existing product range are produced and offered for sale as part of an existing product category.
>
> (Borstrock 2018: 171–87)

The danger here is that this approach further undermines the true value of luxury and the expertise of the designer maker. The continued introduction of automation into the production line within the confines of the luxury brand expedites the production, distribution and sales of products:

> Now, and into the future as Industry 4.0 unfolds, computers are connected and communicate with one another to ultimately make decisions without human involvement. Ultimately, it's the

network of these machines that are digitally connected with one another and create and share information that results in the true power of Industry 4.0.

(Marr 2018: n.pag.)

We could argue that technology may indeed provide the opportunity to enhance the bespoke offer where products are made to the precise requirements of the client, but this is the exception rather than the norm. The common barrier to bespoke goods is generally founded on cost of entry but it is also becoming clear consumer behaviour and expectations are equally important as the cost of customized services fall. The customers' need is already being serviced by the convenience of off – the-peg fashion or being able to experience the car in the showroom. This is particularly relevant as they are increasingly time poor and resistant to the meaningful engagement customized services require.

It is also apparent that as the discerning customer becomes increasingly aware of the impact their actions have on the environment they will repurpose and reuse existing products. The continued growth in rental outlets will undoubtedly contribute to the potentially significant impact circular models have on the production and consumption of goods – they could be seen as contemporary antique markets stocked with newer rather than older products. This rise in prominence is forcing customers to rethink how they shop. Renting and sharing and the reduction of events generating a large carbon footprint are ways in which luxury is being redefined for the future. Gucci, for example, has announced it is reducing the number of runway shows to just two per year. Fashion shows are not only the manifestations of twelve months worth of work by thousands of individuals transforming tonnes of materials into products, but there's also the production of the show itself. The set, lighting, sound and construction needs to be completed in order to welcome the celebrity crowd that flies in from all over the world.

This is not limited to the fashion and accessories market but is extended to the big-ticket items such as planes. Private jet co-ownership and leasing is a growing market. Online apps including flyuberjets, flyxo and flyblackbird offer travellers the opportunity to 'hitch' a ride at very short notice. This market continues to grow. Runway shows and fashion weeks in cities around the world, as a result of the global pandemic, were cancelled. As a result, Yves Saint Laurent no longer shows on a traditional runway show as part of Paris Fashion Week. As a result, we may see this trend continue. This significant change alters the way fashion is shown and sold and has set a precedent for the future of luxury. It suggests live models on a runway are no longer the most innovative way to show clothes and accessories. Digital platforms with avatars can provide a much more immersive experience through which the customer has more control in how they engage with a brand, and in their own time. Virtual realities will be created offering fantastical environments not possible in a physical space. They could be bespoke, further emphasizing the luxury of the experience. There are many possible scenarios: those fully controlled by a luxury brand, where key brand messaging dominates the environment, and another that is much more about the relationship between the maker and the client – the one-on-one experience that will come to define changes in perceptions of luxury.

Purveyors of luxury have always pushed boundaries. Whether it was the manufacture of tapestries by Les Gobelins for the court of Louis XIV, the finely crafted eggs by Fabergé or a gun made by Purdey, a trunk by Louis Vuitton or a garment by Christian Dior. They were all masters of their craft. They pursued a mission of innovation to ensure what they made was of the finest quality using the best materials. They were explorers of sorts who stopped at nothing to provide their clients with the finest goods and service. They were influenced by the world around them, their travels, their clients' travels, other cultures and experiences. They were the modern-day Grand Tour explorers. They were leaders in their respective fields who set examples that influenced those around them and those who came after them, those who adopted their techniques and continue to do so to this day. They provided a future that would inspire the pursuit of craft, a knowledge of materials, construction and engineering.

This idea of luxury has not changed; it is the interpretation of luxury that has changed. It has become a global industry that engages customers through marketing campaigns traditional in their execution and that capture the notion of excess and aspiration in a single image. Today, the product has, to a certain extent, become irrelevant, as it is the image that defines luxury. This however will change as the consumer becomes more divided not only in motivation, but as has been suggested in previous chapters, the wealth divide grows as does the need to be more socially and environmentally responsible. The future of luxury will be determined by a shift in consuming habits partly as a result of global disruption and change and partly because of an increasingly bespoke service offer defined by technological advance and the use of data to personalize the shopping experience.

These different approaches to the way luxury is sold will create further distinction between the mass manufactured luxury brands and the purveyors of luxury goods who follow a different logic. One is defined by fashion, where shopping is an orchestrated experience enhanced through the analysis of data generated by previous shopping patterns, as well as data generated through the use of card spending. It is a transactional approach in which the primary concern is money. But it is beginning to change to include other value propositions, as customers are encouraged to give up more of their data.

The luxury experience will need to be both immersive and responsive and to a certain extent, all encompassing. The virtual reality (VR) and augmented reality (AR) experiences, for example, will provide opportunities for designer makers, luxury brands, indeed all companies, to connect with their customers in new ways. This will also provide brands with the opportunity to further exploit their own and emerging markets. Luxury carmaker Porsche has developed an AR app for smart phones that allows customers to customize and visualize their dream car parked outside their own home. This direct extension of the Porsche brand, albeit virtually, into the customer's living environment connects the carmaker with the user in meaningful and consequently powerful ways. It directly relates to the individual and personal circumstances of the emerging user.

# Does it matter what or how we buy?

Shopping is at once personal and social and can even be seen as a political action, for example, by those committed to only buying sustainable or environmentally friendly clothing, or who refuse to buy from one or another brand based on its labour practices. It is a business endeavour, an important part of the economy and something that has impacted on various facets of social life. As such, responses to shopping are wide ranging from the most conservative and rational approaches to those showing total abandon if not recklessness. Some could be bound to notions of democracy, freedom and self-determination. Others are concerned with issues of sustainability, waste and social responsibility and with issues of equity and diversity. Still more may care about these issues but do not believe they should have to take personal responsibility for their actions. They blame the industry and see change as originating from above. And for some consumers, these issues are not even a consideration.

It is expected as we move forward that consumer responses to fashion and shopping, particularly when it is luxury shopping, will continue to be complex and contradictory. In the new luxury landscape, many aspirational customers will disappear, no longer possessing the economic means despite their wishes to participate in luxury purchasing. This may prove auspicious for over-priced luxury purveyors and for resellers and rental services. If the demand for luxury remains, it may be significantly diminished and carried out in a much more measured manner. Will craftspersons and designers flourish as they develop more personalized relationships with customers? Will bespoke companies that see themselves as outside of the luxury 'industry', a designation that has been rejected by them, emerge as the leaders in a smaller and more genuine luxury enterprise? Is there a possibility for a more democratic practice in luxury to develop, one whose scope is much more diverse and inclusive?

Giorgio Armani wrote about the 'absurd' state of the fashion industry in 2020 in an open letter to industry publication, *WWD* (Zargani 2020b). Referring to the coronavirus, he said the only response the industry could make was 'a careful and intelligent slowdown' (Armani cited in Zargani 2020b: n.pag.). He wrote to Miles Socha, in 2020, congratulating him and his co-authors on an article published a day earlier for taking a 'courageous and necessary' position, which called for a 'new era of slower fashion' with 'fewer collections' suited to the weather and 'fewer markdowns' (Armani cited in Zargani 2020b: n.pag.). In this article, Karl Lagerfeld is cited as an example of luxury taking its cue from fast fashion. Lagerfeld, who died in 2019, released six collections per year and insisted new merchandise be promoted in stores every two months. Armani spoke of a 'criminal nonalignment' between commercial seasons and the weather and an opportunity for a realignment entailing rethinking collections and slowing down. This would lead to a return to 'authenticity' where garments are made to last, where there would be time for developing a 'precise aesthetic code' and where consumers' needs will be considered. Speaking to those in the industry, he expressed his belief this would 'bring value back to our work' (Armani cited in Zargani 2020b: n.pag.).

Other parts of the luxury industry are no different, but few possess the transient nature of fashion. The automotive, watch, aeronautic and antique industries supply products with a longer lifespan, and are more likely to be traded or resold rather than simply discarded. A lesson, as we have discussed in this book, learnt by the fashion industry.

As we suggest, it is clear that luxury as it has come to be defined today will be reassessed. There is the possibility of returning to a notion of genuine exclusivity. As notions of exclusivity continue to be redefined they must include new perspectives and voices from around the world. Luxury's Eurocentric focus needs to be challenged to include a more diverse and inclusive interpretation of luxury.

In a Bain and Company video, two of the authors of a report on the future of luxury – published in 2019 based on research conducted in 2018 – in which predictions are made every year up until 2025, give an update on their findings (see D'Arpizio et al. 2019). Claudia D'Arpizio and Federica Levato (2019) speak about 'sustainability, social responsibility and circular fashion as a new mantra, new vision for the environment, for human labour and animal welfare' (D'Arpizio et al. 2019: n.pag.). And immediately afterwards, they discuss increased production, 'always-on marketing', 'monthly novelties' and 'big data-driven and automated supply chains' (D'Arpizio et al. 2019: n.pag.). This is clearly an indication of a disconnected logic that analysts sometimes fall into where statistics garnered from survey research and industry data stand on their own without an understanding of the driving force behind the data. Either that depth of knowledge is lacking, or there is a belief that merely highlighting results is significant and sufficient. Furthermore, predictions are made many years ahead based on assertions which cannot take into account unforeseen variables. While some of these predictions may be necessary, there is perhaps a greater need to ground one's assertions in reality and in reasonable systems of thought.

## Inertia

As we elaborated in Chapter 8, 'Luxury and the retail environment', new technologies offer fresh directions for luxury brands to engage with their customers and the spaces in which they shop. However, we conclude that when technology is applied to the retail environment, this is generally more visible in very specific details of the store. For example, a magic mirror or a smart display. The relationship between the physical and digital experience has always been loaded with latent tension. Creating a cohesive experience is proving challenging for customers and brands as they attempt to reconcile their experiences. Regardless of how much effort designers put into generating a smart store, with the aim of providing a seamless physical/digital experience to customers, challenges remain. There is always a distinct moment where people need to switch between the space in which they are physically present and the digital space (through their phone or another screen). The desire to price check an item they see in store with online options, or sending a photo of the item to a friend for advice, punctuates the physical experience. This distracts the customer and makes it more difficult for the brand to encourage and maintain complete immersion.

Augmenting a customer's shopping experience is becoming increasingly sophisticated and as a recent survey shows,

> nearly 57 per cent of smartphone and tablet owners use mobile retail applications to gather additional product information, while 24 per cent use mobile grocery apps. It's estimated that by 2020, smartphone retail mobile commerce (mCommerce) will total $268.2 billion, an estimated 31.5 per cent growth in 2019.
> (Kovalchuk 2019: n.pag.)

However, we argue there are still some barriers to overcome in the successful implementation of the technological view promised by the smart and ubiquitous technology gurus/evangelists/visionaries. The view of a seamless technological experience whereby computers disappear in the environment was pioneered by scientists and visionaries such as Mark Weiser (see Weiser et al. 1999), or Pedro Domingos with his *Master Algorithm* (2015), among many others. Weiser's vision of 'technology receding into the background of our lives' (Stanford University 2013: n.pag.) is happening gradually, yet it has a long way to go (cf. Warren 2004). Currently, the consumer recognizes quite clearly when they are dealing with a piece of technology in a retail environment, for example standing in front of a magic mirror or using virtual reality, augmented reality or social media. The main idea of a technology that disappears in the environment would suggest the awareness of using technology could at a certain point diminish and eventually evaporate. Instead of maintaining the clear difference experienced today between humans and machines (technology), we would move towards a situation where machines (and thus the technology underpinning them) are everywhere, embedded in the very fabric of our lives. In this, technology will move from being in the background of people's lives to being indistinguishably on the same plane. Adam Greenfield (2010) provided a very clear description of technology disappearing in the environment coining the term 'everyware'. In his detailed account of everyware,

> the garment, the room and the street become sites of processing and mediation. Household objects from shower stalls to coffee pots are reimagined as places where facts about the world can be gathered, considered and acted upon. And all the familiar rituals of everyday life [...] are remade as an intricate dance of information about ourselves, the state of the external world, and the options available to us at any given moment.
> (Greenfield 2010: 1)

The image of a fluid and invisible technology appeals to all of us and has been depicted in many creative ways in novels and films. In one of the episodes of the HBO sci-fi series *Westworld*, two main characters enter a luxury store to buy a new suit (Series 3, Episode 4) using an advanced version of a magic mirror whereby different outfits and styles can be selected on a tablet and visualized in real-time on people. Such images give us an indication of what people really expect from the luxury fashion industry. They seek a seamless, joyful and effortless experience where garments (and any other luxury products) can be tried on, realistically simulated and to some extent, used, by simply expressing an interest in them. The illustration of this luxury element in this example is the highly personalized, unique and bespoke nature of the experience. This is created in real-time just for that particular customer without them being necessarily aware of the presence of technology.

Technology is today close to offering such an experience. However, it has not yet been embraced by the luxury industry, but rather applied to fields such as medicine and urban infrastructure. A new generation of smart cities is being designed as we write, and they promise to include seamless experiences for their residents. For example, Sidewalk Toronto – the visionary new town developed by Google's Alphabet – promises a new public environment heavily characterized by ubiquitous technologies, sensors and computing. In this, people's mundane burdens like grocery shopping, cleaning or paying bills are automatically taken care of by centralized computers so people have more free time to enjoy other things.

If we compare the intention of providing an effortless and almost unconscious use of technology that Sidewalk Toronto offers with some of the case studies we discussed in Chapter 6, we notice that the former aims to liberate individuals from all those rituals of transition from the physical to the cyber world (e.g. taking a mobile phone from the pocket, unlocking it, opening the app, accessing the brand services) are not realized. Conversely, the latter appear more interested in display and create unique experiences by offering new and unexpected events. In Sidewalk Labs Toronto,

> buildings should be able to accommodate a range of uses and shift quickly and inexpensively from one need to another. The result would be communities where people can live, work, shop, and socialize within a short walk. [...] Within a single neighbourhood people could find affordable space to pursue their professional dreams, whether a single co-working desk to plot out a start-up or a short-term stall to sell a handcrafted confection. Homes could

meet the needs of growing families and single-person house-
holds alike.

(Sidewalk Labs 2019: 236)

Moreover, buildings are designed to be intelligent, where all physical
elements become the interface between people and the data they use
and produce:

> [S]mart buildings must be able to recognize every last room,
> hallway, motion sensor, key fob reader, light bank, thermostat,
> and appliance inside them and to network them together [...].
> Through the development of a metadata schema for buildings,
> [...] [the technological system in Sidewalk Toronto] establishes a
> standardized naming scheme in which all devices are named by
> floor, room number, device type, and an index, so that TVs are
> identified as 19-301-TV-1, 19-302-TV-1, and so forth, while ther-
> mostats could be identified as 19-301- TSAT-1 and 19-302-TSAT-
> 1. Such a naming schema allows a computer to understand which
> room a TV is in and how to control the lights and thermostat in
> that room to prepare for a presentation. [...] Suddenly, a building
> can learn to turn down the heat in a crowded mid-winter board-
> room before the thermostat rises.
>
> (Sidewalk Labs 2019: 317)

We may argue that while a visionary understanding of technology calls
for the technology itself to disappear in the environment, the luxury
industry seems to prefer to use technology to do exactly the opposite:
be visible and unique. A clear example of this could be the branding
strategy devised by Supreme, where the omni-present logo appears to
be a key feature of their image (Kulkarni 2019). This is probably taken
to an extreme where the street brand presented a brick with their logo
on it for the retail price of $30 to respond to street violence and crime
(Leach 2016). The bricks sold out in minutes and have since become
an object for collectors (Khomami 2016).

Because of this different approach, a sort of inertia or resistance
characterizes luxury brands in designing the spatial experience for
their customers. The more technology advocates for becoming invisible, pervasive and staying in the background, the more luxury brands
seem to resist bringing this technology to the fore. They are resisting
making it apparent and turning it into a major feature of their overall
identity. While ubiquitous computing (ubicomp) technology promotes
a seamless transition between physical and digital (or even the elim-
ination of such binaries), the idea of celebrating the digital over the

physical (or vice versa) can create even more distance between these two dimensions.

Such discrepancy further exacerbates circumstances like global crises, temporary lockdowns and global pandemics, where people are forced to spend more time online and cannot access physical stores. In these cases, the customer's relationship with luxury brands suddenly becomes digital-only. The luxury industry, that is heavily invested in a tangible, concrete and generally speaking, physical experience for their customers, may find it difficult to engage with their clientele at the same level as other sectors that promote digital/seamless experiences (e.g. social networks, online markets, digital environments like video games, media service providers, etc.).

In the next decades, technology will become increasingly ubiquitous and its mission to disappear in the environment will be gradually achieved. The retail environment needs to embrace this idea and luxury brands should consider taking a more active role in this development. Instead of trying to incorporate the latest technology into their traditional store, which is scarcely visible, they should start to innovate in the digital environment as they have always done with materials, objects and the physical experience. Looking at the successful example of some of the world-changing tech companies that revolutionized the way in which all of us live and interact, the luxury industry should lead in the pursuit of technological progress. Luxury brands should cast their visionary approach in the digital world, as they have done in the physical, promoting a new generation of (ubiquitous) retail environments.

# Looking ahead

As we made clear from the outset of this book, luxury and its definition has come to be defined and popularized by fashion brands. The changes envisaged, as alluded to by Giorgio Armani, are smaller scale production, something more specialized. And this applies to a vast range of products from timepieces to private yachts and jets. The opportunities for the luxury industry remain in the hands of the makers who will, once again, redefine the luxury landscape. The idea that a smaller designer maker, whose expertise may once again be revered, is something that must be taken seriously. There is much more at stake here than simply promoting craftsmanship. The impact on livelihoods, talent growth, learning skills, cultural and social impact and an acknowledgement and resuscitation of dying skills is the underlying rationale behind reverting to traditional approaches to luxury creation and production.

This is an undeniably exciting future. The focus on craftsmanship for the luxury brands has been on the major European fashion cities, with luxury clientele drawn to goods made in France, Italy, and the United Kingdom. Perhaps the future holds opportunities for a wider range of geographic spaces to be included in the luxury universe. Craft traditions have long been a part of the cultural heritage in many parts of the world, for example Takumi in Japan or master weavers in Ghana, yet these contributions do not receive the recognition they rightfully deserve.

With that in mind one must not lose sight of the hidden costs of mass-producing luxury goods. It is very easy to be swept away by the torrent of super slick imagery that promotes luxury and the luxury lifestyle. The documentary *The True Cost* (2015) focuses on the detrimental impact of fast fashion both on the environment and on garment workers. The luxury industry is largely shielded from such negative attention but in 2016 the documentary film *Merci Patron!* became a box office hit in France. LVMH CEO Bernard Arnault was exposed for having moved luxury production from France to lower wage regions in Europe, such as Poland, leaving impoverished and unemployed French artisans in his wake. While there have been some press exposés about the luxury industry, these are few and far between and not enough to change the consciousness of consumers.

In a McKinsey article (Amed et al. 2019), the 'woke' consumer is discussed. This consumer is identified as mainly belonging to Generation Z and the Millennial demographic and is seen as one who cares about sustainability, the environment and social responsibility. Amed et al. say two-thirds of consumers worldwide will 'switch, avoid, or boycott brands based on their stance on controversial issues' (2019: n.pag.). They argue that because of this, 'a new global ethos is emerging' (Amed et al. 2019: n.pag.). We've heard about the 'woke' consumer who cares about sustainability and ethical consumption but far more consumers 'care' than are willing to buy less, to change their shopping habits or to pay more for products. This conundrum, caring but not fundamentally shifting one's priorities, allows business to continue as usual and for fast fashion brands to flourish.

At the luxury level, we find 'attention' to sustainability (even if without much substance), on the one hand, and unfair labour practices on the other hand. Guerlain, an LVMH owned company, presented a document on social responsibility with its entire focus on the preservation of bees. It states: 'We commit and act in the name of beauty for our clients, in the name of beauty for our creations and in the name of beauty for the planet' (Guerlain n.d.: n.pag.). The list of their ambitions is not without merit. They will, they say, be carbon neutral by 2028 and all products will be eco designed by 2022.

What is evident is a market of halves. There are companies who take some actions to reduce their carbon footprint, reduce the water yield in the production of cotton, reuse old garments and fabrics to manufacture new ones. Others pay lip service to these issues, but essentially continue to operate in the same way they have been doing for decades. The contrast is palpable and confusing. How can one company, LVMH, be so encouraging of wasteful behaviour, and, at the same time, on the surface at least, suggest they take climate change and social responsibility seriously? Surely luxury and the luxury markets are predisposed to longevity? The idea of buying a watch that you do not actually own as popularized by Patek Philippe in their 20+ year long advertising campaign 'You never actually own a Patek Philippe. You merely look after it for the next generation' is at odds with the notion of brands maximizing sales by using fashion trends to encourage consumption. Tim Calkins, professor of marketing at Kellogg School of Management, explains: 'A Patek watch is not a device for telling time. It is an heirloom that transfers values across generations' (Naas 2016: n.pag.).

Stephen Jones, in Chapter 5, speaks as a craftsperson truly engaged in the making of handmade products. His skill is embedded in the things he makes and his personal relationship with his customer connects them to the product itself, allowing them to engage with luxury in a meaningful way. This is in complete contrast to Patek Philippe extracting meaning from an exchange, which is disconnected from any meaningful engagement. The customer typically buys a Patek Phillipe watch in a store and has no connection to the maker. And in most cases, the maker has no real connection to the product. Jones (2010) says:

> Well, the ingredients in luxury; there's craftsmanship, and there is authenticity, and so this whole idea that this thing has been passed down from father to son, and because of that it's a good thing, and it's a connection to a time which was maybe slower or more time was spent in the creation of a beautiful object.

Patek Philippe currently have approximately 200 different styles of watch listed on their website. In an interview on the In Pursuit of Luxury podcast, Richard Mille horologist, Theodore Dhiel, suggests they produce around 65,000 watches a year. They also list 37 authorized retailers in the United Kingdom alone. The idea behind the heirloom advertising campaign is to introduce more customers to the brand, something that appears to have worked very successfully judging by their retail footprint and extensive collection of watches. The value proposition is powerful when pitched to address people's emotions, and has given Patek Philippe no reason to change its

marketing strategy. What this approach does is illustrate the influen-
tial power marketing has over the consumer that contributes to the
success of the brand.

Alison Lloyd (2020), founder of the iconic British fashion company
Ally Capellino, echoes Jones' sentiments, saying:

> People's perception of luxury is also the perception of the knowl-
> edge bound up in that company, the skills involved, the history of
> what's gone before. What they have produced, the knowledge
> that they can do it and what they've built up and even company
> secrets I suppose are things, which are particular to them. And
> probably quite a lot of that is perceived rather than real, I would
> imagine; hard to know, though.

Where products and services are marketed at the top end, the luxury
customer fuels the growth of a story that appeals to, and creates, an
emotional connection with products. Can the luxury industry use this
strategy to address the current sustainability and environmental issues
prevalent in the consumer goods industry, or is this impossible due to
the high cost of entry into this elite club? Luxury goods companies
could be in a fortunate position as consumers begin to re-evaluate
how they spend their money. Consumers concerned with fast fashion's
impact on the environment may turn their attention to luxury brands.
They may decide that luxury products are a better buying decision and
be swayed by a sustainability agenda that is cloaked in a mystique of
aspiration.

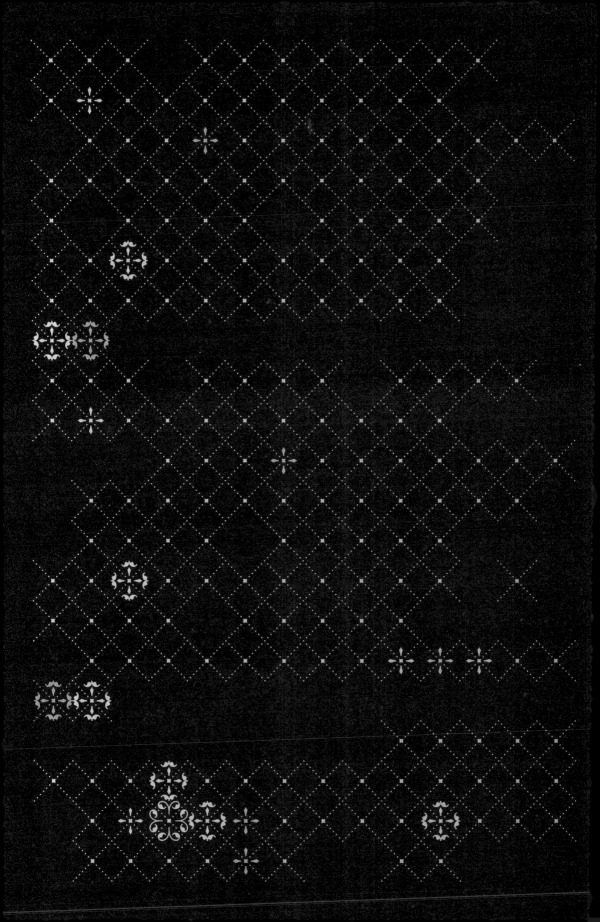

# 10

# Final Thoughts

The premise of this book is to explore different facets of luxury and how they are defined, interpreted and implemented in a constantly changing environment. What is clear is that the term 'luxury' does not necessarily mean the goods or services are in fact luxury; it assumes the goods are of better quality.

As has been discussed extensively, luxury in a contemporary context is most prevalent in the global fashion market. It is the fashion market that has come to define how we see luxury, how we experience it and how we interact with it. The reality, however, is that despite a rethink in terms of how we spend as a result of us having overspent on goods and services that were superfluous to need, we now watch what we spend under the guise of caring for the planet and its resources.

Luxury, it could be said, has been, and is, the catalyst through which the global demand for goods and services has thrived as a result of deliberate campaigns founded on the promotion of aspirational lifestyles. It is the word 'luxury' that has transformed fashion, specifically those brands consumed by four global conglomerates that adopted the term for self-gain. What we attempt in our writing is to illustrate the discrepancies between how luxury is defined. There are so many variances that there comes a point where a true meaning of luxury must be clarified to ensure the makers, who spend their lives honing their skills to the betterment, not only to themselves but also to others, is recognized.

How does one appreciate rarity, skill, craftsmanship and knowledge of materials if there is no distinction in the description? Through an analysis of the practices adopted by both the global corporations and small artisanal designer makers we articulate differences in practice with the intention of clarifying how luxury is perceived.

We acknowledge the role of technology, its adoption in parts of the sector in manufacture, data warehousing, enhancing the shopping experience, distribution and vertical integration. And what is made clear is that there is a distinction to be drawn between the different approaches to luxury. The conglomerates, as we have discussed in great detail – including LVMH, Kering, Richemont and the Prada Group – align themselves with fashion. They utilize the power of heritage to increasingly enhance product offers – despite turning to mass production over a period of 30 odd years to grow their businesses and to capitalize on what was a continuously growing market. This approach blurs the lines. Whereas one can argue, the stable of companies were at one time purveyors of luxury, this is no longer the case. Saying that, a blanket dismissal is unhelpful as there are instances where most of these companies do in fact engage the skills of craftspeople to create products. This may be in the case of a bespoke trunk, haute couture garments, fine jewellery and timepieces. But these examples are the exception rather than the rule. This activity is confined to the top of the pyramid. What happens below approaches what one would expect to find in the realm of designer fashion. Yet if these items are made by the brand, they are consecrated by an honourable heritage motivated less by profit than by excellence and pride. The brands also benefit by the Made In France, Italy or the United Kingdom label, which for many customers is a guarantee of fine craftsmanship, quality, prestige and even ethical standards. This may be more a marketing tool than a genuine sign of what is represented. Many factory workers, as we have seen, are deskilled or never given an opportunity to fully develop the skills of their trade. Some work in low wage factories in Asia or Eastern Europe, others work at home at piece rate wages, such as in Southern Italy for example.

We conclude, luxury is a concept that is demonstrably unstable and is influenced by many factors, bringing value into question. Within this context, value is not limited to financial worth but is attributed to a number of factors adding worth to a product or service. It is evident that labour plays a significant role in contributing to the luxury landscape. Labour may traditionally be associated with factory work but it may be attributed, from the outset, to research and design, sourcing materials, farming the land, producing materials, shipping, cutting, making, packing and selling. Each of these descriptors is loaded with meaning, as each comprises multiple elements that could be further examined. For example, design could refer simply to the designer of something: a product (car, yacht, plane, handbag, watch, etc.), or service (hotel experience, personal shopping, bespoke vacation). But it could also be someone who, as an innovator, uses craft skills as well as technological know-how to pursue a different path in resolving a complex design issue. Within a luxury context the complexity of the work, or labour, comes to define the maker. More often than not they have learnt their skills through apprenticeships, through much trial and error in the application and realization of a 'task'. They hone their skills and apply them to their work; skill is an intrinsic feature used to describe luxury.

We expose the common practices adopted by the luxury conglomerates, the ways in which they utilize data to enhance the shopping experience through their retail environments, social media and the use of technology to disrupt the supply chain to their advantage – in most cases, the implementation of vertical integration is at the cost of the workforce.

We analyse the extent to which the physical space (as the space of consumption, but also the relational space between customer and brands) has changed significantly since the 1980s. Increasingly, stores rely on technology to not only provide a seamless experience for the customer but also to deliver up to the minute data on the availability of product and customer profiles. What we refer to in the book as the retail environment suggests a new dimension where the physical and the digital experiences are merged. More and more customers will experience a two-way relationship with brands where their feedback and comments on the brands' activities is received and acted upon almost in real-time. Underpinned by new technologies, the engagement of customers with new ways to experience shopping, and the continuous adaptation of designers (of products and experience) to these fast-paced changes, we argue that the entire luxury ecosystem is constantly changing, and changing significantly at that. This is leading to the emergence of new types of retail spaces, which are virtual/physical hybrids, and a new generation of designers whose skillset is significantly wider to include, for example, data science, psychology and user experience (UX). The data held in relation to the customer is incredibly valuable and offers an illusory feeling of luxury like a first class, or premium passenger travelling on a commercial airline; the flight manager knows the client, maybe not personally, but through information provided to them.

The shopping experience is one that increasingly adopts technology to further engage with the customer. Despite a relatively slow uptake by the luxury sector, artificial intelligence, augmented and virtual reality are seen as critical components to increase sales through experience. Luxury brands, although reticent, are now being forced into implementing tech systems much more visible to their customers. How we use smartphones and tablets continues to change. Increasingly they are being used as shopping tools as augmented and virtual reality is integrated into the tech and adopted by retailer and customer. The retailers want to attract customers through increasingly sophisticated tech providing unique, interactive and immersive shopping experiences.

Where once it was only Burberry that dipped its toes into the technology water, now Dior, Vuitton et al are also doing so. The rationale behind this drive towards tech may be more sinister than the retailer admits. Of course, having smart mirrors in the changing rooms may enhance the trying on session, touch screens at service points may also be engaging and augmented reality options where available may point to a future where shopping is a completely different experience. But at the heart of all this surveillance is the collection of data and the violation of privacy for financial gain. This non-consensual coercion, where individuals share their data through content they themselves generate with the luxury brands, may prove to be a contentious road to follow. And although this, in theory, may be a capitalist model, those in control are limited to four global players. This is not luxury defined by craftsman, but aspiration defined by corporate power brokers.

The physical stores, those cathedrals of consumption housed on elite boulevards, in trendy shopping districts and on prime real estate in fashion capitals around the globe, glorify the brand. They are designed by the world's leading architects and interior designers who themselves have come to be part of the fashion industrial complex. They speak to their customers in a way that exudes the power of the brand. But this is one experience, one that is defined by fashion for fashion. It is seasonal and changes with the seasons. And luxury brands, all of them, rely on the seasonal change in product offer. This is in stark contrast to the true innovators who push the boundaries in pursuit of excellence.

In this book, we note certain discrepancies between the potential experience new technologies offer and real implementation by luxury brands. New technology proposes the foundations for a completely new customer experience and relationship with the brand. Some aspects of these new dimensions are already a reality and are used by a few enthusiasts around the world (think of the hands-free prototypes for augmented reality to name but one). Others are possible in principle, but not available yet, or not yet implemented to the extent we would like to see. We can observe some of these upcoming technologies in sci-fi films and TV series where technologies are developed to an extreme to change completely the way people interact with each other, as well as with objects and space around them. Series such as *Black Mirror* epitomize the potential that lies behind technological advancement, currently a near-future distance to us. We speculate on this point, offering a critical view on what luxury brands (and the designers and technologists working with them) could offer but, in some instances, they seem to have chosen a more cautious approach. Generalizing, we conclude that luxury brands (and designers) are still to find their own place in this fast-changing environment in order to fully express their true potential and re-establish that unique and ground-breaking experience that once characterized the luxury experience.

Questions one may have to ask revolve around community and how customers might rally around smaller purveyors of luxury goods who they support for their ethical standpoints and trust with their personal data. This data is not only a digital fingerprint but is also a prized commodity and should always be valued to enable experiences true to traditional notions of luxury. The zeitgeist of luxury may be changing and its traditional foundation undermined.

Is a new moment for luxury upon us where humanitarian and egalitarian ideals can become part of its evolving definition as we move forward into an uncertain future?

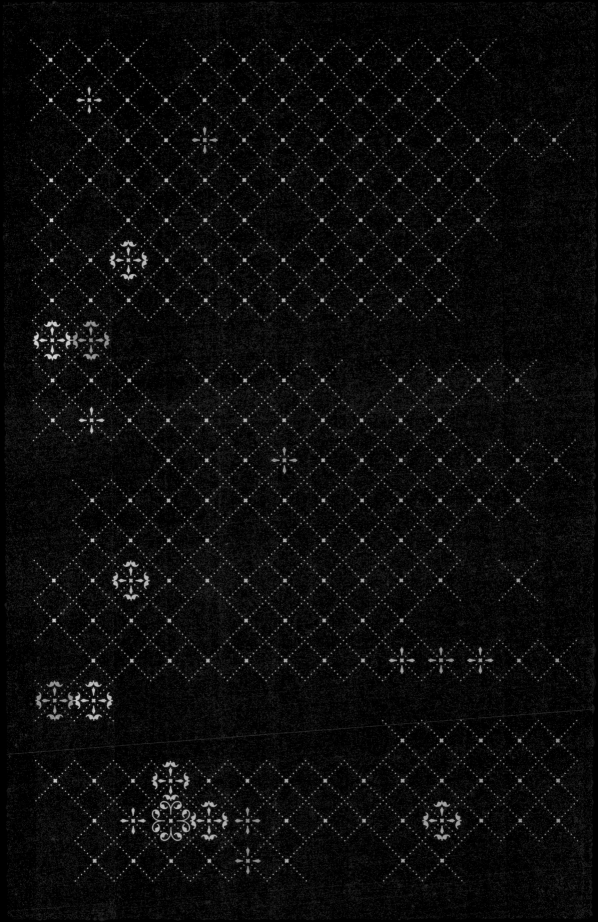

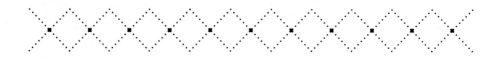

# Notes

1. Millennials, Generation Y, Gen Next born in the late 1980s to the mid 90s and Generation Z born between 1997 onwards.
2. All quotes from Alison Lloyd are from her 2020 interview with Shaun Borstrock (see Lloyd 2020).
3. All quotes from Stephen Jones are from his 2010 interview with Shaun Borstrock (see Jones 2010).
4. All quotes from Theo Fennell are from his 2020 interview with Shaun Borstrock (see Fennell 2020).
5. All quotes from Stephen Jones are from his 2020 interview with Shaun Borstrock (see Jones 2020).
6. All quotes from Jussara Lee are from her 2019 interview with Veronica Manlow (see Lee 2019).
7. All quotes from Beatrice Amblard are from her 2020 interview with Veronica Manlow (see Amblard 2020).
8. All quotes from Steve Doudaklian are from his 2019 interview with Veronica Manlow (see Doudaklian 2019).
9. All quotes are from Veronica Manlow's 2020 interviews with these women.
10. Positive Luxury is the company behind the Butterfly Mark, a unique mark awarded to luxury lifestyle brands in recognition of their commitment to creating a positive impact on our world.

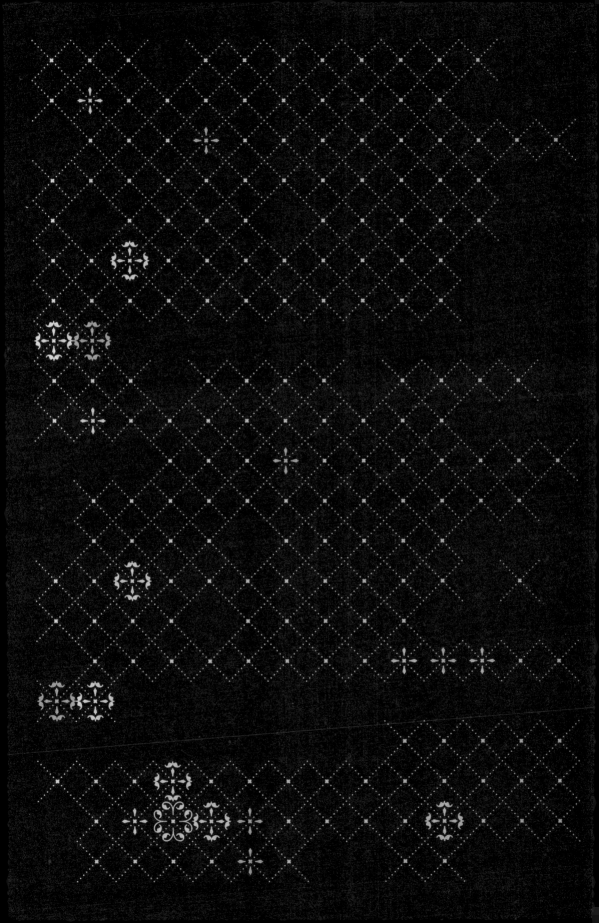

# References

Abboud, Leila (2020), 'LVMH sales hit by Hong Kong protests', 29 January, https://www.ft.com/content/2609b892-41b7-11ea-bdb5-169ba7be433d. Accessed 7 February 2020.

ABI Research (2014), 'Nearly 9 billion wireless connectivity chipsets to ship during 2019 alone', 22 May, https://www.abiresearch.com/press/nearly-9-billion-wireless-connectivity-chipsets-to/. Accessed 9 February 2020.

AFP (2014), 'Embroiderer Lesage (Chanel) acquires a weaving atelier', Fashion Network, 1 December, https://ww.fashionnetwork.com/news/Embroidererlesage-acquires-a-weaving-atelier,446753.html. Accessed 4 March 2019.

Aloisi, Silvia and Spencer, Mimosa (2021), 'Birkin bag maker Hermes tempers expectations after stellar growth', Reuters, 30 July, https://www.reuters.com/business/retail-consumer/sales-birkin-bag-maker-hermes-soar-q2-2021-07-30/. Accessed 1 August 2021.

Alvarez, José-Manuel Benito (2016), 'Middle Paleolithic hand axe: Ancient history encyclopedia', World History Encyclopedia, 20 December, https://www.ancient.eu/image/6195/. Accessed 20 May 2020.

Amblard, Beatrice (2020), telephone interview with V. Manlow, 13 and 15 June.

Amed, Imran, Balchandani, Anita, Beltrami, Marco, Berg, Achim and Rölkens, Felix (2019), 'The influence of "woke" consumers on fashion', McKinsey and Company,

12 February, https://www.mckinsey.com/industries/retail/our-insights/the-influence-of-woke-consumers-on-fashion. Accessed 5 March 2020.

Anon. (2015a), 'Jane Birkin asks Hermès to remove her name from handbag after Peta exposé', The Guardian, 28 July, https://www.theguardian.com/fashion/2015/jul/28/hermes-jane-birkin-handbag-peta-crocodiles. Accesseed 11 November 2021.

Anon. (2015b), 'Saltwater crocodiles: High fashion meets evolutionary design', The Australian, 11 July, https://www.theaustralian.com.au/weekend-australian-magazine/saltwater-crocodiles-high-fashion-meets-evolutionary-design/news-story/5d-d554716513843885959a63afb150f0. Accessed 6 March 2020.

Anon. ([2010] 2017), 'Louis Vuitton ad banned in the UK for misleading customers', Huffpost, [26 May] 6 December, https://www.huffpost.com/entry/louis-vuitton-ad-banned-i_n_590968. Accessed 6 March 2019.

Anon. (2017), 'Fuel of the future: Data is giving rise to a new economy', The Economist, 6 May, https://www.economist.com/briefing/2017/05/06/data-is-giving-rise-to-a-new-economy. Accessed 13 October 2021.

Anon. (2018), 'Burberry burns bags, clothes and perfume worth millions', BBC, 19 July, https://www.bbc.co.uk/news/business-44885983. Accessed 5 April 2020.

Anon. (n.d.), 'Feted then banned: The latest for Louis Vuitton London', *Signature 9*, http://www.signature9. com/style/fashion/feted-then-banne d-the-latest-for-louis-vuitton-london. Accessed 15 May 2020.

APLF (2020), https://www.aplf.com/. Accessed 15 January 2019.

Arendt, Hannah (1958), *The Human Condition*, Chicago: University of Chicago Press.

Armitage, John and Roberts, Joanne (2016), *Critical Luxury Studies: Art, Design, Media*, Edinburgh: Edinburgh University Press.

Arnett, George (2020), 'Luxury brands gear up to deal with massive luxury prob- lem', *Vogue Business*, 16 March, https:// www.voguebusiness.com/companies/ luxury-brands-gear-inventory-loui s-vuitton-prada. Accessed 13 June 2020.

Asylum (n.d.), 'Hublot pop-up store, Singapore (2012)', http://theasylum. com.sg/project/hublot-pop-up-store/. Accessed 10 January 2020.

Avvenice (n.d.), 'Hermès beauty', https:// avvenice.com/en/529_hermes-beauty. Accessed 11 November 2021.

Barry, Laurence and Fisher, Fran (2019), 'Digital audiences and the deconstruc- tion of the collective', *Subjectivity* 12:3, pp. 210–27.

Barthes, Roland (1957), *Mythologies*, Paris: Seuil.

Bastani, Aaron (2019), *Fully Automated Luxury Communism: A Manifesto*, Brook- lyn and London: Verso.

Bataille, Georges ([1949] 1988), *The Accursed Share: Volume 1: Consumption* (trans. R. Hurley), Zone Books: New York.

Baudrillard, Jean (1996), *The System of Objects* (trans. J. Benedict), London and New York: Verso.

Becker, Elizabeth (2020), 'How hard will the coronavirus hit the travel industry?', National Geographic, 2 April, https:// www.nationalgeographic.com/travel/ article/how-coronavirus-is-impacting-th e-travel-industry. Accessed 5 April 2020.

Bekker, Henk (2020), 'Bugatti Chiron production at 250', Car Sales Statistics, 20 February, https://www.nation- algeographic.com/travel/article/ how-coronavirus-is-impacting-th e-travel-industry. Accessed 5 April 2020.

Bentley, Alexander, Horton, Mark and Langton, Philip (2015), 'A history of sugar – the food nobody needs, but everyone craves', *The Conversation*, 30 October, https://theconversation.com/a-history- of-sugar-the-food-nobody-needs- but-everyone-craves-49823. Accessed 7 December 2019.

Berg, Maxine (2005), *Luxury and Pleas- ure in Eighteenth Century Britain*, Oxford: Oxford University Press.

Berluti, Olga (2009), in-person interview with S. Borstrock, London, 15 June.

Bernays, Edward L. (1947), 'The engi- neering of consent', *The Annals of the American Academy of Political and Social Science*, 250:1, pp. 113–20.

Berry, Christopher (1994), *The Idea of Luxury: A Conceptual and Historical Investigation*, Cambridge: Cambridge University Press.

Biondi, Annachiara (2020), 'Fashion and luxury face $600 billion decline in sales', *Vogue Business*, 27 March, https:// www.voguebusiness.com/companies/ bcg-luxury-spending-drop-coronavirus- covid-19. Accessed 30 March 2020.

Blanks, Tim (2020), 'The end of the (fash- ion) world as we know it', *The Business of Fashion*, 24 March, https://www.busines- soffashion.com/opinions/luxury/the-end- of-the-fashion-world-as-we-know-it. Accessed 30 March 2020.

BMW (2014), 'BMW vision future luxury: Modern luxury driven by design and innovation', 20 April, https://www.press.bmwgroup.com/global/article/detail/T0177724EN/bmw-vision-future-luxurymodern-luxury-driven-by-design-andinnovation?language=en. Accessed 10 January 2020.

Bonacich, Edna and Appelbaum, Richard (2000), *Behind the Label: Inequality in the Los Angeles Apparel Industry*, Berkeley: University of California Press.

Boradkar, Persad (2010), 'Design as problem solving', in R. Frodeman (ed.), *The Oxford Handbook of Interdisciplinarity*, Oxford: Oxford University Press, pp. 273–87.

Borstrock, Shaun (2014), 'Do contemporary luxury brands adhere to historical paradigms of luxury?', in J. H. Hancock II, G. Muratovski, V. Manlow and A. Peirson-Smith (eds), *Global Fashion Brands: Style, Luxury & History*, Bristol: Intellect, pp. 231–48.

Borstrock, Shaun (2018), 'Personalisation, customization and bespoke: Increasing the product offer', *Journal of Design, Business and Society*, 4:2, pp. 171–87.

Bourdieu, Pierre (1977), *Outline of a Theory of Practice* (trans. Richard Nice), Cambridge: Cambridge University Press.

Bourdieu, Pierre (1984), *Distinction: A Social Critique of the Judgement of Taste* (trans. R. Nice), Cambridge: Harvard University Press.

Bourdieu, Pierre (1986), 'The forms of capital', in J. Richardson (ed.), *Handbook of Theory and Research for the Sociology of Education*, New York: Greenwood Press.

Bourdieu, Pierre (1990), *In Other Words: Essays Toward a Reflexive Sociology*, Stanford, CA: Stanford University Press.

Bourdieu, Pierre (1993), 'The field of cultural production', in R. Johnson (ed.), *The Future of Cultural Production: Essays on Art and Literature*, New York: Columbia University Press, pp. 29–144.

Bourdieu, Pierre and Passeron, Jean-Clayde (1990), *Reproduction in Education, Society and Culture*, London: Sage.

Bourdieu, Pierre and Wacquant, Loïc J. D. (1992), *An Invitation to Reflexive Sociology*, Chicago, IL: Chicago University Press.

Brownsell, Alex (2010), 'Louis Vuitton "hand made" campaign falls foul of ASA', Campaign, 26 May, https://www.campaignlive.co.uk/article/louis-vuitton-hand-made-campaign-falls-foul-asa/1005786. Accessed 28 September 2021.

Bugatti (2019), 'New head of quality at Bugatti in Molsheim', 15 August, https://www.bugatti.com/media/news/2019/new-head-of-quality/. Accessed 30 August 2019.

Bugatti (n.d), 'History', https://www.bugatti.com/brand/history/. Accessed 10 June 2020.

*Business of Fashion* (2017), 'Hermès boosts French production to meet Asian', 27 April, https://www.businessoffashion.com/articles/luxury/hermes-boosts-french-production-to-meet-asian-demand-as-sales-accelerate. Accessed 29 April 2020.

*Business of Fashion* Team and McKinsey & Company (2020), 'The new normal: A discount mindset will deepen its grip on consumers,' *Business of Fashion*, 14 April, https://www.businessoffashion.com/articles/retail/the-new-normal-a-discount-mindset-will-deepen-its-grip-on-consumers Accessed 6 April 2020.

Burridge, Nicky (2017), 'Artificial intelligence gets a seat in the boardroom, *Nikkei Asia*, 10 May, https://asia.nikkei.com/Business/Artificial-intelligence-gets-a-seat-in-the-boardroom. Accessed 10 May 2017.

Cairns, Graham (n.d.), 'The mediated city', AMPS, https://architecturemps.com/the-mediated-city/. Accessed 14 May 2020.

Cantista, Isabel and Sadaba, Teresa (eds) (2020), *Understanding Luxury Fashion: From Emotions to Brand Building*, New York: Palgrave Macmillan.

Capellino, Ally (2012), in-person interview with S. Borstrock, *The Luxury and Luxury Brand Landscape*, London, 21 November.

Capri Holdings (2019), 'Capri Holdings Limited to acquire Italian shoe manufacturer', 16 December, http://www.capriholdings.com/news-releases/news-releases-details/2019/Capri-Holdings-Limited-to-Acquire-Italian-Shoe-Manufacturer/default.aspx. Accessed 9 March 2020.

Carta, Silvio (2019), *Big Data, Code and the Discrete City: Shaping Public Realms*, Routledge Studies in Urbanism and the City, Abingdon: Routledge.

Carta, Silvio and De Kock, Pieter (2019), 'Reifying luxury, gold to golden: How the showroom became a digital showreel, from object (gold) to experience (golden) – experiencing luxury by abstracting the object', *Journal of Design, Business & Society*, 5:2, pp. 193–206.

Carta, Silvio, Onafuye, Rebecca and De Kock, Pieter (2019), 'Standing out in a crowd: Big data to produce new forms of publicness', in S. Figueiredo, S. Krishnamurthy and T. Schroeder (eds), *Architecture and the Smart City*, London: Routledge, pp. 223–25.

Cassin, Elena (1968), *La Splendeur Divine: Introduction à l'Etude de la Mentalité Mésopotamienne*, Hague: De Gruyter Mouton.

Chamberlain, Gethin (2012), 'Olympic brands caught up in abuse scandal', *The Observer*, 3 March, https://

gethinchamberlain.com/?p=1696. Accessed 23 June 2020.

Chang, Brittany (2019), 'Bugatti's new $18.7 million hypercar was purchased by an anonymous buyer, making it the most expensive new car ever sold', *Business Insider*, 13 August, https://www.businessinsider.com/bugatti-la-voiture-noire-most-expensive-new-car-ever-2019-8?r=US&IR=T. Accessed 2 September 2019.

Chrisafis, Angelique (2015), 'Hermès and Jane Berkin resolve spat over crocodile handbags', *The Guardian*, 11 September, https://www.theguardian.com/fashion/2015/sep/11/hermes-jane-birkin-crocodile-handbag-peta-luxury. Accessed 14 January 2020.

Cloutier, David (2015), *The Vice of Luxury: Economic Excess in a Consumer Age*, Washington, DC: Georgetown University Press.

Craddock, James (ed.) (2016), 'Bugatti, Ettor', *Encyclopaedia of World Biography*, 2nd ed., vol. 36, Detroit: Gale, pp. 110–12.

Crunchbase (2020), 'Kering section acquisitions', 22 February, https://www.crunchbase.com/organization/kering#-section-acquisitions. Accessed 22 March 2020.

Currid-Halkett, Elizabeth (2019), *The Sum of Small Things: A Theory of the Aspirational Class*, Princeton: Princeton University Press.

Curtis, Adam (2002), *The Century of the Self*, UK: BBC.

Daily Mail Reporter (2010), 'Louis Vuitton ads banned after design house misled customers by suggesting its bags were hand-stitched', *Mail Online*, 26 May, https://www.dailymail.co.uk/femail/article-1281443/Louis-Vuitton-ads-banned-suggesting-bags-hand-stitched.html. Accessed 23 June 2019.

Dalton, Matthew (2019), 'Why your next Louis Vuitton bag may hail from Texas', *Wall Street Journal*, 17 October, https://www.wsj.com/articles/why-your-next-louis-vuitton-bag-may-hail-from-texas-11571332220. Accessed 1 December 2019.

Dalton, Trent (2015), 'Louis Vuitton and Hermès turn our saltwater crocodiles into high fashion', *The Australian*, 11 July, https://www.theaustralian.com.au/weekend-australian-magazine/saltwater-crocodiles-high-fashion-meets-evolutionary-design/news-story/5dd554716513843885959a63afb150f0. Accessed 1 June 2020.

Danziger, Pamela N. (2018), '5 brands that reveal the future of luxury online', *Forbes*, 26 February, https://www.forbes.com/sites/pamdanziger/2018/02/26/5-brands-that-reveal-the-future-of-luxury-online/?sh=dcf3cb13c7e3. Accessed 14 April 2020.

Danziger, Pamela N. (2019a), '3 ways millennials and gen-z consumers are radically transforming the luxury market', *Forbes*, 29 May, https://www.forbes.com/sites/pamdanziger/2019/05/29/3-ways-millennials-and-gen-z-consumers-are-radically-transforming-the-luxury-market/?sh=45ed81e7479f. Accessed 19 September 2019.

Danziger, Pamela N. (2019b), 'What LVMH knows that American luxury brands still haven't learned: Outlets are anathema for luxury brands', *Forbes*, 8 December, https://www.forbes.com/sites/pamdanziger/2019/12/08/what-european-luxury-brands-know-that-american-brands-still-havent-learned-outlets-are-anathema-for-luxury-brands/?sh=59d6770249c3. Accessed 8 June 2020.

D'Arpizio, Claudia, Levato, Federica, Prete, Filippo, Del Fabbro, Elisa and Montgolfier, Joëlle de (2019), *Luxury Goods Worldwide Market Study, Fall-Winter 2018*, Bain and Company, https://www.bain.com/contentassets/8df501b9f8d6442e-ba00040246c6b4f9/bain_digest__luxury_goods_worldwide_market_study_fall_winter_2018.pdf. Accessed 27 May 2020.

D'Arpizio, Claudia, Levato, Federica, Fenili, Stefano, Colacchio, Fabio and Prete, Filippo (2020), 'Luxury after Covid-19: changed for (the) good?', Bain & Company, 26 March, https://www.bain.com/insights/luxury-after-coronavirus/. Accessed 8 November 2021.

Davis, Brent (2016), 'Rimowa hiring expanding operations in Cambridge: A story of exceptional Savoir-Faire', 5 February, https://www.therecord.com/business/2016/02/05/rimowa-hiring-expanding-operations-in-cambridge.html. Accessed 12 October 2021.

De Portzamparc, Christian (2020), 'Flagship Dior', Christian de Portzamparc, https://www.christiandeportzamparc.com/en/projects/flagship-dior-seoul/. Accessed 12 February 2020.

Dior (2020), 'Savoire Faire', Instagram, https://www.instagram.com/dior/?hl=en. Accessed 21 February 2020.

Djabali, Nadia (2018a), 'Augmenter les salaires chez Vuitton, c'est pas du luxe', *Force Ouvrière*, 25 February, https://www.force-ouvriere.fr/augmenter-les-salaires-chez-vuitton-c-est-pas-du-luxe?lang=fr. Accessed 25 June 2020.

Djabali, Nadia (2018b), 'Les salaires pas très glamour de la mode', *Force Ouvrière*, 5 March, https://www.force-ouvriere.fr/les-salaires-pas-tres-glamour-de-la-mode?lang=fr. Accessed 28 July 2020.

Dodge, Martin and Kitchin, Rob (2001), 'Flying through code/space: The real virtuality of air travel', *Environment and Planning A*, 36:2, pp. 195–211.

Domingos, Pedro (2015), *The Master Algorithm: How the Quest for the Ultimate Learning Machine Will Remake Our World*, New York: Basic Books.

Domingos, Pedro (2017), 'The next hundred years of your life' YouTube, 18

January, https://www.youtube.com/watch?v=r2YiRiLAUY. Accessed 14 June 2020 [no longer available].

Donnelly, Christopher and Scaff, Renato (2013), 'Who are the millennial shoppers? And what do they really want', *Outlook*, 2, pp. 1–7, https://www.avanade.com/-/media/asset/point-of-view/who-are-millennial-shoppers.pdf. Accessed 27 May 2019.

Doran, Sophie (2013), 'The new luxury is luxury for all, suggests Jean-Noel Kapferer', *Luxury Society*, 22 April, https://www.luxurysociety.com/en/articles/2013/04/the-new-luxury-is-luxury-for-all-suggests-jean-noel-kapferer/. Accessed 2 August 2020.

Doudaklian, Steve (2019), in-person interview with V. Manlow, Falls Church, VA, 20 December.

Doulton, Maria (2020), 'Original thinker: 26 May 15:30 exclusive Theo Fennell interview', 26 May, http://www.thejewelleryeditor.com/jewellery/article/theo-fennell-interview-jewellery-video/. Accessed 15 June 2020.

Dourish, Paul (2017), *The Stuff of Bits: An Essay on the Materialities of Information*, London: MIT Press.

Dourish, Paul and Bell, Genevieve (2011), *Divining a Digital Future: Mess and Mythology in Ubiquitous Computing*, London: MIT Press.

Dourish, Paul and Mazmanian, Melissa (2011), 'Media as material: Information representations as material foundations for organizational practice', Working paper for the *Third International Symposium on Process Organization Studies*, Corfu, Greece, June, vol. 92, https://www.researchgate.net/publication/228467184_Media_as_Material_Information_Representations_as_Material_Foundations_for_Organizational_Practice. Accessed 12 october 2021.

Doyle, Alister (2007), 'Botswana "snake rock" may show stone age religion', *Reuters*, 20 January, https://www.reuters.com/article/science-botswana-snake-dc-idUSL3069331020061130. Accessed 12 March 2020.

DRWF (2018), 'Sugar tax on sugary drinks introduced', 6 April, https://www.drwf.org.uk/news-and-events/news/sugar-tax-sugary-drinks-introduced-nhs-reports-twice-many-people-admitted. Accessed 6 April 2018.

eBay (2020), 'eBay releases "2020: Luxury watch report," offers shoppers up to 30% off top brands', 28 January, https://www.ebayinc.com/stories/news/ebay-releases-2020-luxury-watch-report-offers-shoppers-up-to-30-off-top-brands/. Accessed 28 January 2020.

Edelkoort, Li (2020), 'The BoF podcast: Li Edelkoort says the coronavirus is a representation of our conscience', *Business of Fashion*, 27 March, https://www.businessoffashion.com/podcasts/luxury/the-bof-podcast-li-edelkoort-on-how-covid-19-is-ushering-in-the-age-of-the-amateur. Accessed 20 April 2020.

Ellen MacArthur Foundation (2020), 'Circular economy concept', 12 February, https://ellenmacarthurfoundation.org/topics/circular-economy-introduction/overview. Accessed 17 March 2020.

Emelianov, Valdimir V. (2010), 'On the early history of Melammu: Religion and ideology', in L. E. Kogan, N. Koslova, S. Loesov and S. Tishchenko (eds), *Language in the Ancient Near East: Proceedings of the 53rd Rencontre Assyriologique Internationale*, vol. 1, State College: Eisenbrauns, pp. 1109–19.

*Encyclopaedia Britannica* (2020), 'The editors: Giorgio Armani', https://www.britannica.com/biography/Giorgio-Armani. Accessed 7 July 2021.

Etherington, Darrell (2017), 'Facebook buys computer vision startup focused on adding objects to video', Techcrunch, 11 August, https://techcrunch.com/2017/08/11/facebook-buys-computer-vision-startup-focused-on-adding-objects-to-video/. Accessed 10 December 2019.

Faiers, Jonathan (2016), '"In a galaxy far, far..." C-3PO, mink, and the promise of disruptive luxury', *Cultural Politics*, 12:1, pp. 83–97.

Fennell, Theo (2020), in-person interview with S. Borstrock, London, 20 May.

Fernault, Helene (2014), *Haute Couture Ateliers: The Artisans of Fashion*, New York: The Vendome Press.

Financial Times (n.d.), 'Gamers get virtual access to high fashion and accessories', https://www.ft.com/content/59cb4152-1bf9-11ea-81f0-0c253907d3e0. Accessed 14 October 2021 [behind a paywall].

Frearson, Amy (2011), 'Pacific Place by Thomas Heatherwick', Dezeen, 5 December, https://www.dezeen.com/2011/12/05/pacific-place-by-thomas-heatherwick/. Accessed 18 November 2021.

Friedman, Vanessa (2020), 'Should we still go shopping (online)?', *New York Times*, 26 March , https://www.nytimes.com/2020/03/26/style/coronavirus-shopping.html. Accessed 12 October 2021.

Gaultier, Jean-Paul (2019), interview, *Fashion*,  France 24, 20 November.

Glassman, Jim (2019), 'The true state of the consumer isn't seen in retail sales', JP Morgan, 30 October, https://www.jpmorgan.com/commercial-banking/insights/true-state-of-consumer-isnt-seen-in-retail-sales. Accessed 12 October 2021.

Goldberger, Paul (2002), 'High-tech emporiums: Prada and Toys r Us have much in common, *New Yorker*, 17 March, https://www.newyorker.com/magazine/2002/03/25/high-tech-emporiums. Accessed 19 September 2020.

Goldman Sachs (2016), 'Virtual and augmented reality: The next big computing platform?', 9 February, https://www.goldmansachs.com/insights/pages/virtual-and-augmented-reality-report.html. Accessed 1 February 2020.

Goor, Dafna, Ordabayeva, Nailya, Deinan, Anat and Crener, Sandrine (2019), *The Imposter Syndrome from Luxury Consumption*, Oxford: Oxford University Press on behalf of the *Journal for Consumer Research, Inc.*

Graham, Steve and Marvin, Simon (2002), *Telecommunications and the City: Electronic Spaces, Urban Place*, New York: Routledge.

Green, Emma (2013), 'Innovation: The history of a buzzword', *The Atlantic*, 20 June, https://www.theatlantic.com/business/archive/2013/06/innovation-the-history-of-a-buzzword/277067/. Accessed 29 January 2020.

Greenfield, Adam (2010), *Everyware: The Dawning Age of Ubiquitous Computing*, San Francisco: New Riders.

Greenhouse, Steven (1989), 'A luxury fight to the finish', *New York Time Magazine*, 17 December, https://www.nytimes.com/1989/12/17/magazine/a-luxury-fight-to-the-finish.html. Accessed 15 September 2021.

Grinnell, Sunhee (2015), 'Cartes parfumees: Scented leather card holder collection by Maison Francis Kurkdjian Paris', *Vanity Fair*, 23 October, https://www.vanityfair.com/style/2015/10/parfume-de-la-carte-scented-leather-cardholder-collection-by-maison-francis-kurkdjian-paris. Accessed 29 February 2019.

Groupe Artémis (n.d.), Groupe Artémis, https://en.wikipedia.org/wiki/Groupe_Art%C3%A9mis. Accessed 11 November 2021.

Guerlain (n.d.), 'Our commitment', https://www.guerlain.com/uk/en-uk/c/our-commitment.html. Accessed 15 May 2020.

Guilbault, Laure (2021), 'LVMH rebound continues, driven by Dior and Louis Vuitton', *Vogue Business*, 26 January, https://www.voguebusiness.com/companies/lvmhs-rebound-continues-driven-by-dior-and-louis-vuitton. Accessed 1 February 2021.

Hajer, Maarten (1999), 'The generic city',*Theory, Culture & Society*, 16:4, pp. 137–44.

Harari, Yuval Noah (2015) *Sapiens: A Brief History of Humankind*, London, Vintage.

Harper, Abigail (2019), *Rotten, Bitter Chocolate*, UK: Netflix.

The Harris Poll (2020), 'Poll: Americans are wary about travelling after Covid-19 curve flattens', 21–22 March, https://theharris-poll.com/poll-americans-are-wary-about-traveling-after-Covid-19-curve-flattens/. Accessed 13 August 2020.

Harvey, David (1989), *The Condition of Postmodernity*, Oxford: Blackwell.

Harvey, David (1990), 'Between space and time: Reflections on the geographical imagination', *Annals of the Association of American Geographers*, 80:3, pp. 418–34.

Heatherwick, Thomas (2005), 'Pacific Place', http://www.heatherwick.com/projects/buildings/pacific-place/. Accessed 10 January 2020.

Hebdige, Dick (1979), *Subculture: The Meaning of Style*, London: Routledge.

Heine, Klaus (2012), *The Concept of Luxury Brands: Luxury Brand Management*, 2nd ed., Berlin: Technische Universität Berlin, https://upmarkit.com/sites/default/files/content/20130403_Heine_The_Concept_of_Luxury_Brands.pdf Accessed 12 October 2021.

Hermès (n.d.), 'Leather school: Passing on values and skills', https://artwalkingsticks.com/blogs/blog/what-does-a-cane-symbolize. Accessed 1 February 2020.

Hovailo, Oleksandr (2020), 'What does a cane symbolize?', Art Walking Sticks, 17 April, https://artwalkingsticks.com/blogs/blog/what-does-a-cane-symbolize. Accessed 18 November 2021.

Huddleston Jr., Tom (2019), 'Take a look at the world's most expensive new car – it just sold for $19 million', CNBC, 23 March, https://www.cnbc.com/2019/03/22/take-a-look-bugattis-la-voiture-noire-car-just-sold-for-19-million.html. Accessed 4 June 2020.

Hume, David ([1742] 1875), *Essays Moral, Political, and Literary*, vol. 1, London: Longmans, Green and Co.

Huxley, Aldous (1958), *A Brave New World*, New York: Harper & Brothers.

Indeed (2019a), 'Lesage: Management patriarchal', 24 September, https://fr.indeed.com/cmp/Lesage/reviews. Accessed 12 December 2019.

Indeed (2019b, 'Hermès: Un travail très stressant', 13 November, https://fr.indeed.com/cmp/Herm%C3%A8s-1/reviews. Accessed 19 October 2020.

Indeed (2019c), 'Worst job I ever had', 31 August, https://www.indeed.com/cmp/Louis-Vuitton/reviews/worst-job-i-have-ever-had?id=5fc72a-600cae0685. Accessed 12 September 2019.

Indeed (2019d), 'Demanding stressful work with high goals', 26 June, https://www.indeed.com/cmp/Louis-Vuitton/reviews/demanding-stressful-work-with-

high-goals?id=fee200b08f0540cb.
Accessed 12 September 2019.

Interaction Design Foundation (n.d.), 'What is human-computer interaction', https://www.interaction-design.org/literature/topics/human-computer-interaction#:~:text=Human%2Dcomputer%20interaction%20(HCI)%20is%20a%20multidisciplinary%20field%20of,forms%20of%20information%20technology%20design. Accessed 24 October 2020.

*Italian Shoes* (2017), 'Prada: Beyond fashion', 29 March, https://www.italian-shoes.com/en/prada-beyond-fashion/. Accessed 20 April 2021.

Jackson, Tim (2002), 'International Herald Tribune Fashion 2001 conference review', *Journal of Fashion Marketing and Management*, 6:4, https://www.emerald.com/insight/content/doi/10.1108/jfmm.2002.28406dac.001./full/html. Accessed 1 February 2020.

Jones, Lora (2018), 'Going Solo: The rise of self employment', *BBC News*, 30 July, https://www.bbc.co.uk/news/business-44887623. Accessed 10 May 2021.

Jones, Stephen (2010), interviewed by S. Borstrock, 'The popularisation and democratization of luxury', Ph.D. thesis, Hatfield: University of Hertfordshire.

Joshi, Naveen (2019), 'Retailers have a lot to gain from AR and VR', *Forbes*, 1 October, https://www.forbes.com/sites/cognitiveworld/2019/10/01/retailers-have-a-lot-to-gain-from-ar-and-vr/?sh=60d0c3b57a1c. Accessed 1 February 2020.

Kapferer, Jean-Noël, Kernstock, Joachim, Brexendorf, Tim Oliver and Powell, Shaun M. (eds) (2017), *Advances in Luxury Brand Management*, Cham: Palgrave Macmillan.

Kering (n.d.), 'Crafting tomorrow's luxury', https://www.kering.com/en/sustainability/crafting-tomorrow-s-luxury/. Accessed 22 May 2020.

Khomami, Nadia (2016), 'Red clay brick on sale for up to $1,000 on eBay', *The Guardian*, 30 September, https://www.theguardian.com/technology/2016/sep/30/red-clay-brick-selling-for-up-to-1000-on-ebay. Accessed 31 May 2020.

Kitchin, Rob (2013), 'Big data and human geography: Opportunities, challenges and risks', *Dialogues in Human Geography*, 3:3, pp. 262–67.

Kitchin, Rob and Dodge, Martin (2011), *Code/Space: Software and Everyday Life*, London: MIT Press.

Kitchin, Rob, Lauriault, Tracey P. and Wilson, Matthew W. (eds) (2017), *Understanding Spatial Media*, London: Sage.

KnowTheChain (2018), *2018 Apparel & Footwear Benchmark Findings Report*, https://knowthechain.org/wp-content/uploads/KTC_AF_2018.pdf. Accessed 3 March 2020.

Kollewe, Julia (2018), 'Burberry to stop burning unsold items after green criticism', *The Guardian*, 6 September, https://www.theguardian.com/business/2018/sep/06/burberry-to-stop-burning-unsold-items-fur-after-green-criticism. Accessed 20 May 2020.

Koolhaas, Rem (1995), *Field Trip: A(A) Memoir, SMLXL*, Rotterdam: 010 Publishers.

Kovalchuk, Taras (2019), 'Augmenting the customer retail Experience', Retailcustomerexperience.com, 20 November, https://www.retailcustomerexperience.com/blogs/augmenting-the-retail-customer-experience/. Accessed 28 May 2020.

Krogh, Georg, Nonaka, Ikujiro and Kazuo, Ichijo (2000), *Enabling Knowledge Creation: How to Unlock the Mystery of Tacit*

*Knowledge and Release the Power of Innovation*, Oxford: Oxford University Press.

Krugman, Paul (2020), interview, *Morning Joe*, MSNBC, 1 May.

Kulkarni, Soham (2019), 'The "SUPREME" theory of hype branding', Medium, 7 March, https://medium.com/predict/https-mediu m-com-strategy-insider-the-supreme-theory-of-hype-branding-af3f9acd7fe. Accessed 31 May 2020.

*La Resérve Magazine* (n.d.), 'Atelier Renard: A backstage view of a premier leather atelier artisan', http://www. lareserve-mag.com/atelier-renard-premier-leather-artisan/. Accessed 16 February 2020.

*Le Figaro* (2019), 'Atelier Renard: Pour l'amour du cuir', 18 March, http:// adresses-incontournables.madame.lefi-garo.fr/shopping-boutiques/atelier-renar d-pour-lamour-du-cuir/. Accessed 15 March 2020.

Lee, Jussara (2019), in-person interview with V. Manlow, New York, 11 and 15 November; 21 January.

Leach, Alec (2016), '8 possible reasons Supreme made an actual brick this season', Highsnobiety, 18 August, https://www.highsnobiety.com/p/supreme-brick/. Accessed 31 May 2020.

Leitch, Luke (2020), 'Stephen Jones crafted his new couture collection in collaboration with the digital influencer Noonoouri', *Vogue*, 14 June, https://www.vogue.com/slideshow/stephen-jones-couture-collection-noonoouri. Accessed 20 June 2020.

Lembke, Alexandra (2017), 'Revealed: The Romanian site where LV makes its Italian shoes', *The Guardian*, 17 June, https://www.theguardian.com/business/2017/jun/17/revealed-th e-romanian-site-where-louis-vui tton-makes-its-italian-shoes. Accessed 17 July 2019.

Li, Jane (2018), 'Eight-day strike at China factory making Michael Kors bags ends as workers' pension and wage demands met', *South China Morning Post*, 18 March, https://www.scmp.com/busi-ness/china-business/article/2137548/eight-day-strike-china-factory-making -michael-kors-bags-ends. Accessed 1 June 2019.

Lindt & Sprüngli (2020), 'Farming program', 25 March, https://www. farming-program.com/en#the-lindt--spr%C3%BCngli--promise. Accessed 20 May 2020.

Lipovetsky, Gilles and Roux, Elyette (2003), *Le Luxe Eternel: De L'Age du Sacré au Temps de Marques*, Paris: Gallimard.

LLFOURN (2018), 'A brief history of ledgers', *Unraveling the Ouroboros*, 15 February, https://medium.com/unraveling-the-ouroboros/a-brie f-history-of-ledgers-b6ab84a7ff41. Accessed 21 July 2019.

Lloyd, Alison (2020), in-person interview with S. Borstrock, London, 25 January.

London Fashion Week (2020), 'Stephen Jones millinery "Analogue Fairydust"', 12–14 June, https://londonfashion-week.co.uk/schedule/67/stephen-jone s-millinery-analogue-fairydust. Accessed 20 June 2020.

Louis Vitton (n.d), 'Keepall 55', https://uk.louisvuitton.com/eng-gb/products/keepall-55-monogram-canvas-000697. Accessed 25 March 2020.

*L'Usine Nouvelle* (2011), 'Louis Vuit-ton, l'industriel', 7 July, https://www.usinenouvelle.com/article/louis-vuitton-l-industriel.N155197. Accessed 1 May 2020.

LVMH (2011), 'LMVH to jointly own and control Heng-Long, one of the world's leading and most renowned tanneries of crocodilian leather together with its founding family', Louis Vuitton, 7 October, https://www.lvmh.com/news-documents/press-releases/lvmh-to-jointly-own-and-control-heng-long-one-of-the-worlds-leading-and-most-renowned-tanneries-of-crocodilian-leather-together-with-its-founding-family/. Accessed 22 March 2020.

LVMH (2019), 'Ahead of its sustainability roadmap, LVMH announces new commitments for environment and biodiversity', 26 September, https://www.lvmh.com/news-documents/press-releases/en-avance-sur-sa-feuille-de-route-lvmh-prend-de-nouveaux-engagements-en-faveur-de-lenvironnement-et-de-la-biodiversite/. Accessed 12 October 2021.

LVMH (2020), 'EllesVMH: Social and environmental responsibility', https://www.lvmh.com/group/lvmh-commitments/social-environmental-responsibility/ellesvmh-initiative-lvmh/. Accessed 22 December 2020.

LVMH (2021a), 'LVMH partners with other major luxury companies on Aura, the first global luxury blockchain', 20 April, https://www.lvmh.com/news-documents/news/lvmh-partners-with-other-major-luxury-companies-on-aura-the-first-global-luxury-blockchain/. Accessed on 29 April 2021.

LVMH (2021b), 'Investors: LVMH, the world's leading luxury products group, gathers 75 prestigious brands, with 44.7 billion euros revenue in 2020 and a retail network of over 5,000 stores worldwide', https://www.lvmh.com/investors/. Accessed May 2021.

LVMH (n.d.), 'Leadership & entrepreneurship', https://www.lvmh.com/group/lvmh-commitments/leadership-entrepreneurship/. Accessed 12 October 2021.

Mackenzie, Adrian (2002), *Transductions: Bodies and Machines at Speed*, London: A&C Black.

Mackenzie, Adrian (2003), 'Transduction: Invention, innovation and collective life draft', Protocolo disponível, http://www.lancs.ac.uk/staff/mackenza/papers/transduction.pdf. Accessed 13 June 2020.

Mackenzie, Adrian (2010), *Wirelessness: Radical Empiricism in Network Cultures*, Cambridge: MIT Press.

Maheshwari, Sapna and Friedman, Vanessa (2020), 'The death of the department store: "Very few are likely to survive"', *New York Times*, 21 April, https://www.nytimes.com/2020/04/21/business/coronavirus-department-stores-neiman-marcus.html. Accessed 5 May 2020.

Manovich, Lev (2013), *Software Takes Command*, London: A&C Black.

Manuelli, Sara (2006), *Design for Shopping: New Retail Interiors*, London: Laurence King.

Mark, Joshua J. (2011), 'Writing', *Ancient History Encyclopaedia*', https://www.worldhistory.org/writing/. Accessed June 2019.

Marr, Bernard (2018), 'What is industry 4.0?', Bernard Marr & Company, https://bernardmarr.com/what-is-industry-4-0-heres-a-super-easy-explanation-for-anyone/. Accessed 1 June 2020.

Marx, Karl ([1844] 2009), *Economic and Political Manuscripts of 1844*, https://www.marxists.org/archive/marx/works/download/pdf/Economic-Philosophic-Manuscripts-1844.pdf. Accessed 28 May 2019.

Matsuda, Naoki (2020), 'China's retailers face hard truth: If you reopen, they won't come', *Financial Times*, 12 April, https://www.ft.com/content/07bd5ad6-6979-400f-a26e-bb0eefac1e6d. Accessed 17 May 2020.

Mattham, Kate (2019), 'France moves to ban the destruction of unsold luxury goods in favor of recycling', *Forbes*, 6 June, https://www.forbes.com/sites/

katematthams/2019/06/06/france-moves-to-ban-the-destruction-of-unsold-luxury-goods-in-favor-of-recycling/?sh=-2068be45334e. Accessed 12 February 2020.

McDowell, Maghan (2021), 'The blockchain playbook: From LVMH's aura to arainee', *Vogue Business*, 26 April, https://www.voguebusiness.com/technology/the-blockchain-playbook-from-lvmhs-aura-to-arianee. Accessed 12 May 2021.

McIntyre, Megan (2017), 'The private-label companies you never realized were making your favorite beauty products', *Fashionista*, https://fashionista.com/2017/06/private-label-beauty-products-cosmetics. Accessed 22 December 2019.

McKinsey and Company (2017), *The State of Fashion 2018*, https://www.mckinsey.com/~/media/mckinsey/industries/retail/our%20insights/renewed%20optimism%20for%20the%20fashion%20industry/the-state-of-fashion-2018-final.ashx#:~:text=The%20McKinsey%20Global%20Fashion%20Index%20forecasts%20industry%20sales%20growth%20to,the%20end%20of%20an%20era. Accessed 12 January 2020.

McKinsey and Company (2020), 'A perspective for the luxury-goods industry during and after-coronavirus', 1 April, https://www.mckinsey.com/industries/retail/our-insights/a-perspective-for-the-luxury-goods-industry-during-and-after-coronavirus. Accessed 10 June 2020.

Mead, George Herbert (1934), *Mind, Self and Society: From the Standpoint of a Social Behaviorist* (intro. C. W. Morris), Chicago: University of Chicago Press.

Media Publications (2019), '2019 true-luxury global consumer insight', BCG, 17 April, http://media-publications.bcg.com/france/True-Luxury%20Global%20Consumer%20Insight%202019%20-%20Plenary%20-%20vMedia.pdf. Accessed 12 June 2020.

Memomi (2020), 'The world's most advanced digital mirror', https://memory-mirror.com/. Accessed 1 February 2020.

Mills, C. Wright ([1956] 2000), *The Power Elite*, New York: Oxford University Press.

Moody's Investors Service (2019), 'Moody's assigns first time A1 rating to LVMH: Stable outlook', 3 July, https://www.moodys.com/research/Moodys-assigns-firsttime-A1-rating-to-LVMH-stable-outlook--PR_401714. Accessed 4 June 2020.

Moody's Investors Service (2020), 'Moody's affirms LVMH A1 rating: Outlook stable', 31 March, https://www.moodys.com/research/Moodys-affirms-LVMHA1-rating-outlook-stable--PR_421728. Accessed 10 June 2020.

Munro, Chelsea (2021), 'Shocking new investigation reveals the horror behind Hermès-owned crocodile farms', PETA UK, 2 September, https://www.peta.org.uk/blog/hermes-crocodile-kindness-project/. Accessed 30 November 2021.

MVRDV (2020), 'Crystal Houses', MVRDV, https://www.mvrdv.nl/projects/240/crystal-houses. Accessed 10 January 2020.

Naas, Roberta (2016), 'Patek Philippe celebrates 20 years of its iconic advertising campaign', 9 December, https://www.forbes.com/sites/robertanaas/2016/12/09/patek-philippe-celebrates-20-years-of-its-iconic-advertising-campaign-you-never-actually-own-a-patek-philippe/?sh=4eadae13475b. Accessed 25 February 2020.

Nagarajan, Shalini (2020), 'French luxury brand Hermès pulls in $2.7 million in a day at a flagship store in China as wealthy shoppers splurge after the coronavirus lockdown', *Business Insider*, 15 April, https://www.businessinsider.com/wealthy-chinese-shoppers-slurge-at-hermes-store-in-china-2020-4?r=US&IR=T. Accessed 13 July 2020.

Neufeld, Dietmar (2009), 'Sumptuous clothing and ornamentation in the Apocalypse', *Hervormde Teologiese Studies*, 58, pp. 664–89.

Nicoletti, Susanna (2018), 'Bugatti is a global brand, not a French one', The Luxury Society, 17 September, https://www.luxurysociety.com/en/articles/2018/09/bugatti-global-brand-not-french-one. Accessed 10 April 2019.

NielsenIQ (2020), 'NielsenIQ investigation: "Pandemic pantries" pressure supply chain amid Covid-19 fears', NielsenIQ, 2 March, https://nielseniq.com/global/en/insights/analysis/2020/nielseniq-investigation-pandemic-pantries-pressure-supply-chain-amid-covid-19-fears/. Accessed 10 April 2020.

NRF (n.d.), 'Economy: Retail jobs', National Retail Federation, https://nrf.com/insights/economy/about-retail-jobs. Accessed 14 June 2020.

O'Connell, L. (2020), 'LVMH stores', Statista, 24 February, https://www.statista.com/statistics/245854/total-number-of-stores-of-the-lvmh-group-worldwide/. Accessed 10 October 2020.

Okonkwo, Uché (2007), *Luxury Fashion Branding: Trends, Tactics, Techniques*, London: Palgrave Macmillan.

OMA (2002), *Harvard Design School Guide to Shopping* (eds R. Koolhaas, C. J. Chung, J. Inaba and S. T. Leong, Harvard University GSD, https://www.gsd.harvard.edu/publication/harvard-design-school-guide-to-shopping/. Accessed 15 September 2021.

Paris, Mario (ed.) (2017), *Making Prestigious Places: How Luxury Influences the Transformation of Cities*, New York: Routledge.

Partridge, Joanna (2020), 'New car sales in UK plunge by 44% as coronavirus bites', *The Guardian*, 6 April, https://www.theguardian.com/business/2020/apr/06/car-plant-shutdowns-may-cost-auto-industry-more-than-100bn-covid-19. Accessed 22 May 2020.

People for the Ethical Treatment of Animals (PETA) (2019), 'Exposed: Crocodiles and alligators factory-farmed for Hermès luxury goods, https://investigations.peta.org/crocodile-alligator-slaughter-hermes/. Accessed 16 May 2020.

People for the Ethical Treatment of Animals (PETA) (n.d.), 'Beauty brands that you thought were cruelty free but aren't', https://www.peta.org/living/personal-care-fashion/beauty-brands-that-you-thought-were-cruelty-free-but-arent/. Accessed 14 May 2021.

Perinbanayagam, Robert S. (1985), *Signifying Acts: Structure and Meaning in Everyday Life*, Carbondale, IL and Edwardsville, IL: Southern Illinois University Press.

Pine II, Joseph (1999), *Mass Customisation: The New Frontier in Business Competition*, Boston: Harvard Business School Press.

Prada Group (2018), *Company Profile*, February, https://www.pradagroup.com/content/dam/pradagroup/documents/Group_Profile/Company%20profile%20Prada%20Group_ENG.pdf. Accessed 22 May 2020.

Rawal, Amit (2017), 'Burberry's new AR experiment with apple – a fad or a signpost for the future?', Linkedin, 13 October, https://www.linkedin.com/pulse/burberrys-new-ar-experiment-apple-fad-signpost-future-amit-rawal-. Accessed 1 February 2020.

The Research Council of Norway (2006), 'World's oldest ritual discovered -- worshipped the python 70,000 years ago', *Science Daily*, 30 November, https://www.sciencedaily.com/releases/2006/11/061130081347.htm. Accessed 16 July 2020.

Research Gate (2015), 'Luxury branding: The industry, trends, and future conceptualisations', *Asia Pacific Journal of Marketing and Logistics*, 27:1, pp. 82–98, https://www.researchgate.net/publication/273167542_Luxury_branding_The_industry_trends_and_future_conceptualisations. Accessed 18 May 2021.

Retail Economics (2020), 'UK retail stats and facts', https://www.retaileconomics.co.uk/library-retail-stats-and-facts. Accessed 12 June 2020.

Reuters staff (2017), 'LVMH cuts ties to crocodile farms criticized by animal rights groups', Reuters, 13 January, https://www.reuters.com/article/us-lvmh-crocodiles/lvmh-cuts-ties-to-crocodile-farms-criticized-by-animal-rights-group-idUSKBN14X23B. Accessed 20 March 2020.

Reuters staff (2020), 'BMW sees demand falling further after 1st quarter sales plunge due to coronavirus', Reuters, 6 April, https://www.reuters.com/article/us-health-coronavirus-bmw-deliveries/bmw-sees-demand-falling-further-afterfirst-quarter-sales-plunge-due-tocoronavirus-idUSKBN21O0M0. Accessed 14 September 2020.

Richemont (n.d.), 'Sustainability: Our approach', https://www.richemont.com/en/home/sustainability/our-approach/. Accessed 22 May 2020.

Ripe.io (2020), '#knowyourfood', https://www.ripe.io/about. Accessed 22 March 2020.

Romagnoli, Rumble (2020), 'Smart digital marketing ideas adopt your luxury brand', The Drum, 31 July, https://www.thedrum.com/opinion/2020/07/31/smart-digital-marketing-ideas-adopt-your-luxury-brand-2020. Accessed 13 May 2021.

Ryan, Carol (2020), 'Got a Birkin bag to sell? That's a problem for Hermès *Wall Street Journal*, 28 February, https://www.wsj.com/articles/got-a-birkin-bag-to-sell-thats-a-problem-for-hermes-11582885805. Accessed 14 May 2020.

Sansome, Ian (2011), 'Great dynasties of the world: The Bugattis', *The Guardian*, 9 April, https://www.theguardian.com/lifeandstyle/2011/apr/09/bugatti-cars-jewellery-jeremy-clarkson?CMP=gu_com. Accessed 28 March 2020.

Schooley, Skye (2021), 'What is corporate social responsibility', *Business News Daily*, 18 March, https://www.businessnewsdaily.com/4679-corporate-social-responsibility.html. Accessed 2 April 2021.

Sekora, John (1977), *Luxury: The Concept in Western Thought, Eden to Smollett*, Baltimore: Johns Hopkins University Press.

Selter, Emily (2017), '11 things you didn't know about Birkins', *Town & Country*, 8 August, https://www.townandcountrymag.com/style/fashion-trends/g10262999/hermes-birkin-bag-facts/. Accessed 19 May 2020.

Sennett, Richard (2008), *The Craftsman*, New Haven: Yale University Press.

Seo, Yuri and Buchanon-Olivier, Margo (2015), 'Luxury branding: The industry, trends, and future conceptualisations', *Asia Pacific Journal of Marketing and Logistics*, 27:1, pp. 82–98.

Serdari, Thomaï (2020), *Rethinking Luxury Fashion: The Role of Cultural Intelligence in Creative Strategy,* New York: Palgrave Macmillan.

Sherman, Lauren (2020), 'Winner take all: How LVMH and Kering will extend their supremacy post pandemic', *Business of Fashion*, 26 May, https://www.businessoffashion.com/articles/luxury/winners-take-all-how-lvmh-and-kering-will-extend-their-supremacy-post-pandemic. Accessed 27 May 2020.

Sidewalk Labs (2019), *Toronto Tomorrow: A New Approach for Inclusive Growth,* https://storage.googleapis.com/sidewalk-toronto-ca/wp-content/uploads/2019/06/23135715/MIDP_Volume2.pdf. Accessed 31 May 2020.

Silver, Jocelyn (2020), 'Is it okay to online shop during a pandemic', *Paper*, 1 April, https://www.paper-mag.com/online-shopping-durin g-coronavirus-2645611815.html. Accessed 21 April 2020.

Simmel, Georg ([1904] 1957), 'Fashion', *The American Journal of Sociology*, 62:6 (May), pp. 541–58.

Starling Bank (n.d.), 'Our ethiics state-ment', https://www.starlingbank.com/ about/ethics-statement/. Accessed 26 September 2021.

Stanford University (2013), 'Ubiquitous computing', 3 April, https://hci.stanford. edu/courses/cs376/2013/lectures/2013-04-03-ubicomp-intro/CS376-2013-intro-ubicomp.pdf. Accessed 1 September 2019.

Statista (2020), 'Luxury goods USA', https://www.statista.com/outlook/cmo/ luxury-goods/united-states. Accessed 13 May 2021.

Statista (2021), 'Global brand value of Hermès from 2010 to 2020', 12 February, https://www.stati-sta.com/statistics/985435/ hermes-brand-value-worldwide/. Accessed 19 May 2021.

Stephen Jones Millinery (n.d.), 'History', http://www.stephenjonesmillinery.com/ History. Accessed 13 June 2020.

Suhrawardi, Rebecca (2019), 'The big issues facing fashion in 2019', *Forbes*, 16 January, https://www.forbes.com/ sites/rebeccasuhrawardi/2019/01/16/ the-big-issues-facing-fashion-in-2019/?sh=7527923423a9. Accessed 12 June 2019.

Sun, Lena H. (2020), 'CDC director warns second wave of coronavirus is likely to be even more devastating', *The Washington Post*, 21 April, https://www.washington-post.com/health/2020/04/21/coronaviru s-secondwave-cdcdirector/. Accessed 22 May 2020.

Swartz, David (1996), 'Bringing the study of culture and religion: Pierre Bourdieu's political economy of symbolic power', *Sociology of Religion*, Special Issue/ Section: 'Sociology of Culture and Society of Religion', 57:1 (Spring), pp. 71–85.

Szymkowski, Sean (2020), 'Q1 car sales plummet in the US due to coronavi-rus outbreak', CNET Roadshow, 13 April, https://www.cnet.com/roadshow/ news/car-sales-q1-coronavirus-covi d-19-automakers-us/. Accessed 13 August 2020.

Taub, Eric A. (2020), 'This car's yearly tune up costs as much as a civic', *New York Times*, 25 May, https://www. nytimes.com/2020/05/25/business/ bugatti-chiron-price.html. Accessed 30 June 2020.

Taylor, Frederick Winslow (1913), *The Principles of Scientific Management*, New York and London: Harper & Brothers Publishers.

TFL (2015), 'Hermès has acquired yet another one of its suppliers', *The Fashion Law*, 15 November, https://www.thefash-ionlaw.com/herms-has-acquired-ye t-another-one-of-its-supplier/. Accessed 3 December 2019 [no longer available].

Theo Fennell (n.d.), 'The Theo Fennell story', https://www.theofennell.com/ theo-fennell-story/. Accessed 12 Decem-ber 2019.

Thomas, Dana (2016), *Gods and Kings: The Rise and Fall of Alexander McQueen and John Galliano*, New York: Penguin Books.

Thomas, Dana (2007), *Deluxe: How Luxury Lost its Lustre*, New York: Penguin Books.

Todd, Laura May (2020), 'The making of Prada's most iconic bag', *New York Times*, 13 May, https://www.nytimes. com/2020/05/13/t-magazine/ prada-handbag-making-of.html. Accessed 13 May 2020.

Todd, Sarah (2019), 'Luxury is embarrassing', *Quartz*, 27 December, https://qz.com/1776106/why-americans-are-embarrassed-by-luxury/. Accessed 28 December 2019.

Toussaint, Kristin (2019), 'If your shoes were made specifically for you, would you care more about who made them?', *Fast Company*, 17 December, https://www.fastcompany.com/90441638/if-your-shoes-were-made-specifically-for-you-would-you-care-more-about-who-made-them. Accessed 16 January 2020.

Tso, Karen (2020), 'Op Ed: The luxury sector is bracing for the worst sales in numbers in its history', CNBC, 7 April, https://www.cnbc.com/2020/04/06/op-ed-the-luxury-sector-is-bracing-for-the-worst-sales-in-its-history.html. Accessed 13 May 2020.

Tugui, Alexandru (2004), 'Calm technologies in a multimedia world', Ubiquity, 5: 4, 16–23 March, https://ubiquity.acm.org/article.cfm?id=985617. Accessed 15 September 2021.

Twitchell, James B. (2002), *Living it Up: Our Love Affair With Luxury*, New York: Columbia University Press.

UNStudio (n.d.a), 'Hanjie Wanda Square', https://www.unstudio.com/en/page/11931/hanjie-wanda-square. Accessed 10 January 2020.

UNStudio (n.d.b), 'P.C. Hooftstraat 138', https://www.unstudio.com/en/page/12901/p.c.-hooftstraat-138. Accessed 10 January 2020.

Van Dijck, José (2014), 'Datafication, dataism and dataveillance: Big data between scientific paradigm and ideology', *Surveillance & Society*, 12:2, pp. 197–208.

Vanarama (2020), '4 ways augmented reality will revolutionise the automotive industry', https://www.vanarama.com/blog/cars/4-ways-augmented-reality-will-revolutionise-the-automotive-industry. Accessed 15 September 2021.

Veblen, Thorstein ([1899] 1953), *The Theory of the Leisure Class: An Economic Study of Institutions*, The Mentor Edition (ed. and intro. C. Wright Mills), New York: The Macmillan Company.

Vogt, Yngv (2012), 'World's oldest ritual discovered: Worshipped the python 70,000 years ago' (trans. A. L. Belardinelli), *Appolon*, 1 February, https://www.apollon.uio.no/english/articles/2006/python-english.html. Accessed 28 November 2019.

Warren, P. W. (2004), 'From ubiquitous computing to ubiquitous intelligence, *BT Technology Journal*, 22, pp. 28–38, https://link.springer.com/article/10.1023%2FB%3ABTTJ.0000033468.54111.2a. Accessed 23 June 2019.

Waugh, Robert (2018), 'Tech is killing the high street – but can it save it?', *The Telegraph*, 21 June, https://www.telegraph.co.uk/business/ready-and-enabled/retail-technology/. Accessed 15 February 2020.

Weber, Max (1978), *Economy and Society: An Outline of Interpretive Sociology*, Berkeley: University of California Press.

Weiser, Mark (1994), 'Ubiquitous computing', *22nd ACM Conference on Computer Science*, 8–10 March, 418:10, New York: Association for Computing Machinery, pp. 1145.

Weiser, Mark and Brown, John Seely (1997), *Beyond Calculation: The Coming Age of Calm Technology*, New York: Springer, pp. 75–85.

Weiser, Mark, Gold, Rich and Brown, John Seely (1999), 'The origins of ubiquitous computing research at PARC in the late 1980s', *IBM Systems Journal*, 38:4, pp. 693–96.

Wesler, Kit W. (2012), *An Archaeology of Religion*, Lanham: University Press of America.

White, Katherine, Habib, Rishad and Hardisty, David J. (2019), 'How to SHIFT consumer behaviors to be more sustainable: A literature review and guiding framework', *Journal of Marketing*, 83:3, pp. 22–49.

White, Sarah (2019), 'Vuitton to hire more French handbag makers as Chinese sales boom', Reuters, 5 September, https://www.reuters.com/article/us-france-vuitton/vuitton-to-hire-more-french-handbag-makers-as-chinese-sales-boom-idUSKCN1VQ1T5. Accessed 18 April 2021.

Williams, Robert (2017), 'Hermès invests in France as Macron, Le Pen joust over jobs', 27 April, Bloomberg, https://www.bloomberg.com/news/articles/2017-04-27/hermes-first-quarter-sales-beat-estimates-on-strong-asia-demand. Accessed 28 July 2019.

Williams, Robert (2019), 'Louis Vuitton commits to French supply chain with new factory', 4 October, Bloomberg, https://www.bloomberg.com/news/articles/2019-10-04/louis-vuitton-just-opened-a-new-factory-in-france. Accessed 8 February 2020.

Willsher, Kim (2020), 'Landmark French law will stop unsold goods being thrown away', 30 January, *The Guardian*, https://www.theguardian.com/world/2020/jan/30/france-passes-landmark-law-to-stop-unsold-goods-being-thrown-away. Accessed 4 April 2020.

Woman 1 (2020), in-person interview with V. Manlow interview, Texas, 30 January.

Woman 2 (2020), in-person interview with V Manlow interview, Texas, 31 January.

Woman 3 (2020), in-person interviews with V Manlow interview, Texas, 31 January.

Woman 4 (2020), in-person interview with V Manlow interview, Texas, 31 January.

Wu, Sarah (2015), 'Simple pleasures: Leather wallets that make your money smell sweeter', *Forbes*, 5 October, https://www.forbes.com/sites/sarahwu/2015/10/05/simple-pleasures-leather-wallets-that-make-your-money-smell-sweeter/?sh=375c-7b19709a. Accessed 28 July 2019.

Yotka, Steff (2010), 'In defense of the banned Louis Vuitton ad', *Fashionista*, 28 May, https://fashionista.com/2010/05/in-defense-of-the-banned-louis-vuitton-ad. Accessed 9 November 2021.

Youngs, Jeff (2020), 'Mercedes-Benz coronavirus relief and new incentives', J. D. Power, 10 April, https://www.jdpower.com/cars/shopping-guides/mercedes-benz-coronavirus-financial-relief-and-new-car-incentives. Accessed 18 April 2020.

Za, Valentina (2014), 'Italian fashion house Prada buys French tannery', 8 October, Reuters, https://www.reuters.com/article/us-prada-tannery/italian-fashion-house-prada-buys-french-tannery-idUSKCN-0HX1S020141008. Accessed 10 December 2020.

Zargani, Luisa (2020a), 'Miuccia Prada shares outlook, views on sustainability', *WWD*, 12 January, https://wwd.com/fashion-news/fashion-scoops/miuccia-prada-shares-outlook-views-on-sustainability-1203421330/. Accessed 26 March 2020.

Zargani, Luisa (2020b), 'Giorgio Armani writes open letter to *WWD*', *WWD*, 3 April, https://wwd.com/fashion-news/designer-luxury/giorgio-armani-writes-open-letter-wwd-1203553687/. Accessed 30 November 2020.

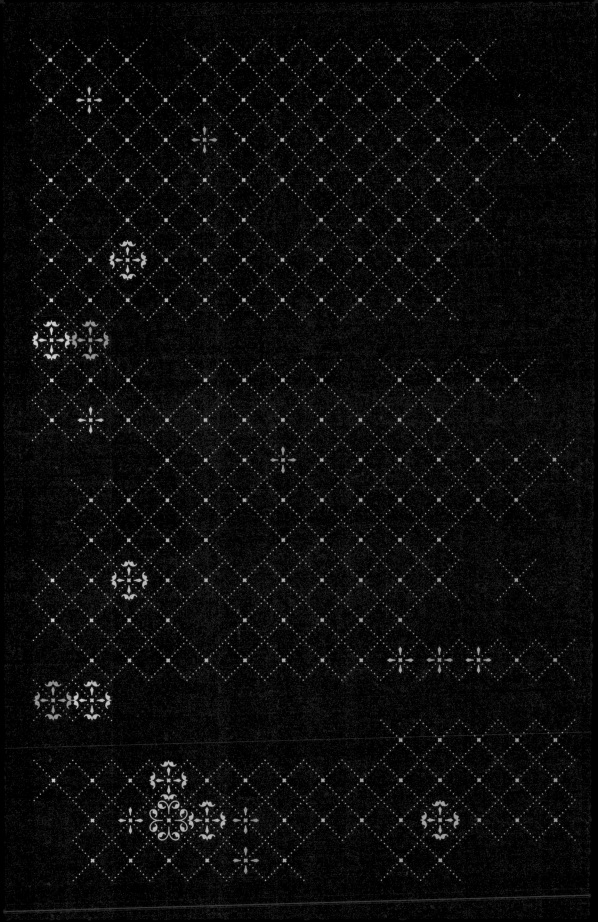

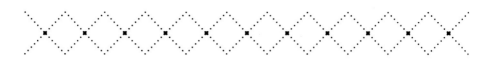

# Index

Entries within Tables are shown as **bold** page numbers. Endnotes are indexed as 189nxx.